Short Essays

MODELS FOR COMPOSITION   SECOND EDITION

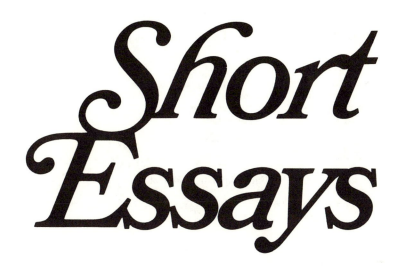

Short Essays

MODELS FOR COMPOSITION SECOND EDITION

Gerald Levin

The University of Akron

HARCOURT BRACE JOVANOVICH, INC.

New York   San Diego   Chicago   San Francisco   Atlanta

London   Sydney   Toronto

ISBN: 0-15-580914-8

Library of Congress Catalog Card Number: 79-89736

Printed in the United States of America

preface

As in the first edition, nearly all these 59 short essays appear here for the first time in a freshman reader. The majority are three to five pages long—about the length usually assigned in composition classes. For this reason they are especially appropriate in classes where a detailed discussion of the essay is a necessary preliminary to writing. Students of all abilities probably find it easiest to study the organization and development of ideas by reading short essays, but instructors who want longer examples will find a number of them in this book, including those by Huggins, Yablonsky, Engle, Hills, Bourjaily, Wicker, Kendall, and McGinley.

The essays are concrete, contemporary, and pertinent to the world and interests of freshmen. They present an intellectual challenge to students of all writing abilities, without presenting the complex reading problems that prevent many essays from being useful models for composition. Many topics are represented, such as urban and rural living, sports, changing values in American life, and growing up. Nine of the essays deal with work, and the new Dialog concerns job prospects and the choice of a college major. Another important feature of this book is the large number of argumentative essays on contemporary issues of interest to freshmen.

The essays are presented complete. The following are self-contained sections from chapters of books, and several are complete chapters: Angelou, Kendall, Huggins, Updike, Trillin, Deford, the section from *The Foxfire Book,* Stuart, Sandoz, Craig, and Dillard. New to the second edition are the essays by Heckscher, Nelson, Krents, Huggins, Sandoz, Borland, Yagoda, Bourjaily, Allen, Fischer, Emerson, Hoffer, Prinz, Raspberry, Stuart, Engle, Perrin, McKenzie, Apple, and Atkinson.

An alternative table of contents shows how the essays may be grouped thematically. A second alternative table of contents (in the *Instructor's Manual*) groups the essays according to type: narration, description, exposition, and argument and persuasion. Each essay illustrates rhetoric topics other than the one under which it is included, and instructors may want to switch essay and topic to fit the needs of their classes. The *Instructor's Manual* includes many such alternative combinations. Many of the Suggestions for Writing in the text and the Suggestions for Teaching in the *Instructor's Manual* offer possibilities for comparison of ideas and rhetorical development. Each essay is followed by a Comment on the rhetorical principles that the essay illustrates. The Questions generally begin with the content and rhetoric of each essay, developing points made in the Comment, and conclude with the student's response to the essay's ideas and experiences. The Vocabulary Study is designed to supplement these questions, to teach the uses of a dictionary in reading and writing, and to emphasize the importance of context.

I wish to thank the many instructors who commented on the first edition—particularly Andrea A. Lunsford, University of British Columbia, and Ann Raimes, Hunter College of the City University of New York, for their criticism of the original manuscript and their many useful suggestions for revision. I owe thanks also to William A. Francis, Bruce Holland, Alice J. MacDonald, Sally K. Slocum, and Arlene A. Toth, all of the University of Akron, for many years of discussion on topics of composition; and, for their helpful comments and suggestions, to John A. R. Dick, the University of Texas at El Paso, and Susan Hill, Southern Vermont College. My wife, Lillian Levin, assisted me in preparing the manuscript for publication. Eben W. Ludlow and Natalie Bowen, both of Harcourt Brace Jovanovich, encouraged this book from its inception to its completion, and I am grateful to them for their help.

GERALD LEVIN

contents

THEMATIC
TABLE OF CONTENTS

AMERICAN LIFE

SPORTS

PEOPLE

NATURE

LANGUAGE

VALUES

ISSUES AND CONTROVERSIES

Short Essays

MODELS FOR COMPOSITION   SECOND EDITION

thesis

The main idea of an essay is the one that organizes the many smaller ideas and details. In the expository essay—the essay that explains ideas—this main idea is called the *thesis*. Essays of personal experience and other kinds also may be organized through a controlling idea or impression.

Occasionally the thesis of an essay appears in the first sentence:

> Parents want two opposite things at once: they want their children to excel, and they want their children to be docile. But the two don't go together and never have.—Sydney J. Harris, *Parents Must Make Up Their Minds*

This practice occurs often in newspaper editorials and magazine articles that try to be brief. Because such a beginning can seem abrupt and may not be clear to the reader without an introduction, writers often build to the thesis—presenting it later in the first paragraph or later in the essay. Introductory comments and details place the reader in the world and ideas of the writer, as in this brief opening paragraph that leads up to the thesis, the last sentence of the paragraph:

> Revolutions are not made by fate but by men. Sometimes they are solitary men of genius. But the great revolutions in the eighteenth century were made by many lesser men banded together. What drove them was the conviction that every man is master of his own salvation.—Jacob Bronowski, *The Drive for Power*

Sometimes the thesis is not stated until the end of the essay. One reason for this delay is that the idea will not be clear without considerable explanation and examples. Another reason is that the idea gains special emphasis when it is placed toward the end of the essay, because the closing paragraph, like the opening paragraph, is a place of natural emphasis. The more controversial the thesis, the later in the essay it may appear, for the writer may wish to make the reader receptive to it before actually stating it.

In some essays the writer may not state the thesis but will let details suggest or imply it. This is one of many effective ways to make the reader give attention to the idea.

GOING MY WAY

Martin L. Krovetz

When Martin Krovetz wrote this essay, he was the assistant principal of Carmel High School in Carmel, California; he is now the principal of Harbor High School in Santa Cruz, California. His personal essay draws some interesting and important conclusions from his own experience concerning the decisions some Americans have been making about how to live their lives.

[1] We live in an age of change and mobility. The person who has had the same job for twenty years and has lived in the same house for that time may have trouble understanding my thoughts expressed here.

[2] Until I was 15 years old I lived in Rochester, N.Y. During that time I attended three elementary schools, one junior high school and one high school. My last two years of high school were in Miami Beach. I then attended a large state university for four years to earn my B.A., followed by four more years at a second large university where I earned my Ph.D. I spent no more than four years at any one of these eight schools. I am employed in my third major job. I left the other two voluntarily after three years each and went on to something new. Now after two years in my present position I'm actively considering what should come next.

[3] Everything has come in two-, three- or four-year cycles. No

roots here, no roots there. Upward mobility is the theme. What's next, what's right to get there, thinking more of the future than the present . . .

[4] I was an excellent student in school. My Phi Beta Kappa key reminds me that I played by most of the rules. I realize now, as many people do, that most of the book learning has slipped my mind, but the messages given by the teachers all those years still ring loud and strong. Elementary school prepares you for junior high school. Junior high school prepares you for high school. High school prepares you for college. College prepares you for graduate school. Graduate school prepares you for a job. (There are a lot of Ph.D.'s unemployed these days, I hear.) If you work hard enough at the first job, the second job will offer more prestige, power and pay. If you work hard at the second job . . . The endless cycle of a prosperous and *worthwhile* life. What better example of Marshall McLuhan's "the medium is the message."

[5] Somewhere a part of me has been lost. There have been many whos at each stop, but it gets harder and harder to give of myself to others when I know that the relationship will be shortlived, based on the life-style I have chosen for myself to date. I tell myself that the next stop may not be lasting, but it will be longer. The next stop is where the roots will grow and flourish. I sound too much like the aspiring law student who plans to play by all the rules until he is president of the General Motors Corp. and will then change the world.

[6] Every year, I try to get back to Florida to visit with my father, sister, grandparents, nieces and nephew, aunts and uncles and two people who have been my closest friends since the first days of college. Two weeks out of 52 my extended family is a reality. A couple of times a year I correspond with friends from graduate school. We are spread all over North America now, but over the last four years I have seen several of them once or twice during someone's vacation. At the same time, if I'm not moving, someone else probably is. As an educator, I have become close friends with many of my past students. Their lives too are spent in two-, three- and four-year cycles. They too are now spread all over North America.

[7] Needless to say, I'm not sure that I want to change my life-style. I have an advantage that reportedly a majority of Americans do not have: I like my work. Each change of jobs has been stimulating and has caused me to grow as a person. I am away from my extended family, but I spend a lot of time with my nuclear family

and find my relationship with my wife and three children to be very rewarding. I have made friends all along the way. I have hated to leave any of them, but I have enjoyed watching us change and grow with each move and with each new group of friends. Life is a learning process and by living in a number of places in the United States I have come to recognize and appreciate the pluralism within this country. Also, intellectually at least, I allow myself to think that I am somewhat of a free thinker, a person who will take risks and state his views even if it happens to endanger his job security; I pride myself on this, in fact.

[8] The dilemma facing me is at least somewhat clear. Do I choose the professional and personal satisfaction that I perceive comes from a life-style characterized by mobility, or do I choose the shelter and satisfaction that come from choosing a more stable life-style and then try to find ways to achieve the other satisfactions? I notice as I write this that the ingrained biases are evident to me; I cringed slightly as I wrote the word "shelter." Protection and shelter have negative connotations for me; strength, power and fame are positive. I am not at all sure that these ideas are mutually exclusive; I know that the valences are questionable, but I will need to reevaluate my value system in order to be able to make a valid judgment.

[9] I suppose that I see the world as made up of "them guys" who choose to not take chances, to work 40 hours a week at a boring job, drink lots of beer and watch "Let's Make a Deal" on television; and "us guys" who are willing to take chances, speak up, move, drink wine, eat cheese and read lots of newsmagazines. Along the way a number of "them guys" have been my friends, and they have admitted that they are jealous of the way I choose to approach life. I now wonder if I'm a little jealous of some of what they have as well.

[10] I suspect that I will allow this dilemma to be waged inside me for a few more years and perhaps through several more moves. At some point, however, I shall choose to at least try to look at my new house and new community as *home*. In the long run I still might choose to remain there for only three or four years; but once at least I should allow myself to think that the soil is rich and permit my roots to grow.

COMMENT

Krovetz begins with an observation about American life: "We live in an age of change and mobility." He then develops it through his personal experience. For him as for other Americans, life is experienced in "two-, three- or four-year cycles," the result being the loss of "shelter" and stability. Krovetz says at the beginning of paragraph 5 that "Somewhere a part of me has been lost." This statement is his controlling idea or thesis: the opening four paragraphs build to it. The remainder of the essay develops this idea through his experiences and his thoughts about their advantages and disadvantages. The final sentence restates it—adding a partial solution to the problem. Krovetz reminds the reader of his controlling idea in his references to his visits home, to his new jobs, and to the "several more moves" he probably will make. At no point does he stray to an unrelated topic. Notice also that Krovetz divides the essay into two parts: the first part states a problem; the second explores a solution.

QUESTIONS FOR STUDY AND DISCUSSION

1. What general problem concerns Krovetz? Why is the solution suggested at the end only partial? Is Krovetz saying he *will* grow roots?

2. What personal qualities does Krovetz stress in explaining his way of living? How do these qualities show the ways in which he is different from "them guys"?

3. Does Krovetz suggest that the disadvantages of his way of living outweigh the advantages—or the reverse? Or does he consider the advantages and disadvantages equal?

4. Was "upward mobility" the theme of your education, or were you taught other values? Were you taught the same values at home and at school?

5. Do you agree that the world is made up of "them guys" and "us guys," or do you distinguish attitudes toward work and personal relationships in other ways?

6. How closely do your present values and goals resemble Krovetz's?

VOCABULARY STUDY

1. Krovetz states that the words *protection* and *shelter* have "negative connotations" for him, that is, unpleasant associations. What other words in the essay probably have negative connotations for him too?

2. Notice his statement that *strength, power,* and *fame* have positive connotations for him. Think of three or four other words that probably also would seem positive to him.

3. Rewrite paragraph 8 in your words. In particular find substitute words and phrases for *dilemma, mobility, ingrained, biases, valences, reevaluate,* and *valid.*

SUGGESTIONS FOR WRITING

1. Write your own essay on the topic "Going My Way." Introduce your thesis or controlling idea in your opening paragraph and keep it before your reader in the whole essay. You may wish to organize the essay as Krovetz does—presenting a problem and exploring a solution.

2. Compare two of your friends through their attitudes toward change and mobility. You might wish to compare them to Krovetz or discuss whether they are "them" or "us" guys. Use your comparison to make a point, and underline this controlling idea.

3. Discuss what experiences you want now in a job, or will want later. You might discuss the influence of your friends on your attitude toward work. Build the discussion to a statement of your controlling idea in your final paragraph. You might introduce yourself and the topic of the essay in your opening paragraph.

PICKING COTTON

Maya Angelou

Maya Angelou was born in St. Louis in 1928, and grew up in Stamps, Arkansas, where she was raised by her grandmother, who operated the only black general store in town. In 1940 she moved to San Francisco to live with her mother. She later studied dancing and taught it in Italy and Israel, after performing professionally. Angelou has served as an official of the Southern Christian Leadership Conference, and she has traveled and lived in Africa, teaching school and writing for newspapers in Egypt and Ghana. Returning to the United States, she worked in the theater and taught writing. Her description of cotton pickers in Stamps is a complete section of an early chapter of her auto-biography, *I Know Why the Caged Bird Sings* (1969).

[1] Each year I watched the field across from the Store turn cat-erpillar green, then gradually frosty white. I knew exactly how long it would be before the big wagons would pull into the front yard and load on the cotton pickers at daybreak to carry them to the remains of slavery's plantations.

[2] During the picking season my grandmother would get out of bed at four o'clock (she never used an alarm clock) and creak down to her knees and chant in a sleep-filled voice, "Our Father, thank you for letting me see this New Day. Thank you that you didn't allow the bed I lay on last night to be my cooling board, nor my blanket my winding sheet. Guide my feet this day along the straight and narrow, and help me to put a bridle on my tongue. Bless this house, and everybody in it. Thank you, in the name of your Son, Jesus Christ, Amen."

[3] Before she had quite arisen, she called our names and issued orders, and pushed her large feet into homemade slippers and across the bare lye-washed wooden floor to light the coal-oil lamp.

[4] The lamplight in the Store gave a soft make-believe feeling to our world which made me want to whisper and walk about on tiptoe. The odors of onions and oranges and kerosene had been mixing all night and wouldn't be disturbed until the wooded slat was removed from the door and the early morning air forced its way in with the bodies of people who had walked miles to reach the pickup place.

[5] "Sister, I'll have two cans of sardines."

[6] "I'm gonna work so fast today I'm gonna make you look like you standing still."

[7] "Lemme have a hunk uh cheese and some sody crackers."

[8] "Just gimme a coupla them fat peanut paddies." That would be from a picker who was taking his lunch. The greasy brown paper sack was stuck behind the bib of his overalls. He'd use the candy as a snack before the noon sun called the workers to rest.

[9] In those tender mornings the Store was full of laughing, jok-ing, boasting and bragging. One man was going to pick two hundred

pounds of cotton, and another three hundred. Even the children were promising to bring home fo' bits and six bits.

[10] The champion picker of the day before was the hero of the dawn. If he prophesied that the cotton in today's field was going to be sparse and stick to the bolls like glue, every listener would grunt a hearty agreement.

[11] The sound of the empty cotton sacks dragging over the floor and the murmurs of waking people were sliced by the cash register as we rang up the five-cent sales.

[12] If the morning sounds and smells were touched with the supernatural, the late afternoon had all the features of the normal Arkansas life. In the dying sunlight the people dragged, rather than their empty cotton sacks.

[13] Brought back to the Store, the pickers would step out of the backs of trucks and fold down, dirt-disappointed, to the ground. No matter how much they had picked, it wasn't enough. Their wages wouldn't even get them out of debt to my grandmother, not to mention the staggering bill that waited on them at the white commissary downtown.

[14] The sounds of the new morning had been replaced with grumbles about cheating houses, weighted scales, snakes, skimpy cotton and dusty rows. In later years I was to confront the stereotyped picture of gay song-singing cotton pickers with such inordinate rage that I was told even by fellow Blacks that my paranoia was embarrassing. But I had seen the fingers cut by the mean little cotton bolls, and I had witnessed the backs and shoulders and arms and legs resisting any further demands.

[15] Some of the workers would leave their sacks at the Store to be picked up the following morning, but a few had to take them home for repairs. I winced to picture them sewing the coarse material under a coal-oil lamp with fingers stiffening from the day's work. In too few hours they would have to walk back to Sister Henderson's Store, get vittles and load, again, onto the trucks. Then they would face another day of trying to earn enough for the whole year with the heavy knowledge that they were going to end the season as they started it. Without the money or credit necessary to sustain a family for three months. In cotton-picking time the late afternoons revealed the harshness of Black Southern life, which in the early morning had been softened by nature's blessing of grogginess, forgetfulness and the soft lamplight.

COMMENT

Angelou's description begins with her grandmother's rising at four o'clock in the morning; it ends with a picture of workers mending their sacks under coal-oil lamps at night. The details at the beginning suggest a softness of life: "The odors of onions and oranges and kerosene had been mixing all night and wouldn't be disturbed until the wooded slat was removed from the door"; the sounds and smells of morning "were touched with the supernatural," she tell us in a later passage. In contrast to the morning, the late afternoon is harsh and ordinary, and she gives details of that world in the remaining paragraphs. The concluding sentence of the essay combines these impressions and states a thesis. Angelou is writing for an audience that perhaps holds a stereotype of the Southern black; that audience must be immersed in the sounds and feelings of the real Southern black world if it is to lose that stereotype. Angelou saves her thesis for the end of the essay as a way of involving the reader in the real world, intellectually and emotionally.

QUESTIONS FOR STUDY AND DISCUSSION

1. What details in the essay suggest "nature's blessing of grogginess, forgetfulness and the soft lamplight"? Why are these a blessing? What other details suggest the "features of the normal Arkansas life"?

2. How does Angelou suggest the child's view of that world? How do you know that an adult, and not a child, is describing it?

3. How does Angelou suggest the influence of that world on her feelings about her race?

4. How do the details contradict a stereotype of the Southern black? How does Angelou remind us of that stereotype? What other stereotypes is she possibly criticizing?

5. What stereotypes—perhaps of teenagers or older sisters or high-school athletes—could you attack through a similar presentation of details? What stereotypes have affected your life and image of yourself?

VOCABULARY STUDY

1. Some of the words in the essay are colloquial (words used conversationally and informally) and some are dialect (words restricted to a

particular group or part of the country. Look up the following words to find out how your dictionary defines and classifies them: *hunk, bib, bit* (as in *six bits*), *vittles.*

2. Look up *paranoia.* Is Angelou using the word in its technical or general sense in paragraph 14? How would you state this idea?

SUGGESTIONS FOR WRITING

1. Describe a childhood experience that tells your reader something important about your upbringing. Build your details to a statement of your controlling idea.

2. Describe a childhood experience from two points of view—that of the child and that of the young adult remembering the experience. Then comment on the differences between what the child experiences and what the adult understands. Use these differences to state a thesis.

3. Discuss a stereotype that shaped your view of other people or of yourself. Explain how you came to hold this stereotype, and how you discovered its falseness.

DOING CHORES

August Heckscher

August Heckscher, who was born in 1913 in Huntington, New York, worked for many years as a newspaper editor and was an editorial writer for the *New York Herald Tribune.* He has served as director of the Twentieth Century Fund, president of the Woodrow Wilson Foundation, and administrator of recreation and cultural affairs for New York City. His writings include numerous books on public affairs, the latest of which is *Open Spaces: The Life of American Cities* (1977).

¹I have been doing chores, being for a brief spell alone in a house that recently was astir with bustle and echoed with the voices of a gathered family. For those who may be in some doubt as to the nature of chores, their variety, their pleasures and their drudgery, I am prepared to deliver a short disquisition.

²The first point about chores is that they are repetitive. They come every day or thereabouts, and once done they require after a certain time to be done again. In this regard a chore is the very opposite of a "happening"—that strange sort of event which a few years back was so much in fashion. For a happening was in essence unrepeatable; it came about in ways no one could predict, taking form from vaporous imaginings or sudden impulse. Chores, by contrast, can be foreseen in advance; for better or worse, I know that tomorrow I must be re-enacting the same small round of ritualistic deeds; and they arise, moreover, from practical necessities, not from poetic flights.

³A second point about chores is that they leave no visible mark of improvement or progress behind them. When I am finished, things will be precisely as they were before—except that the fires will have been set, the garbage disposed of, and the garden weeded. In this, they are different from the works which optimistically I undertake. Ozymandias may have been presumptuous, but he was essentially right when he looked about him and said: "*See how my works endure!*" A work, once achieved, leaves a mark upon the world; nothing is ever quite the same again. The page of a book may have been printed or a page of manuscript written; a sketch, a poem, a song composed; or perhaps some happy achievement reached in one of the more evanescent art forms like the dance or cooking. All these have an existence of their own, outside of time, and at least for a little while live on in the mind of their creator and perhaps a few of his friends.

⁴The well-meaning wife, seeing her husband about his chores, will miss the character of his performance. "Henry loves to cut wood," she will say; "he positively dotes on controlling the flow of waste from dinner-table to compost heap." The wife is perhaps trying to appease an unnecessary sense of guilt at seeing her spouse engaged in such mundane efforts. The fact is, he doesn't love doing chores. But neither does he feel humiliated or out of sorts for having to do them. The nature of a chore is that it is neither pleasant nor unpleasant in itself; it is entirely neutral—but it is obligatory.

[5]Neutral—and yet I must confess that with their repetition, and perhaps because of their very inconsequence, chores can in the end evoke a mild sort of satisfaction. Here, as in more heroic fields of endeavor, a certain basic craft asserts itself. To do what must be done neatly, efficiently, expeditiously—"without rest and without haste"—lights a small fire deep in the interior being and puts a man in good humor with the world. Santayana described leisure as "being at home among manageable things"; and if he was right we who are the chore-doers of the world are the true leisure classes. At least one can be sure that no chore will defeat us; none will raise insuperable obstacles, or leave us deflated as when the divine muse abandons her devotee.

[6]A man I know became seduced by the minor pleasure of doing chores—or at any rate by the absence of pain which they involve— and could be seen from morning till nightfall trotting about his small domain, putting everything in order, setting everything to rights that the slow processes of time had disturbed. He was perhaps going too far. To season chores with work, and to intersperse them with a few happenings, is the secret of a contented existence. Fortunate the man or woman who achieves a just balance between these three types of activity—as I have been able to do by good chance, and for a little space of time.

COMMENT

Where Angelou writes concretely about the experience of work in an Alabama community, Heckscher writes in general terms. His purpose is to define one kind of happiness. That definition, coming in the final paragraph, takes the form of a general comment on the three activities discussed in the essay—chores, work, and happenings: "To season chores with work, and to intersperse them with a few happenings, is the secret of a contented existence." Heckscher builds to this thesis instead of beginning with it, because his point about these activities would not be clear without his having defined and illustrated them.

QUESTIONS FOR STUDY AND DISCUSSION

1. What are the differences between chores and work? Has Heckscher given a meaning to *work* different from your own? Do you ordinarily describe chores as work?

2. How does Heckscher introduce the essay? Does he merely state the subject—or does he also hint at his thesis?

3. Could the second point about chores (paragraph 3) have been discussed before the first?

4. Is Heckscher writing to a general audience or to a special one—perhaps husbands who perform weekend chores? What is his purpose in writing—to reflect on his personal experience, to inform his readers about work and chores, or to persuade them to change their thinking about work or their way of performing it?

5. Do you agree that chores can provide "a mild sort of satisfaction"?

VOCABULARY STUDY

1. Read Shelley's poem "Ozymandias," and in a short paragraph discuss Heckscher's use of it in his essay.

2. Compare the dictionary meaning of the italicized word with the word following it in parentheses. Be ready to explain how the parenthesized word changes the meaning of the sentence:
   a. paragraph 1: a short *disquisition* (sermon)
   b. paragraph 2: the same small round of *ritualistic* (habitual) deeds
   c. paragraph 3: Ozymandias may have been *presumptuous* (conceited)
   d. paragraph 3: one of the more *evanescent* (changing) art forms
   e. paragraph 4: "he positively *dotes on* (enjoys)
   f. paragraph 4: such *mundane* (ordinary) efforts
   g. paragraph 4: it is entirely *neutral* (uninteresting)
   h. paragraph 5: what must be done neatly, efficiently, *expeditiously* (speedily)
   i. paragraph 5: leave us *deflated* (tired) as when the divine muse abandons her *devotee* (fan)
   j. paragraph 6: his small *domain* (household)

SUGGESTIONS FOR WRITING

1. Discuss how accurately Heckscher's definitions fit the various kinds of work you perform at home. In the course of your essay, discuss how closely your idea of happiness agrees with Heckscher's.

2. Discuss daily activities at home and at school that you do not consider chores, and explain why.

3. About chores, Heckscher states: "Here, as in more heroic fields of endeavor, a certain basic craft asserts itself." Discuss the "basic craft" of a chore that you perform regularly. Contrast this "craft" with work that you also perform regularly.

4. Write your own definition of a contented existence, comparing your ideas and experiences with Heckscher's if you wish.

topic sentence

The *topic sentence* of a paragraph is what its name suggests—the statement of the subject or topic of the paragraph, sometimes in the form of a phrase or brief transitional sentence at the beginning:

> Christmas time! That man must be a misanthrope indeed, in whose breast something like a jovial feeling is not roused—in whose mind some pleasant associations are not awakened—by the recurrence of Christmas.—Charles Dickens, *Sketches by Boz*

> Now comes the moral of the story—for it has a moral after all.—Dickens, *Sketches*

Usually the topic sentence is the central or controlling idea of the paragraph, a miniature thesis, which the various details and idea of the paragraph develop. Here are topic sentences that open paragraphs in George Orwell's essay "Politics and the English Language":

> In our time, it is broadly true that political writing is bad writing.

> In our time, political speech and writing are largely the defense of the indefensible.

> But if thought corrupts language, language can also corrupt thought.

Placed at the beginning of the paragraph, the topic sentence gains prominence and guides the reader's attention. The topic sentence, however, may appear anywhere in the paragraph—at the beginning, the middle, or the end. On occasion it may be divided between two sentences, as in this passage from the same Orwell essay:

> As I have tried to show, modern writing at its worst does not consist in picking out words for the sake of their meaning and inventing images in order to make the meaning clearer. It consists in gumming together long strips of words which have already been set in order by someone else, and making the results presentable by sheer humbug.

In the remainder of the paragraph that these sentences introduce, Orwell illustrates his topic idea through a long series of examples.

In many paragraphs a series of details builds to the topic sentence. Here is Orwell's description of his leaving the English public school he attended:

> Bingo [the headmaster's wife] shook hands to say goodbye. She even gave me my Christian name for the occasion. But there was a sort of patronage, almost a sneer, in her face and in her voice. The tone in which she said goodbye was nearly the tone in which she had been used to say *little butterflies*. I had won two scholarships, but I was a failure, because success was measured not by what you did but by what you *were* [*topic sentence*]. I was "not a good type of boy and could bring no credit on the school. I did not possess character or courage or health or strength or money, or even good manners, the power to look like a gentleman." [*explanation of topic idea*]—*Such, Such Were the Joys*

FAST FOOD

Elaine Kendall

Elaine Kendall has written extensively about American life for numerous magazines, including *Harper's* and *Saturday Review,* and in such books as *The Upper Hand* (1965) and *Peculiar Institutions* (1975). The essay printed here is part of a chapter in *The Happy Mediocrity* (1971), her book about American eating habits and other customs. Though McDonald's and other fast-food chains have changed somewhat since 1971, Kendall's essay still sheds light on American attitudes toward food.

[1]The recent boom in the food franchising business amounts to a rare and almost perfect example of American historical inevitability at work. The public companies that have been formed during the past ten years to purvey hamburger, fried chicken, and hot dogs to America have been the glamor stocks of the 1960's, and their track records make old champions like AT&T, General Motors, and electronics look lame by comparison. In a single year some of the food franchisers have shown price increases so huge as to be incredible— McDonald's up 346 percent from 1967 to 1968; Kentucky Fried Chicken up 700 percent; Lum's, essentially a frankfurter operation, up 1,280 percent. Nineteen seventy was a letdown. Lum's earnings rose only 165 percent, Kentucky Fried a mere 26 percent; McDonald's was up 30 percent. Everyone got hurt in 1970, but the investor who was up to his elbows in fast food seems to have escaped with relatively slight first-degree burns. In each case the triteness of the food contrasts sharply with the novelty of the stock quotations. Nothing much is new except the figures. The successful franchisers all work on the same fundamental principle, which is to sell their formulas, their names, and generous helpings of psychological support to individual entrepreneurs across the country. To emphasize their slight difference from their antecedents in the catering business, the franchisers like to refer to themselves as "systems," a word that hints at a new direction in American gastronomy. As the market reports prove, these "systems" are still all go. Every one of these companies is built on certain basic American attitudes toward food, attitudes that have been plain enough all along, but have suddenly become considerably plainer and almost certainly irreversible. The wonder is only that it took so long to happen.

[2]As befits a prototype, the McDonald's Hamburger Empire illustrates these attitudes beautifully. Although Ray Kroc, the president of McDonald's, doesn't attribute his success to anything as vague or chancy as historical inevitability, he certainly hasn't sold more than five billion hamburgers without a profound understanding of his market and the forces that shaped it.

[3]Fifty seconds is regarded as the optimum length of time to

prepare a McDonald's meal, which typically consists of a hamburger, a milk shake, and an order of french fries. McDonald's stores have an eerily exaggerated resemblance to seventeenth-century New England dining rooms. Most contain no chairs, though a few experimental units with seating have been tested. "Things change," says Mr. Kroc, "and so do we." When and if America ever becomes a nation of two- or three-minute epicures, Mr. Kroc will be ready, but for the time being, the Puritan code is strictly enforced. Adults as well as children stand to feed, and there's no lolling around a McDonald's. "We never allow a jukebox, a cigarette machine, a vending device, a pinball game, or a telephone in a McDonald's restaurant," says Mr. Kroc. The lack of these amenities is intended to discourage teen-agers, a group that McDonald's can easily do without. The company even prefers not to hire waitresses, thereby reducing the temptation still further. When Mr. Kroc looks for a site, he counts "church steeples, signs of substantial family neighborhoods." This policy was widely publicized toward the end of 1968, just as Mr. Kroc was embarking on his second thousand set of stands.

[4] The ideal location for a McDonald's is the "above-average residential area." "We want young families," say the McDonald's scouts, and unlike the older highway drive-ins, which relied heavily on a snack trade, McDonald's attracts and gets a family dinner business. If they don't choose to lean against the bare walls inside for the time it takes to swallow the food, Mom, Dad, Sis, and Junior can sit in their car, depreciating their own upholstery, running their own heater, and listening to the radio. For 19 cents they get the hamburger, but customers are encouraged to supply their own shelter and ambience. McDonald's, however, serves an important side dish of security with each order. Every burger is guaranteed to be just like every other. The possibility of variation has been finally routed, thereby averting invidious comparisons with burgers past, as well as eliminating squabbling among the children for the biggest, the rarest, or the best. A McDonald's burger puts a moratorium on that kind of table (or back-seat) talk forever. The last one and the one before that, all the way back to 1955, were identical in every respect. The roast beef sandwich has been discontinued completely. It had an unfortunate tendency to deviate from a single standard.

[5] Each stand must be managed by a certified graduate of McDonald's "Hamburger University" where the curriculum consists of courses in Q.S.C.—Quality, Service, and Cleanliness. "We at

McDonald's," says Mr. Kroc, "believe in these fundamentals and really live by them." Although Hamburger University has a limited catalogue, it maintains an active research and development program. For instance, by the end of 1970, the company had adopted a scoop that delivers the same number of french-fried potato pieces every time, regardless of who is running the machine or where. The company laboratories, of course, have long since arrived at the perfect meat-fat ratio, the perfect size ($3\frac{1}{2}$ inches by $\frac{3}{16}$ inch B.C.— Before Cooking), and the perfect roll measurement ($3\frac{3}{4}$ inches), thus assuring a bun surround of no less than $\frac{1}{4}$ inch. The university seems to have a strong science and math department.

[6]There is still another, subtler factor that contributes to the success of these plans. Franchise shops are not dependent on that rare and mercurial personage, the chef. The chef's place in this country has always been awkward and ambiguous—a man doing woman's work, a kind of super-servant who has to be treated like an artist or, at least, a craftsman. Few people have ever been attracted to so dubious a profession, but lots of Americans are available and willing to press buttons and work levers. There is nothing effeminate about that. Franchised food is manufactured, rather than "cooked" in any true sense. Its components are delivered to the shop already blended, assembled and portioned. The store only heats it. The methods have been scientifically developed, and the serving is done according to the assembly-line principles that we approve. The new food is simply bought and consumed, out of stock. The identical recipe serves everyone.

[7]The bespoke meal, like the bespoke suit or shoe, seems destined to become a special privilege for the quirky few. The trend is clearly away from the custom restaurant, and although a few such places may linger in the cities for some time to come, it is doubtful whether Americans will put up with so costly, so complex, and so essentially undemocratic an institution much longer. The franchisers have something far more appropriate to offer, something that Alexis de Tocqueville hinted at when he said that "the majority possesses a power which is physical and moral at the same time; it acts upon the will as well as upon the actions of men, and it represses not only all contests, but all controversy. . . ." In 1835, of course, the only kind of despotism De Tocqueville really feared was political.

[8]The food that Americans eat at home has been thoroughly branded, standardized, and nationalized for more than fifty years,

and it should have been obvious that the public would welcome—would eventually *demand*—the same sort of reassurance and the same monotony in the food they consumed elsewhere. The chain restaurants like Howard Johnson's recognized the mood long ago, but a chain is only as strong as its weakest link. Howard Johnson's was a great plan, but it stopped short of the ideal. Twenty-eight flavors of ice cream are twenty-six flavors too many, when 90 percent of the people are content with chocolate or vanilla. Howard Johnsons are cluttered with tables, chairs, rest rooms, telephones, and banks of vending machines. They employ waitresses, a proved and expendable hazard. While the newer outlets along the turnpikes are considerably more functional, they are apparently not as austere as America would like. Some HoJos even serve whiskey, a practice known to encourage talking and lingering over meals, slowing down turnover, and contributing to wear and tear on the premises. For Howard Johnson it's almost too late to change, and it seems destined to become the sybarite's chain. The germ of franchising was there from the start, but it was not fully exploited. Howard Johnson's had a distinctive quasi-Colonial architectural style; it had the limited menu, the moderate price, and a central commissary to assure the public that variation in the appearance and quality of HoJo food would be held to a minimum. All the choicest locations were theirs, and by the end of the 1950's when most of the turnpikes were complete, there was hardly anywhere else to eat without taking a long and time-wasting detour. HoJo grew and thrived, but not as dramatically as the franchising companies have done. The reason is simple and economically sound. Howard Johnson's continued to spend company money every time a new store opened. The franchisers do not. The required capital is put up by the franchisee, a refinement which allows corporations like McDonald's, Lum's, and the various chicken systems to proliferate at a far more rapid rate than any old-fashioned chain could hope to do. The franchisers are thus in a position to crowd everyone else right off the map. McDonald's, for example, receives an infusion of $97,000 every time a new outlet opens. By September 30, 1970, there were 1,481 of them, and the home office has a perpetual waiting list of 100 people with funds in hand, marking time until there is an available seat in Hamburger University. There are no scholarships in HU. Every student not only pays his own way, but actually *endows* the institution.

[9]Ninety-seven thousand dollars is double or even triple the

amount of capital the other franchisers require, but the McDonald's franchisee, like the Harvard freshman, is a very special person. He is, according to corporate records, between thirty-five and fifty years old with a solid business background. (Failures do not accumulate or borrow ninety-seven grand very readily.) He has, in many cases, tried the Organization Life and rejected it. Unlike the product he merchandizes, the McDonald's man tends to be a strong individualist. He's not afraid of hard work. The stands are open all day seven days a week until late in the evening. A McDonald's franchisee, in fact, seems to represent something close to the early American business tradition. Each candidate is assured that he can count on an annual revenue of $300,000—approximately five times the average for drive-in restaurants and considerably more than can be realized by investing $97,000 somewhere else. Once the shop is under way, 10 percent of this gross goes right back to the parent company for "counseling services," local and national advertising, and rental of the premises. These appropriations are rigidly fixed. The initial investment buys the sign, the university course, the recipe, and the right to the magic name. After that, the acceptee is on his own, though troubleshooters from Papa Kroc's regional offices are readily available for advice and support. The lease is for twenty years, and it represents a thoroughgoing commitment to cheap hamburgers, as well as a promise to the American public that this is no mere fad. There's every assurance that McDonald's will be with us in 1990. So far there are no officially acknowledged instances of a McDonald's stand having failed, though there are undoubtedly some that have changed hands or even reverted to the parent company. McDonald's maintains a few hundred house shops so that radical innovations like chairs, apple pie, and larger hamburgers may be tried at no risk to the private investor. The triple-decker Mighty Mac was launched this way and is now considered a major factor in McDonald's stability during otherwise lean 1970.

[10] Most of the other franchisers use the McDonald's system as a paradigm, though often on a more limited scale. Even if the investment is only half what McDonald's requires, however, there is bound to be "education," advice, and continuing control. McDonald's may get particularly solvent types—"former dentists, retired Navy officers, and even a man who was once former assistant Secretary of Labor," but such impressive credentials are not required for a Lum's, a Chicken Delight, a Colonel Sanders', a Burger Chef, Min-

nie Pearl's, a Denny's a Nathan's Famous, a Big Boy, a Dairy Tastee, King, Queen, or Freeze, or the pizza establishments. (There are, after all, not enough ex-dentists, naval officers, or Labor Department assistants in the country to buy into all these places.) In general, the franchisee is a man who would like to be on his own but still needs the special props: the moral support and business assistance that the franchising companies can provide. He has usually accumulated $30,000 to $50,000 and wants an assurance that he's not jeopardizing it. He is looking for a tested, accepted, certified, sure thing, and the franchisers seem to have it.

[11] These success stories thoroughly disprove the notion that the American people dine out in order to have something that they can't get at home. The franchisers sell only those items that can be prepared quickly and easily by anyone. The food is comparatively cheap, but you can still have a bigger, juicier hamburger for your 19 cents if you divide a pound of ground meat into quarters. The burger systems get *ten* to a pound, a ratio rarely approached by even the most grudging housewife. What the franchisers seem to be selling is the antithesis of warmth, charm, atmosphere, social life—or even nourishment. They are actually anti-restaurants, judged by any of the usual definitions.

[12] If these places existed only to cater to people caught on the road at mealtime, they'd be readily explainable, but that's not the case. The fact that they often serve that purpose is really quite incidental to the whole idea. They are on the road because America is mostly road, but as Mr. Kroc says, and the others agree, residential and business neighborhoods make the most desirable locations. The idea is for someone in the office to bring back a bag of hamburgers for the steno pool or for Dad to pick up dinner while the family waits in the car or in front of the TV. That sort of trade accounts for two-thirds of the total volume. Between-meal business is just lagniappe.

[13] The fried chicken franchisers of which there are now dozens, rely almost entirely upon a regular mealtime trade. A bucket of fried chicken is hardly anyone's idea of a mid-morning, after school, or bedtime snack, and it's not something that an officeworker can keep on the desk while getting through the paper work. The chicken shops go far beyond the hamburger and shake concept, which, despite its newer refinements (or lack of refinements), can still be an impulse purchase. The 19-cent hamburger is small enough not to spoil the appetite, and despite the hoopla about secret recipes and

carefully guarded formulas, there's not much you can do with 1.6 ounces of anything. Fried chicken is different. It constitutes a genuine meal, both in price and in substance. Morever, chicken does take some time to prepare, and the differences between methods of frying chicken can be noticeable. The chicken systems are not as dependent on the car as the hamburger empires. Chicken Delight will even deliver a bucketful to your very door in less time than it takes to warm up the oven. Chicken Delight is actually selling a total freedom package—from the hot stove, the freezer, the supermarket, the automobile, and the decision. This variation of the idea is essentially foreign in origin, though that fact is not stressed in any publicity. Nevertheless, in India and many other "emerging" countries of the Orient, peddlers push barrows down the poorer streets selling hot meals to those who have no cooking or food storage facilities. The notion that such a technique would work in America, where kitchen equipment is the grandest and most elaborate in the world, is delightfully provocative. We may be working not only toward the antirestaurant, but toward the antikitchen as well.

[14] The capital of the takeout chicken business is Nashville, Tennessee, the home of Kentucky Colonel Sanders, Eddy Arnold's Tennessee Fried, and the recently formed Mahalia Jackson System, aimed at what is euphemistically known as the "ethnic" market. Minnie Pearl's is in Nashville too, but that one has not got very far out. To get ahead in chicken franchising, it apparently helps to be able to carry a tune. (Ballplayers have not proved to be as handy in the kitchen.) Both Eddy Arnold and Minnie Pearl are *Grand Ole Opry* stars, and Mahalia Jackson can belt out a song better than either of them. Kentucky Colonel Sanders, however, is an important exception. He seems to have created his coast-to-coast $35,000,000 business entirely on the strength of his snow-white mustache, his secret blend of herbs and spices, and his two-step cooking process, which involves tenderizing the chicken under pressure before frying it. Singing may help, but it isn't the *sine qua non*. Neither, apparently, is chicken itself. The Kentucky Colonel sells everything to its franchisees *except* the chicken. The parent company supplies all the real essentials—the special cooking equipment, the signs, the napkins, the paper pails with the colonel's instantly recognizable likeness, and the precious blend of seasonings. The franchisee must find the chickens wherever he can. Under the circumstances, the acces-

sories become crucial to the entire operation, because chicken has a disconcerting tendency to vary in taste and quality. Some are bound to be better or worse than others. The illusion of sameness therefore rests heavily on the paper goods and the equipment. People do not buy just "chicken"—they buy Colonel Sanders' chicken, and it has to be dependable every time, spring, fall, summer, and winter. These accessories do for all those different chickens what the McDonald's laboratory technicians do for the hamburger—make it all look, smell, and taste the same. How wonderful for an American riding around Cuernavaca to come upon Colonel Sanders' pink and white face on the sign and know that while he may be getting a Mexican chicken, it will be a naturalized Kentucky Fried Mexican chicken, wrapped in a virtual affidavit proving that it's not some unknown, foreign *pollo*. The future of the franchising business, in the day of the 747 jets, really bends the mind. The franchisers are enlarging their Hamburger Universities and Fried Chicken Colleges, their Pizza Institutes and their Frankfurter Prep Schools, and accepting exchange students from all over the world. Colonel Sanders, always a leader, has recently entered into an agreement with Mitsubishi to establish Japanese Kentucky Chicken outlets.

[15] Wall Street has many experts on this newest of the wonder businesses, and while these sages agree that "quality issues of franchising stock are no longer on the bargain counter," they are still considered reasonably sound long-term investments, less speculative than a lot of more venerable industries. Donald Trott, of Jas. H. Oliphant and Company, says, with some restraint, that "the franchise stocks should eventually prove highly rewarding, as earnings continue to build up at about twenty to fifty percent annually." Of course, Mr. Trott suggests some caution. Scores of undercapitalized fly-by-night imitations have arrived on the scene, and they have presented a serious threat to the concept. A franchiser needs time to set up his university and find a qualified faculty. He must have good locations, and he must avoid obvious mistakes like offering too broad a menu. Certain food items are inherently unsuitable for franchising. It is important to settle on something that is totally accepted by the entire American population, and the quality must be either controllable, as in the case of hot dogs or hamburger, or disguisable, as with fried chicken. Corned beef, for instance, would be a very poor risk because it varies tremendously from one cut to another. Nathan's Famous, however, is experimenting with it on a

small scale. Tacos and enchiladas go well in California and the Southwest, but research has demonstrated that upstate New York is not yet ready for them. Fish-and-chips is doing well. Generally speaking, the item to be franchised should represent a general consensus of taste. A company that takes a gamble on something "ethnic," like Chinese egg rolls, pizza, or kosher delicatessen, usually finds that it must modify the product drastically—less garlic in the salami, process cheese in the pizza, no shrimp in the egg roll. Another consideration that works against the novel or unusual is that the franchised food has to be inexpensive, durable, and reasonably easy to manage. Beef bourguignonne or lobster Newburg would be absurd for those reasons. The few people who want something so eccentric for dinner don't usually care to eat standing up or in the car. They're difficult types, often insisting on candlelight, wine, waiters, dishes, linen, and other overhead-raising fripperies. So, while the outlook for food franchising is still bright for the stock market investor and the franchisers, for ex-dentists and retired naval officers, it is somewhat dim for the hungry nonconformist in search of an interesting meal.

[16] Although the business is only ten years old, the franchised chains of eleven or more units now purchase 25 percent of all goods—food as well as the extras—currently sold to commercial restaurants of any kind. Not even the horseless carriage caught on that quickly. There isn't much doubt that the chicken systems and the Mighty Macs are here to stay. Moreover, the transitional period of coexistence, during which we will have both "regular" restaurants and the franchisers, just as we once had horses and autos, will be short. By February, 1969, those franchisers that had already become public companies were operating more than 8,000 outlets. The huge remainder remain truly uncountable, and there is no law to say that a franchiser has to go public and publish his figures. Most of them do not. One of the unique features of this particular business is that it can expand indefinitely without ever issuing stock for general sale. The smaller, privately held corporations, of course, will imitate their better known predecessors on the big board, capitalizing upon the established popularity of the same proved items. Multiplicity will not give us variety, but rather its direct opposite. In many medium-sized American cities and in most suburbs, hamburger, hot dog, pizza, and chicken stands are the only restaurants. An entire generation of children has already grown up

thinking that McDonald's is the word for hamburger the way Kleenex is the word for tissue and that "fried" always modifies "chicken."

[17] The automobile alone doesn't wholly explain the success of the franchising concept, although it's certainly central to it. Still, if it were just a case of getting into the car and going to eat or grabbing a quick bite once you *were* out driving, there would be no need for micromeasurements, secret formulas, tamper-proof safes for the spice blends, specially designed ovens, patented potato scoops, and endless guarantees of uniformity. Mere cheapness isn't the answer either, because by the time everybody has had the shake, the burger, and the appropriate "complementary" foods, the meal isn't really for pennies after all. Adults can never be satisfied with 1.6 ounces of hamburger in any case, so bare subsistence level is obviously two or three. The answer is not to be found in the swinging atmosphere, the soft lights, the jukebox, or the good-looking waitress with the long legs and the heart of gold because those things aren't presented. Change of scene can't be a factor because the franchise restaurant is the supreme example of "seen one, you've seen 'em all." Taste? There's no accounting for or disputing that, but it doesn't seem likely that a formula like the Kentucky Colonel's (devised to turn millions of different chickens into a single, archetypical chicken) can leave the consumer much to remember. And if the franchise dinner isn't cheap, fun, exciting, novel, tasty, or even especially convenient, where is its power?

[18] It seems clear that the American people yearn to be told what to eat, long to have that particular decision made for them. Only half a dozen options are available from these places, out of all the thousands of edibles that can be raised, grown, processed, and marketed in this huge, temperate, rich, and fertile country. We have narrowed the choices down to a nearly irreducible minimum. We, the most various collection of people ever assembled into a single nation, have agreed that we will be satisfied with these rigid limitations and that we all will stay satisfied from the time we can first be propped into a car seat until long after we're eligible for Medicare. If we have a widening generation gap, irreconcilable racial discord, or a new sense of individuality, no one would ever know it from the menu at the franchise shop. There the whole experience of eating has been completely drained of every last personal, social, and sensual aspect. You never have to give it a second thought.

COMMENT

Kendall builds to her thesis statement at the end of paragraph 1: the fast food companies have been "built on certain basic American attitudes toward food." Each of the paragraphs that follow deal with these attitudes, the topic sentences usually identifying or referring to them in some way. In paragraphs 3–6, which concern a typical fast food chain, Kendall moves from the more obvious practices that have made McDonald's a success to the less obvious ones. In paragraphs 7–8, she compares McDonald's with other chains before discussing other widely imitated practices of McDonald's. After drawing a few preliminary conclusions about American attitudes (paragraphs 11–12), she turns to the fried chicken chains, which represent a different attitude toward fast food and different practices. The concluding paragraphs of the essay draw conclusions about the fast-food industry and American attitudes. In general, Kendall moves from specific examples to general ideas—using her topic sentences to focus the discussion of each paragraph and to clarify her organization.

QUESTIONS FOR STUDY AND DISCUSSION

1. Paragraph 2 is transitional, connecting the thesis statement of paragraph 1 to the illustration that follows, and providing the topic sentence for paragraph 3. How does this topic sentence fit the examples of paragraph 3?

2. Which of the other topic sentences make direct reference to the concluding sentence of the preceding paragraph, as a means of transition?

3. How many opening sentences of Kendall's paragraphs state the central or controlling idea?

4. How does the whole essay illustrate "American historical inevitability at work"? What qualities of Americans is Kendall concerned with?

5. How are the various fast-food chains different from one another? What do they have in common? Are these similarities and differences equally important to the thesis of the essay?

6. Is Kendall merely illustrating a trait of American life, or is she seeking to persuade readers to change their attitude toward food and to change their eating habits?

VOCABULARY STUDY

Complete the following sentences, using the italicized words in one of their dictionary meanings:

a. The *triteness* of her statements is shown by
b. The *prototype* for the sons of the family was
c. There is no use in *depreciating*
d. He made an *invidious* comparison between
e. The *ambiguity* in the directions is shown by
f. His *mercurial* temper is best revealed in
g. The *innovations* in her design for the building were
h. There is no reason to *jeopardize*
i. The *antithesis* of democracy is
j. The difference between an *ethnic* neighborhood and a mixed one is
k. One *sensual* pleasure to be found in winter hikes is

SUGGESTIONS FOR WRITING

1. Describe your tastes in and attitude toward fast food. Use your description to state your agreement or disagreement with Kendall's ideas.

2. Compare your eating habits in different places—home, the school cafeteria, a fast-food store, for example. Use this comparison to state a thesis.

3. Discuss your agreement or disagreement with one of the following statements:
   a. "Multiplicity will not give us variety, but rather its direct opposite."
   b. "It seems clear that the American people yearn to be told what to eat, long to have that particular decision made for them."
   c. "We have narrowed the choices down to a nearly irreducible minimum."

4. McDonald's has changed in many ways since this essay was written; for example, most of the restaurants now have seating areas. Discuss how this and other changes at McDonald's reflect new attitudes toward fast food and toward patrons. If you believe that the attitudes Kendall describes still prevail, despite the changes, explain your reasoning and support it with examples.

THE DESK

Michael Nelson

Michael Nelson, born in 1951, teaches political science at Vanderbilt University. He previously worked as a VISTA volunteer in the Georgia Legal Services Program, as television moderator in Augusta, Georgia, and as editor of The Washington Monthly. He has written numerous magazine articles on American government and politics, and is a frequent contributor to the Washington Post Magazine and the Baltimore Sun.

[1]When editorial writers and politicians discuss bureaucracy, they talk about it with a capital B—the massive, faceless, red-tape-clogged Bureaucracy of chamber of commerce after-dinner speeches. But when I think of bureaucracy, I think of Martha.

[2]Martha is a retired woman who lives in Augusta, Ga. She survives, but barely, on a small social-security retirement check. A friend once told her that because her income was so low, Martha was also eligible for Supplemental Security Income (SSI). Reluctantly—she is a proud woman—Martha applied.

[3]There is a desk in the Augusta Social Security Administration office; Martha sat down on the "client's" side of it. She was, she timidly told the caseworker who sat opposite her, at her wit's end. She just couldn't make ends meet, not with today's prices. She had never asked anyone for charity before—he had to understand that—but she needed help and had heard that she was entitled to some.

[4]The caseworker understood. Gently, he asked Martha the questions he needed to fill out her application. Everything was in order—except why did she have this $2,000 savings account? For her burial, she told him. She had always dreaded dying as a ward of the state, so for almost 50 years she had saved—a dollar a week when she had it—to finance her own funeral.

[5]But, the caseworker said, we aren't allowed to give SSI to people with more than $1,500 in the bank; that's the law. Don't be silly; the law couldn't apply to burial money, said Martha, scared and

defensive in her embarrassment. The caseworker saw her point, but there was nothing he could do; the law did not—and realistically could not—distinguish between money for funerals and money for high living. Anxious to help, he advised her to go out and blow $500 on a color television—on anything—just to bring her savings down to $1,500. Then, he said, she would be eligible for SSI. Appalled by this perverse advice, Martha left.

[6] Martha is one of several dozen people I have talked to over the past three years, ordinary people from a variety of regions, classes and backgrounds. I talked with them because, as a political scientist and a political journalist, I was interested in finding out what the world of government and politics looks like from the citizens'-eye view. To my surprise, that world contained little of the issues and personalities that pollsters ask about and pundits fulminate about. Instead, it was a world dominated by bureaucracy—not Bureaucracy, mind you, but rather the specific government agencies that these citizens had to deal with in their personal lives—too often, they felt, and with too little satisfaction.

[7] Most ironic was the image of government that was born of these experiences. As any scholarly treatise on the subject will tell you, the great advantage bureaucracy is supposed to offer a complex, modern society like ours is efficient, rational, uniform and courteous treatment for the citizens it deals with. Yet not only did these qualities not come through to the people I talked with, it was their very opposites that seemed more characteristic. People of all classes—the rich man dealing with the Internal Revenue Service as well as the poor woman struggling with the welfare department— felt that the treatment they had received had been bungled, not efficient; unpredictable, not rational; discriminatory or idiosyncratic, not uniform; and, all too often, insensitive, rather than courteous. It was as if they had bought a big new car that not only did not run when they wanted it to, but periodically revved itself up and drove all around their yards.

[8] Are they right? Would that things were that simple. But we taxpayers can't even make up our minds what the problem is with bureaucrats: are they lazy do-nothings, snoozing afternoons away behind the sports section, or wild-eyed do-everythings who can't *ever* sleep unless they have forced some poor soul to rearrange his life to conform with one of their crazy social theories?

[9] As for the bureaucrats, they seem no less blinded by anger

than we. Frequently, they dismiss the unhappy citizens they deal with as sufferers of what one political scientist calls "bureausis"—a childish inability to cope with even the simplest, most reasonable rules and regulations. Like children, they add, we demand a lot but expect somebody else to pay.

[10] Yet there are no callous bureaucrats or "bureautics" in Martha's story, nor were there in most of the stories I heard. What there is, though, is a desk. On one side of it sits the citizen—a whole person who wants to be treated as a whole person. Special consideration? Of course. Bend the rules a little? Certainly, I'm unique. And she is unique, as is every other person who approaches government from her side of the desk.

[11] Across from her sits the bureaucrat. His perspective is entirely different. He is there not as a friend or neighbor, but purely as the representative of his agency, an agency whose only business is to execute the law. His job is to fit this person across the desk into a category: legally eligible for the agency's services or not; if so, for what and on what terms? He cannot, *must* not, look at the whole person, but only at those features that enable him to transform her into a "case," a "file," a "client" for his agency. That way she can count on getting exactly what any other citizen in her category would get from the government—nothing more, nothing less. And do we really want it any different? Would we rather that low-level bureaucrats had the power to give or refuse public services purely as they saw fit?

[12] The desk, whether physical or metaphorical, is there in every encounter between Americans and their government. It turns unique and deserving citizens into snarling clients, and good-hearted civil servants into sullen automatons. More than anything else, I suspect, it explains why we and our government are at each other's throats—why taxpayers pass Proposition 13s and public employees strike like dock workers. *It* is the bureaucracy problem, and if what I heard from the people I talked with is representative, the bureaucracy problem is the crisis of our age.

[13] I only wish I had the solution.

COMMENT

Some of Nelson's topic sentences state the *subject* of the paragraph; the rest state the central or controlling idea. Those of paragraphs 2 and 3 do the first; those of 9 and 10 do the second. A reading of only the topic sentences will show that they contain the ideas of the essay in miniature: the reader discovers not only what the essay is about but also what conclusions Nelson draws from the episode he describes. The whole essay builds from an experience—which Nelson considers representative of bureaucracy and its effects—to general conclusions. Notice that he does not claim to have the solution to the problem of bureaucracy. Identifying the problem is sometimes a step toward a solution; such an identification is his purpose in writing.

QUESTIONS FOR STUDY AND DISCUSSION

1. What other topic sentences merely state the subject of the paragraph? What others state the central or controlling idea?

2. Do any of the topic sentences state the thesis of the essay? What is that thesis?

3. How does Nelson establish his authority on the subject of bureaucracy? How does he seek to persuade you that Martha's experience is a typical one?

4. What does Nelson mean by *bureaucracy*? Does he define this word formally, or does the episode with Martha, together with other details in the essay, provide an indirect definition?

5. Look up the word *metaphorical*. What does Nelson mean by the statement that the desk is both physical and metaphorical?

6. What distinction is Nelson making in paragraph 6 between *bureaucracy* and *Bureaucracy*? What would the second kind of bureaucracy constitute?

7. Do you believe Nelson is right in saying that "the bureaucracy problem is the crisis of our age"? Have you personally experienced such a problem, whether in government or at school? Do you find similar bureaucratic actions or treatment in institutions outside the government—in school offices, or the public library, and the like?

8. What other current social or political issues has Nelson raised in the course of examining government bureaucracy?

VOCABULARY STUDY

1. Explain the difference in meaning in the contrasted words in the following sentence: "People of all classes—the rich man dealing with

the Internal Revenue Service as well as the poor woman struggling with the welfare department—felt that the treatment they had received had been *bungled,* not *efficient; unpredictable,* not *rational; discriminatory* or *idiosyncratic,* not *uniform;* and, all too often, *insensitive,* rather than *courteous.''*

2. Explain how the word in parentheses changes the meaning of the original sentence:
   a. *Appalled* (surprised) by this *perverse* (mistaken) advice, Martha left.
   b. Most *ironic* (contradictory) was the image of government that was born of these experiences.
   c. Across from her sits the bureaucrat. His *perspective* (attitude) is entirely different.
   d. It turns *unique* (special) and deserving citizens into *snarling* (angry) clients, and good-hearted civil servants into *sullen automatons* (sleepy officials).

SUGGESTIONS FOR WRITING

1. Describe an experience with a government agency or official that shaped or changed your attitude toward government in general. Build from the experience to a statement of its effect on you. Draw some conclusions about the problem of government and the citizen, as Nelson does.

2. Describe a series of experiences that shaped your present attitude to the college you now attend. Vary these experiences as much as you can, instead of writing about only positive or only negative ones. Comment on the motives of the people you encountered.

3. Nelson does not state solutions for the problem, but he does imply some. Discuss what these solutions are—and also any other solutions you would propose.

order of ideas

Ideas can be presented in various ways. In reporting an experience or describing a process, we usually present the facts or steps in the order they occur. In describing how to bake a cake, we would list the ingredients before telling how to combine them, and we would give the steps in the order of performance. To a person learning to drive we would not explain how to turn corners until we had explained how to brake and control the steering. We can change this chronological order if we wish, maybe starting with the final step to give the reader a sense of purpose. But in doing so, we must be sure that the reader understands the natural order.

In descriptive writing the order of ideas may be *spatial*— moving from background to foreground, from sky to earth, from north to south. If we are giving reasons for supporting a political candidate, we can state them in the order of *importance,* or we can move from *specific* actions (the candidate's voting record) to *general* attitudes and philosophy. The principle of order usually will depend on the needs of clear exposition and the reader's knowledge of the subject. In describing the care of an automobile, we would probably discuss simple procedures before complex ones—especially if our readers are new car-owners. In training mechanics in the repair of new engines, we might proceed from the most common to the most unusual problems that mechanics are likely to encounter.

We will shortly consider kinds of analysis—comparison and

contrast, example, cause and effect—that provide other important ways of ordering ideas in the whole essay as well as in the paragraph.

DARKNESS AT NOON

Harold Krents

Harold Krents suffered eye damage following birth and at the age of nine became totally blind. He nevertheless graduated from Scarsdale High School, in New York, and later from Harvard College. He received law degrees from Oxford University and Harvard Law School, and has been practicing law since 1971. Krents served as the prototype of the blind boy in Leonard Gershe's play (and the later film) *Butterflies Are Free*. He has long been active in organizations and government agencies concerned with the employment of handicapped people, and the essay reprinted here reflects this interest.

[1] Blind from birth, I have never had the opportunity to see myself and have been completely dependent on the image I create in the eye of the observer. To date it has not been narcissistic.

[2] There are those who assume that since I can't see, I obviously also cannot hear. Very often people will converse with me at the top of their lungs, enunciating each word very carefully. Conversely, people will also often whisper, assuming that since my eyes don't work, my ears don't either.

[3] For example, when I go to the airport and ask the ticket agent for assistance to the plane, he or she will invariably pick up the phone, call a ground hostess and whisper: "Hi, Jane, we've got a 76 here." I have concluded that the word "blind" is not used for one of two reasons: Either they fear that if the dread word is spoken, the ticket agent's retina will immediately detach, or they are reluctant

to inform me of my condition of which I may not have been previously aware.

[4]On the other hand, others know that of course I can hear, but believe that I can't talk. Often, therefore, when my wife and I go out to dinner, a waiter or waitress will ask Kit if "*he* would like a drink" to which I respond that "indeed *he* would."

[5]This point was graphically driven home to me while we were in England. I had been given a year's leave of absence from my Washington law firm to study for a diploma in law degree at Oxford University. During the year I became ill and was hospitalized. Immediately after admission, I was wheeled down to the X-ray room. Just at the door sat an elderly woman—elderly I would judge from the sound of her voice. "What is his name?" the woman asked the orderly who had been wheeling me.

[6]"What's your name?" the orderly repeated to me.

[7]"Harold Krents," I replied.

[8]"Harold Krents," he repeated.

[9]"When was he born?"

[10]"When were you born?"

[11]"November 5, 1944," I responded.

[12]"November 5, 1944," the orderly intoned.

[13]This procedure continued for approximately five minutes at which point even my saint-like disposition deserted me. "Look," I finally blurted out, "this is absolutely ridiculous. Okay, granted I can't see, but it's got to have become pretty clear to both of you that I don't need an interpreter."

[14]"He says he doesn't need an interpreter," the orderly reported to the woman.

[15]The toughest misconception of all is the view that because I can't see, I can't work. I was turned down by over forty law firms because of my blindness, even though my qualifications included a cum laude degree from Harvard College and a good ranking in my Harvard Law School class.

[16]The attempt to find employment, the continuous frustration of being told that it was impossible for a blind person to practice law, the rejection letters, not based on my lack of ability but rather on my disability, will always remain one of the most disillusioning experiences of my life.

[17]Fortunately, this view of limitation and exclusion is beginning to change. On April 16, the Department of Labor issued regulations that mandate equal-employment opportunities for the hand-

icapped. By and large, the business community's response to offering employment to the disabled has been enthusiastic.

[18] I therefore look forward to the day, with the expectation that it is certain to come, when employers will view their handicapped workers as a little child did me years ago when my family still lived in Scarsdale.

[19] I was playing basketball with my father in our backyard according to procedures we had developed. My father would stand beneath the hoop, shout, and I would shoot over his head at the basket attached to our garage. Our next-door neighbor, aged five, wandered over into our yard with a playmate. "He's blind," our neighbor whispered to her friend in a voice that could be heard distinctly by Dad and me. Dad shot and missed; I did the same. Dad hit the rim: I missed entirely: Dad shot and missed the garage entirely. "Which one is blind?" whispered back the little friend.

[20] I would hope that in the near future when a plant manager is touring the factory with the foreman and comes upon a handicapped and nonhandicapped person working together, his comment after watching them work will be, "Which one is disabled?"

COMMENT

Krents wants to do more than state and describe the difficulties of being blind: he wants his reader to understand these difficulties as fully as possible. The essay is organized with this purpose in mind. The three misconceptions about blindness might have been presented in a different order: the order Krents chooses helps us to appreciate the bizarre situation of losing one's sight and being treated as if speech and hearing were lost too. Like Krovetz, Krents moves from problem to solution: this is the general principle of organization in the essay. A notable quality is the proportion of examples to discussion—just enough are provided to illustrate each of the ideas. Krents selects his details carefully, for they must be striking enough to make his points vividly and clearly.

QUESTIONS FOR STUDY AND DISCUSSION

1. In what paragraph does Krents state the basis for his ordering of the three misconceptions? How does this order help us to appreciate the bizarre situation created by blindness? How does the change in tone in paragraph 15 accord with the order of ideas?

2. What is his thesis? Does he state it directly, or is it implied?

3. What are the implied causes of the problems described? Does Krents state or imply a solution for them?

4. What attitudes and feelings does Krents express in the final anecdote?

5. Do you find the organization of ideas successful, or would you have organized them in a different way?

VOCABULARY STUDY

Use each of the following words in a sentence that suggests its exact dictionary meaning: *narcissistic, vain, conceited, proud.*

SUGGESTIONS FOR WRITING

1. Discuss the personal qualities that Krents reveals in his essay. You might begin with qualities he directly refers to in the opening paragraph.

2. Discuss the effect that a permanent or temporary handicap or disability has had on your life, or discuss problems you have observed in the life of a disabled or handicapped friend or relative. You may want to organize your essay as Krovetz and Krents do—working from a problem to a solution. Note that the solution may be partial only; you may want to discuss the extent to which the problems described can be solved.

THE RUPTURE AND THE ORDEAL

Nathan Irvin Huggins

Nathan Irvin Huggins is a professor of history at Columbia University, and has written widely on slavery and the black experience in America. His books include *Voices from the Harlem Renaissance* (1971) and *Black Odyssey* (1977), from which this section of a chapter has been taken. Huggins traveled and did research in Senegal, Ghana, Nigeria, and other African nations to gather material for this book on slavery.

[1] Thinking back on the African's capture and forced migration to America, we tend to focus on the pain and brutality, the great physical suffering, captives must have undergone. There is testimony enough to credit our wildest fantasies about the horrors and inhumanity of the slave trade—the cross-country coffles, the infamous middle passage. Or we think about the loss of freedom that defined the slave's status, imagining people, once free, who through the agency of the slaver were placed in bondage.

[2] We are thus distracted from what is more profound and personal in the experience. We tend to see only the surface of what was, perhaps, the most traumatizing mass human migration in modern history. Pain, suffering, and brutality, much as they are feared and avoided, are part of the imagined possibilities of everyone, everywhere. Any normal social context has within it the potential for misfortune, pain, oppression, and victimization. One sees around oneself those who have fallen victim to disease or crippling accident or criminality or impoverishment. Normal existence makes one conscious of such possibilities, and therefore we become conditioned to living with such personal disaster without questioning the fundamental ground on which we stand.

[3] But what of that catastrophe that spins one outside the orbit of the known universe, that casts one into circumstances where experience provides neither wisdom nor solace? What if the common ground one shared with the sound and the infirm, the rich and the poor, the clever and the dull, the quick and the dead, fell away and one were left isolated in private pain with no known point of reference? Would not, then, the pain itself be the slightest of miseries?

[4] Similarly, to be unfree would of itself amount to little more than misfortune if the terms by which one lived with one's fellow men and the calculus by which one was valued remained unchanged. After all, freedom, as we think of it, is a modern and Western notion—somewhat a fiction even so—and neither European nor African involved in the slave trade would have presumed freedom to have been the natural state of man. The African, certainly, and probably the European, would have questioned the desirability of a freedom that described an independent person having slight social and political restraints and responsibilities.

Unfreedom, and even slavery, was conceivable to the African as a normal state of mankind. The African had even seen slaves about him, those of his father and of other men. At the worst, it was a misfortune, or sometimes a circumstance that a clever slave could work to his advantage. But the transatlantic slave trade was outside that experience; it was something radically new and unimaginable. In a process that could only be related to a witch's spell, one was transformed from person to thing.

[5] Two edges of the slave trade—the rupture of the African from the social tissue that held all meaning for him and his conversion into a marketable object—cut the deepest and touched each to the quick. All other horrors attending to the trade were merely external and superficial cruelties. With luck they might abate in time or be mitigated by circumstance. But these two shocks reverberated to the very foundation of the African's being, changing forever the framework of his life. Thus, those few who suffered these shocks but somehow managed to escape the Atlantic crossing were so altered by the experiences, so set adrift, that they could never find their way back into the world from which they had been torn.

[6] Such experiences do not happen with a single blow. Certainly the mind cannot take in, whole, such devastating events. Rather, as in an earthquake, which begins with tremors, building to catastrophe, each shock deeper and broader than the last, one is finally left alone among other moving creatures, stunned, wounded, and isolated amid the shambles of the known world. In such a disaster, it is impossible for the survivor to fix the point of the most telling blow and to completely rediscover himself after its enormity has passed. So, too, the African was engulfed in a process, the end of which was impossible to see from its onset and its precise beginnings lost forever to recall.

[7] The first capture might have come suddenly, without warning. One might have traveled that way beyond the village many times before—to trade at nearby market villages or on business for the family. Always, beyond the village, in small groups or alone, the air was charged with fear and anticipation of the unexpected, for outside the known and safe precincts, the simplest task could become adventure. There had been stories enough of people, alone, being taken by evil men who might devour them or feed them to some insatiable spirit. Men and women were known simply to vanish without a trace. No warning and no anticipation, however, was

sufficient to prepare for the moment when it came—when unknown men appeared, as if from nowhere, with awful faces and terrible noises, turned one around, beat him to his knees, and pulled him bound and dazed along an unknown trail into emptiness.

[8] Or the blow may have come with more warning, one of a series of raids on neighborhood villages by men who seemed to want only to take people. Straggling wanderers might have brought first word of danger, refugees who had missed death and capture, now seeking some tattered end of family and clan to which to attach themselves. As well, the village may have heard drums telling of violence in the country. The village would be electric with the tales of disaster striking so near at hand, and children would sense the fear as it quivered in the adult whisperings or showed in the quick, nervous movements of heads and eyes as they strained for the first sight or sound that would signal the coming blow.

[9] All the warning and expectation might mean little to a simple farming village. The men and boys might gather their knives and spears. But such tools and such men were better at clearing land and killing wild beasts than fighting off men who had become specialists in battle. The village might seek to evoke spirits, retell the tales of ancient glories and valiant men of the past to awaken the dormant martial sense, to encourage the men in the possibilities of overcoming aggression. For had not their fathers, far before their own time, shown the way? Yet, there might linger the suspicion— as some would counsel—that the best thing might be to move away, out of the path of those who raid, because like all things, this too would pass, the storm would have run its course, and life would go on as it had. Indeed, much time had passed since the last report of a raid in the neighborhood, and that was further away than the time before. Even now, the danger might well have passed.

[10] There could never have been preparation enough when the blow finally fell. The drums may have foretold it. The nerves of all may have been stretched taut awaiting the first sign. But when the screaming, wild-faced men spilled into the village, their stick-weapons rivaling drums with their noise, fire with their smoke, and blowing down people as if by magic; when old men and women were cut down, and children ran like screeching chickens through the village streets: no warning, no preparation, could have been enough. Farmers' weapons and peasants' courage seemed feeble against the onslaught. Death and blood were all around. Huts and compounds,

large and small, crackled under the torch. In the chaos that raged and swirled, some might sneak away unnoticed and fly like the wind to find a place to hide. But most would be swept up and bound together that they might watch the smoldering ruins of their lives.

[11] Some reasoned that security and safety lay in attacking first. To sit back quietly attending fields was the way of disaster. Better to sharpen the instruments of battle and call upon martial ancestors to accompany them into war. Better to exchange their captives with those who hungered for men, exchange them for those sticks of war that blew all down before, better to be so aggressive, so formidable, so frightening, that others would not dare attack.

[12] Such was one way to security, but it necessarily fed the monster that threatened and unsettled the land. And such forays did not always go as planned. The battle, once begun, surged in its own course. The warrior would look up to find himself separated from his fellows, isolated, with no way back. One who had sought to capture was now captive.

[13] Or he might have been spit out from among his people. Some twist or turn in his thought had caused him to see things differently from others, had made him hold too lightly the community's proscriptions against disorder. He took things that were not properly his own. He destroyed things or sacred objects or family peace. Or his view worked so perversely against all positive force that he appeared possessed by those spirits that were against life. He, indeed, had come to feel inhabited by snakes and commanded by another will. Whatever, the village had come to believe that he was an instrument of evil forces, that recent misfortunes could be laid at his feet, that he had become a threat to public peace. Was it not better, then, to vomit up such a creature than to harbor and nurture him in one's bowels until the whole body sickened with corruption? So he, and perhaps some of his kin, would be set out on a path, the end of which no one knew.

[14] Stolen, captured, or rejected, African men, women, and children had no means to save themselves. Pleading and crying availed not, for pity was not the issue. Promises of goods the family would exchange availed not, for these people were items worth more than the cloth or animals or things they knew to be of value. Evoking the spirits availed not, for it seemed in one act there was an emptiness where all familiar spirits had turned their backs, closed their ears. Even then, it was only a hint of what was to follow. Being captured

or taken was not really to be abandoned: there remained points of reference that were familiar. They knew something of the land around and the peoples nearby. They were not really far from their own people, they would be missed, someone would come to get them. At worst, they would be taken as slaves into someone's household.

[15] Quite often, indeed, a captive would be held for short periods in several villages along the way to the large coastal trading centers. One worked at such moments in someone's family; there was a heartening familiarity. The work and the conditions remained within the realm of the conceivable. Perhaps, from such places, one could get word to one's own people to bargain for release. Despairing in that, at least one could make the best of bad fortune, casting one's lot among a new people.

[16] That would have been an unhappy result, but anything would be better than marching along a trail to nowhere. Each step would take one further from home, and each turn or twist would make the way back the more baffling.

[17] One might stay in such way stations a month, no more. The time would come when he would be bound together with others, and the march would continue. After repeated stops, hope waned that the trek would ever end. Onward the road turned, meeting rivers that flowed further still. At some moment, all one's imprecations, all one's pleas to ancestors, all one's evoking of spirits, sound in the ears as the hollowness of one's voice. At such a moment, he would sense the most dreadful meaning in what had happened. He was alone, abandoned by all he knew that could have given him support and anchor: village, family, and even his gods.

[18] As he stumbled and was dragged across space, clues to the future came to him as fearful tales, like fantasies and wild dreams— all was possible now that this was possible: rivers so vast that there was no other side; an end to the earth where one would fall off; men whose skins were the color of plucked chickens, whose hair was as string; men like monsters who ate nothing but other men. Such tales buzzed through his head; such visions swam before his eyes.

[19] From the beginning there were signs to tell the captive he was no longer the same. Before, he could say his name, claim his family and clan, and all would know without further explanation who he was and what weight he had among others. But now his name meant nothing to those who held him, yet he meant something to them: he was important.

[20] He might have sensed this unknown thing in the eyes and voices of his captors. They were pleased with him; they liked him. He was young and strong. Things were upside down because the old were not honored and respected but treated like the sick and feeble. Little was done to see that they ate or rested. Rather, they were driven along until they dropped. Then they were left to die. But all eyes were on him.

[21] At each place when there was a changing of hands, the same flashes of understanding crossed the faces of those who brought them and those who received them. It was like in the market, where the women bargained in trade. There were the looks of depreciation, the haggling back and forth until a trade was made: "I have just so much for these you have brought, no more; that is my final price." So the captive was like a thing to be bartered in the market.

[22] It resembled the market, yet was different, for the stranger did not look at the captive and say: "Here is just the strong one I need to clear my fields; he will meet my needs" or "Yes, this woman will serve my household properly and do my wives' bidding." Here, the buyer did not have a need of his own; rather, he sought to judge the trade in terms of a need of someone else, further on; a need that he could not fully comprehend. *"They* are paying *thus* and *so* for such a one as this," he seemed to say. He merely wanted to make the best bargain so that he, in his turn, would find the trade to his advantage.

[23] The captive thus was dislodged not only from his accustomed place and home. He was also severed from his intrinsic value. He became an abstraction; real and tangible though he was, his meaning to others had nothing to do with the immediate, real, or essential. Little wonder he was likely to believe he would, in time, be eaten.

[24] The sense of personal tragedy and private misfortune was diluted and washed away as one became mixed with many others. Captives like himself but different in language and manner were bound together in the coffles, which strung their agonizing way toward the coast. At the end of the long march or the cascade in war canoe, he would be stuffed and packed with countless others— nameless, now selfless others—in the dungeons of slave castles or the corral-like barracoons. All, a sea of the miserable and lost.

[25] Like a ritual of renaming, a rite of new identity, he and the

others, each in turn, were forced to kneel, and a mark or letter was burned into their flesh with a branding iron. The cry and the pain were brief, nothing new in what had become a litany of wails and moans. But the ritual symbolized a new initiation.

[26] As far as the pain went, it was not so great as circumcision, more intense and long-lasting than that which followed scarification. But with that earlier pain, he had been brought into manhood, made to feel himself in common fellowship with his brothers and other men of the tribe. He had suffered that pain and through it found his selfhood enhanced by new status. But the fire of the brand was to burn out of him who he was and to mark him as property and a thing. Name mattered not, family mattered not, ancestral glories mattered not. He was what the mark on his shoulder said he was, a thing belonging to a company, no more and no less.

[27] It was the company's mark, and the company had need to know how good a physical specimen it had come by. So the captives stood before white men—perhaps seeing them for the first time and finding in their skins verification for some of the rumors. The white men and their African helpers went over their bodies with attention to detail: they felt their wounds and scars, opened their mouths and noticed their teeth, looked into their noses and eyes, and passed them along. The company cared that no one who was healthy would injure or kill himself. Forced to eat if they would not, they would live despite their will. Their lives had value to the company even if they ceased to have meaning to themselves.

[28] Anonymity seemed achieved. The rupture of the web rendered them atoms, not part of a living tissue. They had been wrenched from all ties and known things, and they had been transformed from persons into items of commerce. It merely remained for them to be packed into the bowels of ships and carried across the Atlantic, where they were destined to profit others and build an empire.

COMMENT

Huggins states his thesis at the end of paragraph 4: "But the transatlantic slave trade was outside that experience; it was something radically new and unimaginable. In a process that could only be related to a witch's spell, one was transformed from person to thing." He builds to this statement through a discussion of mistaken ideas we hold about freedom and slavery; thus his exposition is guided—as all exposition must be—by the writer's measure of the reader's knowledge about the subject. Huggins does not assume that his readers will understand exactly what it means for a West African to be changed from a person to a thing. In the remaining paragraphs he develops his thesis concretely—explaining and illustrating the "two edges of the slave trade" that produced this change. Huggins deals with these chronologically: first "his conversion into a marketable object." Notice that each of these considerations has its own order of ideas. Paragraphs 7–14 present the three ways the African was enslaved—through theft, capture, and rejection. Paragraphs 15–27 trace the process by which the African acquired "anonymity." The final paragraph restates the thesis in new words, according to the details of the process just described.

QUESTIONS FOR STUDY AND DISCUSSION

1. What are the misconceptions people hold about freedom and slavery? How does Huggins expose these misconceptions?

2. What is gained by discussing theft and capture before rejection, in paragraphs 7–14? Which of these contributes most to the transformation of the African into a thing?

3. In what sense was the African originally a person? What exactly did the African lose in the process of enslavement? In what sense did he become a thing?

4. To what extent do you hold the misconceptions about freedom and slavery that Huggins exposes? How different is the society of the West African from the world you know? Are there ways in our society in which persons lose their sense of belonging to the community?

VOCABULARY STUDY

Explain the meaning of the following words in the sentences in which they appear: *traumatizing, context* (paragraph 2); *calculus* (paragraph 4); *abate, mitigated* (paragraph 5); *shambles, enormity, engulfed* (paragraph 6); *dormant* (paragraph 9); *taut, onslaught* (paragraph 10); *forays* (paragraph 12); *proscriptions* (paragraph 13); *evoking* (paragraph 14); *haggling* (paragraph 21); *abstraction, tangible* (paragraph 23); *enhanced* (paragraph 26); *anonymity* (paragraph 28).

SUGGESTION FOR WRITING

1. Huggins discusses the ways in which people were rejected by the West African communities he describes. Discuss ways in which a person can be rejected by a group of friends in your neighborhood or the high school you attended. Compare these ways with those described by Huggins.

2. Huggins shows that our understanding of the feelings and the state of mind of people depends on our knowing their history and the circumstances of their present lives. Discuss how you came to understand a friend better through similar knowledge.

3. Discuss how ideas and concepts that you learned in a high school or college history or sociology course increase your understanding of the experiences Huggins describes, or similar ones in which people lose their identity or sense of belonging to their family or community.

unity

In our everyday conversation there is usually some disunity, for we move from one topic to another quickly, and we may return suddenly to a previous one. Confusion seldom arises, at least with friends with whom we share assumptions and knowledge; but when it does occur we can clear it up easily by repeating or explaining our statements. We can repeat ourselves in writing, too, but the more backtracking we do, the more reminders we have to give, and the harder the essay is to read.

By contrast, in a *unified* essay all ideas and details connect to the thesis or controlling idea. The reader sees their connection at every point, and experiences them as a unity, as in music where different sounds are heard together developing a single theme. To achieve unity when we write, we must decide on a single purpose, a controlling idea, and an order of ideas. In short, we must be sure what ideas we want to begin with and why. We must also have a sense of what the reader knows about the subject and how soon the reader will be ready for the statement of the thesis or controlling idea. If we decide to digress from our main idea, we must be sure the reader knows that we are doing so. In general, unity means "one thing at a time," with the reader guided from idea to idea by the writer's single purpose. Once an idea is introduced, it should be discussed fully and without interruption, unless there is good reason to digress.

ON SUMMER

Lorraine Hansberry

Lorraine Hansberry was born in Chicago in 1930. She moved to New York City in 1950 after studying painting in Chicago and Mexico. Her play *Raisin in the Sun* opened in New York in 1959; a later play, *The Sign in Sidney Brustein's Window*, appeared in 1964. She died in 1965. The play *To Be Young, Gifted, and Black* (1969) is about her life and is drawn from her writings, including the essay printed here.

¹It has taken me a good number of years to come to any measure of respect for summer. I was, being May-born, literally an "infant of the spring" and, during the later childhood years, tended, for some reason or other, to rather worship the cold aloofness of winter. The adolescence, admittedly lingering still, brought the traditional passionate commitment to melancholy autumn—and all that. For the longest kind of time I simply thought that *summer* was a mistake.

²In fact, my earliest memory of anything at all is waking up in a darkened room where I had been put to bed for a nap on a summer's afternoon, and feeling very, very hot. I acutely disliked the feeling then and retained the bias for years. I came actively to associate displeasure with most of the usually celebrated natural features and social by-products of the season: the too-grainy texture of sand; the too-cold coldness of the various waters we constantly try to escape into, and the icky-perspiry feeling of bathing caps.

³It also seemed to me, esthetically speaking, that nature had got inexcusably carried away on the summer question and let the whole thing get to be rather much. By duration alone, for instance, a summer's day seemed maddeningly excessive; an utter overstatement. Except for those few hours at either end of it, objects always appeared in too sharp a relief against backgrounds; shadows too pronounced and light too blinding. It always gave me the feeling of walking around in a motion picture which had been too artsily-craftsily exposed. Sound also had a way of coming to the ear without that muting influence, marvelously common to winter, across patios

Reprinted by permission of Robert Nemiroff.

or beaches or through the woods. I suppose I found it too stark and yet too intimate a season.

[4] My childhood Southside summers were the ordinary city kind, full of the street games which other rememberers have turned into fine ballets these days and rhymes that anticipated what some people insist on calling modern poetry:

> Oh, Mary Mack, Mack, Mack
> With the silver buttons, buttons, buttons
> All down her back, back, back
> She asked her mother, mother, mother
> For fifteen cents, cents, cents
> To see the elephant, elephant, elephant
> Jump the fence, fence, fence
> Well, he jumped so high, high, high
> 'Til he touched the sky, sky, sky
> And he didn't come back, back, back
> 'Til the Fourth of Ju-ly, ly, ly!

[5] Evenings were spent mainly on the back porches where screen doors slammed in the darkness with those really very special summertime sounds. And, sometimes, when Chicago nights got too steamy, the whole family got into the car and went to the park and slept out in the open on blankets. Those were, of course, the best times of all because the grownups were invariably reminded of having been children in rural parts of the country and told the best stories then. And it was also cool and sweet to be on the grass and there was usually the scent of freshly cut lemons or melons in the air. And Daddy would lie on his back, as fathers must, and explain about how men thought the stars above us came to be and how far away they were. I never did learn to believe that anything could be as far away as *that*. Especially the stars.

[6] My mother first took us south to visit her Tennessee birthplace one summer when I was seven or eight, I think. I woke up on the back seat of the car while we were still driving through some place called Kentucky and my mother was pointing out to the beautiful hills on both sides of the highway and telling my brothers and my sister about how her father had run away and hidden from his master in those very hills when he was a little boy. She said that his mother had wandered among the wooded slopes in the moonlight

and left food for him in secret places. They were very beautiful hills and I looked out at them for miles and miles after that wondering who and what a *master* might be.

[7] I remember being startled when I first saw my grandmother rocking away on her porch. All my life I had heard that she was a great beauty and no one had ever remarked that they meant a half century before. The woman that I met was as wrinkled as a prune and could hardly hear and barely see and always seemed to be thinking of other times. But she could still rock and talk and even make wonderful cupcakes which were like cornbread, only sweet. She was captivated by automobiles and, even though it was well into the Thirties, I don't think she had ever been in one before we came down and took her driving. She was a little afraid of them and could not seem to negotiate the windows, but she loved driving. She died the next summer and that is all that I remember about her, except that she was born in slavery and had memories of it and they didn't sound anything like *Gone with the Wind*.

[8] Like everyone else, I have spent whole or bits of summers in many different kinds of places since then: camps and resorts in the Middle West and New York State; on an island; in a tiny Mexican village; Cape Cod, perched atop the Truro bluffs at Longnook Beach that Millay wrote about; or simply strolling the streets of Provincetown before the hours when the cocktail parties begin.

[9] And, lastly, I do not think that I will forget days spent, a few summers ago, at a beautiful lodge built right into the rocky cliffs of a bay on the Maine coast. We met a woman there who had lived a purposeful and courageous life and who was then dying of cancer. She had, characteristically, just written a book and taken up painting. She had also been of radical viewpoint all her life: one of those people who energetically believe that the world *can* be changed for the better and spend their lives trying to do just that. And that was the way she thought of cancer; she absolutely refused to award it the stature of tragedy, a devastating instance of the brooding doom and inexplicability of the absurdity of human destiny, etc., etc. The kind of characterization given, lately, as we all know, to far less formidable foes in life than cancer.

[10] But for this remarkable woman it was a matter of nature in imperfection, implying, as always, work for man to do. It was an

enemy, but a palpable one with shape and effect and source; and if it existed, it could be destroyed. She saluted it accordingly, without despondency, but with a lively, beautiful and delightfully ribald anger. There was one thing, she felt, which would prove equal to its relentless ravages and that was the genius of man. Not his mysticism, but man with tubes and slides and the stubborn human notion that the stars are very much within our reach.

[11] The last time I saw her she was sitting surrounded by her paintings with her manuscript laid out for me to read, because, she said, she wanted to know what a *young person* would think of her thinking; one must always keep up with what *young people* thought about things because, after all, they were *change.*

[12] Every now and then her jaw set in anger as we spoke of things people should be angry about. And then, for relief, she would look out at the lovely bay at a mellow sunset settling on the water. Her face softened with love of all that beauty and, watching her, I wished with all my power what I knew that she was wishing: that she might live to see at least one more *summer.* Through her eyes I finally gained the sense of what it might mean; more than the coming autumn with its pretentious melancholy; more than an austere and silent winter which must shut dying people in for precious months; more even than the frivolous spring, too full of too many false promises, would be the gift of another summer with its stark and intimate assertion of neither birth nor death but life at the apex; with the gentlest nights and, above all, the longest days.

[13] I heard later that she did live to see another summer. And I have retained my respect for the noblest of the seasons.

COMMENT

Hansberry begins with a general observation about summer: "For the longest kind of time I simply thought that *summer* was a mistake." She explains why; then, without transition, she mentions a series of experiences associated with summer—childhood experiences in Chicago, a visit to her mother's birthplace in Tennessee and her first meeting with her grandmother, places visited in later years, her acquaintance with a woman dying of cancer. Unexpectedly she has returned to the idea she began with, for the dying woman taught her to look at summer in a new way. The essay seems to be unified only by its subject; we seem to be given a series of disconnected experiences and thoughts associated with summer. But a theme does connect these: happiness, and how we come to discover its meaning and value. We discover happiness at the point of losing something valuable: that is the author's controlling idea. She has moved from superficial reasons for disliking summer to deeper reasons for valuing it.

QUESTIONS FOR STUDY AND DISCUSSION

1. What reasons does Hansberry give for disliking summer? What in the opening section tells us these are superficial reasons that she may later forget or overcome?

2. Could the sections on the summers in Chicago and the visit to Tennessee have been interchanged? Or is there an implied order of ideas?

3. What do the details about the grandmother contribute to the controlling idea of the essay?

4. Later in the essay Hansberry returns to the stars mentioned in the second section. Why does she? How does she return to attitudes introduced in the first section and for what purpose?

5. Hansberry observes the rule of unity—"one thing at a time." How does she do this, at the same time managing to return to earlier experiences and thoughts?

6. What personal qualities does the author reveal about herself through these thoughts about summer?

VOCABULARY STUDY

1. With the help of the dictionary explain the following phrases. Be ready to discuss how much your understanding of the phrase depends on the context—on its use in the sentence or paragraph: *cold aloofness* (paragraph 1); *esthetically speaking, muting influence* (paragraph 3); *negotiate the windows* (paragraph 7); *radical viewpoint, the stature of tragedy, inexplicability of the absurdity of human destiny* (paragraph 9); *without despondency* (paragraph 10); *pretentious melancholy, frivolous spring, life at the apex* (paragraph 12). Notice that some of these phrases are used to represent superficial or pretentious attitudes toward living and dying.

2. The author refers to the poetry of Edna St. Vincent Millay, who lived

in and wrote about New England. Read several of Millay's poems to discover how her language expresses the sounds and sights of New England and perhaps contributed to Hansberry's view of that world.

SUGGESTIONS FOR WRITING

1. Write a series of paragraphs describing experiences associated with a season of the year. Make your final paragraph connect with your first, perhaps showing how your later experiences modified or changed earlier impressions and feelings.

2. Compare Hansberry's thoughts and experiences of summer with your own. You might discuss experiences similar to hers that led to similar or different feelings and thoughts.

3. Discuss what you learned about happiness through a relative or acquaintance who had overcome or was suffering hardship.

BASEBALL

Tom Wicker

Tom Wicker was born in Hamlet, North Carolina, in 1926, and studied journalism at the University of North Carolina, graduating in 1948. He worked as a journalist and editor for several Southern newspapers, including the *Nashville Tennessean,* and began working for the *New York Times* in 1960. He was chief of the *Times* Washington bureau from 1964 to 1968 and has been associate editor since 1968. Recent books of his include *A Time to Die* (1975) and *On Press* (1978).

[1] One hot night in the summer of 1949, I climbed to my usual perch in the cramped press box above the wooden stands of the baseball park in Lumberton, North Carolina. As telegraph editor, general reporter and all-around handyman for the afternoon *Robeson-*

ian of that city, I had appointed myself sports editor, also, and regularly covered the home games of the Lumberton Auctioneers, a farm club of the Chicago Cubs playing in the Class D Tobacco State League. *The Robesonian* paid me not a cent more for spending my summer evenings keeping notes and score, but *The News and Observer* of Raleigh, the state-capital daily, paid me three dollars a game—as I recall it—for filing each night's box score by phone to its sports pages.

² The '49 Auctioneers were undistinguished by anything, including success, except a locally famous first baseman named Turkey Tyson. A stoop-shouldered slap hitter with a reputation for zaniness and getting on base, Tyson derived his nickname from a gobbler-like sound of derision he made when he pulled up at first after one of the frequent singles he poked through opposing infields. The Turkey had played with more minor-league teams than probably exist today and was at the end of the line in Class D; his future was ten seasons behind him and he was old enough to be the father of most of the post-high-school kids he played with and against.

³ One exception—I recall only that his first name was Mike—was a burly, blue-bearded outfielder the Auks (as I labeled them in the headlines over my stories) had obtained somewhere in midseason. He could play ball, or something resembling it, when infrequently sober, had traveled the minor leagues from coast to coast, and although younger than Tyson was also down and about to be out in Class D. (Neither got much closer to the majors than the Game of the Day on radio.) Mike had some difficulty handling the ball, except at the plate; he swung a bat the size of one of the telephone poles that held up the dim lights in the outfield. When he connected he could hit the ball over those lights. More often, he took three mighty swings and hurried back to the bench for a quick swig.

⁴ I had noticed a little something about Mike and that morning in *The Robesonian* had unburdened myself of some inside dope for the avid readers, I liked to imagine. Mike, I told them, was a first-pitch swinger, and the other Tobacco State League clubs were onto him; if he'd lay off that first pitch, I suggested, and wait for *his* pitch, his average would go up and so would the Auks'.

⁵ There was a good crowd on hand that night and in the first inning Turkey Tyson rewarded his fans with his specialty—a ground single about two inches out of reach of a flat-footed second baseman who was probably getting eighty dollars a month and meal

money and might someday make it to the Piedmont League, Class B. *Gobble-gobble* went the Turkey triumphantly from first, and Auks fans cheered. But that was nothing to the roar that went up when barrel-chested Mike, batting cleanup, strode to the plate, thumped his telephone pole twice upon it, then turned his back to the pitcher and pointed that huge bat straight up at the press box and me.

[6] I can only imagine what it was he yelled at me, but I learned one thing—those fans had read my article in *The Robesonian.* That roar told me everyone in the park knew Mike would defy my first-pitch edict. I prayed for the pitcher to throw him the deepest-breaking curve or the fanciest knuckle ball in the history of Abner Doubleday's cow-pasture creation. But somehow I knew, and the crowd knew—as Mike turned back to the plate, hunched over it, waved his war club menacingly, and waggled his rump at the world—exactly what was going to happen.

[7] It did. That pitcher came in with a fast ball that would have bounced off a windowpane. I can still see that mighty swing, hear the crack of the bat connecting, watch the ball soar into outer darkness. As one of the Auks said later, "Mike just disappeared it."

[8] I can still hear that crowd, too, roaring not just for Mike but *at* me, isolated as I was under the single light bulb in my press-box perch. In the open stands down the first- and third-base lines, they stood and pointed upward and howled with glee, as Mike showboated around the bases behind Turkey Tyson and reached the plate again, jumped on it with both feet and bowed low to the press box. Cowering above him in that naked light, I did the only thing I could do; I stood up and bowed, too, and the crowd howled some more. I thought there must be for Mike, in that moment of defiance and triumph, a certain compensation for all those long bus rides through the minor leagues, that long decline of hope and youth down to the smelly locker rooms of Class D. And I *knew* I was never going to make a sportswriter.

[9] And I didn't, although I later did an unavoidable hitch in the sports department of the Winston-Salem *Journal* before I could escape to politics. I don't even see many baseball games these days.

[10] Some idle evenings, I may pick up an inning or two on television, but that's not really baseball on the screen—only part of a reasonable facsimile of the sport I've loved all my life. Maybe I'll get

out to Shea Stadium two or three times a season, but somehow that doesn't seem like the real thing either.

[11] It's not just that the game, at least the way a fan sees it, has changed. It has, but it's not fundamentally different from Turkey Tyson's game, or Babe Ruth's, for that matter. All the old symmetry is there—the innings and outs in their orderly multiples of threes, the foul lines radiating out to the stands, the diamond in its classic dimensions, the exact sixty feet and six inches between the pitching rubber and home plate. The ageless rituals seem never to change— the ball tossed around after an infield out, the coaches waggling and patting their impenetrable signals, the pitcher's sidewise stance with a man on first, the dash and whirl of the pregame infield practice, that solemn conclave of managers and umpires at the plate just before *The Star-Spangled Banner.*

[12] Astroturf, designated hitters, Disneyland scoreboards, salad-bowl stadiums, and Batting Glove Day can't change all that. Nothing seems really to change the game itself: the spectacular individual effort on which it depends; the lack of violence but the sense of menace in the thrown ball, the slashing spikes, the swinging bat; the sudden splendid bursts of action—a runner going from first to third, or even home, on a single, sliding in inches ahead of or behind a perfect peg; the suspense of pitcher vs. hitter in a late-inning rally, with the winning runs on base; all the straight-faced exchanges of "strategy" between managers pulling the same hoary maneuvers John McGraw did, or Connie Mack; the power and the glory of an overwhelming pitcher in his prime; the art and cunning of an experienced pitcher past his prime; the swagger of a big hitter at the plate.

[13] All that is still there for the seeing, even in stadiums like Shea or Chavez Ravine, where the players look like pygmies on a foreign field—even on Astroturf, which senselessly abolishes the clay crescent of the infield, which should be as much a part of the game as knee pants and billed caps.

[14] No, the reason I don't see much baseball today has little to do with the game itself. The problem is that all that's really left is the big leagues and the Little League, and I don't trace back to either. I go back to small-town baseball before television and the suburbs. I loved the game on the vacant lots of childhood, with pickup teams from the neighborhood, someone's dime-store ball coming apart at

the seams, and—in the railroad town where I grew up—sometimes a brake stick for a bat.

[15] Later, in high school and the unending hot summer days of youth, baseball in the dust of skinned infields was life itself to me. Catching for my high-school team, I took a throw from the outfield and put the tag on a runner coming in spikes up, but not before he ripped my thigh open for six inches above the knee. I lay on the ground by the plate while they poured iodine or something on me and it didn't hurt much, because I knew that runner was out and I hadn't ducked away from his spikes. And then I saw my father leaning over me, down from the stands to check on his little boy's wounds, and for the first time in my life I cursed him, told him to go away. I thought I was no kid to be fretted over. That was the spring of '44 and before the year was over one of my teammates was dead in the Battle of the Bulge.

[16] After school was out, we shifted annually to American Legion Junior Baseball, on the same skinned infields, before the same wooden grandstands, in the concession stands of which the ladies of the American Legion Auxiliary sold icy Cokes and peanuts and "bellywashers"—the local name for Royal Crown Cola. The first time I played baseball under lights it was with the Richmond County American Legion Juniors. We played a preseason game in Greensboro, a big city to Richmond County kids, and got stomped; I remember Coach Bill Haltiwanger taking out his fourth pitcher of the night, a rawboned left-hander out of the cotton mills, who had just given up something like five runs after striking out the first batter he faced.

[17] "Well, Lefty," Coach Haltiwanger said, taking the ball from him, "you almost had 'em."

[18] Later on, I tried out for college baseball and got cut the first day of practice. No arm. Even later, I tried to stage a comeback in the Peach Belt League, a semipro circuit in North Carolina, but I didn't last long. Still no arm, and that was a pretty fast league. I remember one elderly Peach Belt pitcher, about Turkey Tyson's vintage, who had been knocking around the semipro and mill-town leagues as long as I'd been living. He had one pitch, a jug-handle curve that came in from the general direction of third base, and he could throw it through a keyhole at about the speed of ice melting. I've seen husky young men who could have broken him in two break their backs instead, trying to hit that jug-handle. He would stand

out there and spit tobacco juice, not infrequently on the ball, and throw it past them for nine innings, or as long as the game went on. And I'd have sold my soul just to be able to throw out a runner at second maybe once or twice a game.

[19] We were not, of course, unaware in those days of the major leagues, although we got a lot more news about the Charlotte Hornets of the Piedmont League, a Washington Senators farm club. I pored daily over the box scores from the big leagues, particularly the Dodgers and the Giants, and never missed a Game of the Day if I could help it. Other forms of life stopped during the World Series, while people huddled at the radio. In the main, however, the big leagues were far away and second fiddle to the American Legion Juniors—although I had seen a major-league game from the bleachers of old Griffith Stadium once when my family made a tourist trip to Washington. Dutch Leonard pitched and a good ole Georgia boy, Cecil Travis, got a couple of hits. Most of life has been downhill since that day.

[20] So baseball for a lot of people is the memory of Joe DiMaggio in center field, or the Gashouse Gang, or Lou Gehrig's farewell to Yankee Stadium, or all those Dodger-Yankee Series of the Fifties (those magic names! Gionfriddo, Podres, Mantle, the Duke, Berra, Robinson, Campanella, Ford). I remember all that, too. I remember Bobby Thomson's home run, and the first televised Series I saw— Durocher's Giants swept Cleveland. I remember Don Larsen's perfect game and Ernie Lombardi's swoon and I have a dim memory of my father boasting about somebody he called the Goose—Goslin, of course, of the Senators. I hit Hubbell's screwball in my dreams.

[21] But all that is secondhand to me, baseball once removed, the perfect baseball I never really saw or knew. Maybe it's age, maybe it's change, maybe it's wounds deeper than the one that left the scar I still bear on my thigh; but baseball to *me* is the skinned infield of my youth, the wooden grandstands, the despair of being washed up with no arm at age twenty-one, the recollection of a fast-ball pitcher who was throwing it past me until I choked the bat, stepped forward in the box and put it almost down his throat, just over second for a single. Baseball to me is the remembered taste of an ice-cold belly-washer sneaked between innings, against all rules. The railroad embankment was just beyond right field and the trains went by, whistling us on. It was always summer, and this season we were solid up the middle, we could win it all.

²² I like to think that thirty years ago baseball in America was something we had to hold on to, to hold us together—solid, changeless, universal, at one and the same time peculiarly *ours* and yet part of the great world beyond us. You pulled off the double play the same way for the Richmond County Juniors, the Auks or the White Sox. When I was in the press box in Lumberton or dying with shame when they stole second on me five times in Carthage, baseball was a common denominator; it had rules, symmetry, a beginning and an end, it challenged and rewarded, you could play or watch, it was the same one day as the next, in one town as in another.

²³ But now the minor leagues and the semipros and country baseball are all but gone, and in the suburbs they put kids of ten and twelve in expensive Little League uniforms to play on perfectly proportioned fields and in the smaller cities the old lopsided parks have been torn down for housing developments and shopping centers. If anything holds us together now, our hometown teams playing in surrounding leagues, those leagues part of the widening circle of all the leagues—if anything holds us together that way now, it isn't baseball, concentrated as it is in the major leagues, the Chavez Ravines of this amortized world, concerned as it is with tax shelters and reserve clauses and player strikes and antitrust, relying as it does on Bat Days and boom-boom superstars with salaries triple their batting averages. It isn't baseball that holds us together in 1976—not baseball in the Astrodome, on artificial grass, foreshortened by television, enlivened by organ music and computerized scoreboards that can simulate fireworks and joy.

²⁴ The game may be the same, but it's been taken away from the country and the towns and given to the accountants and the TV producers and the high rollers. Turkey Tyson and Mike, the home-run hitter of the Auks, couldn't find a place to play today. Class D doesn't exist. To me, Shea Stadium is a poor substitute.

COMMENT

In the course of the essay Wicker talks about his childhood and high school baseball experiences, his experiences in college and as a newspaperman, and those in later years, the changes in baseball, and the meaning of these changes for American life. But he does not talk about these topics in this order. Because he is writing to an audience unfamiliar with his world, he begins with what happened on a hot night in 1949.

This extended episode not only immerses the reader in the actions and feelings of a different world, but also introduces the personality and feelings of the author. Thus we discover what baseball was like through people like Turkey Tyson and Mike. So thorough is the detail that Wicker is able to make a brief comment about the changes in baseball (paragraphs 11 and 12), then turn to a short account of his earlier and later experiences. These later paragraphs lead to a review of these experiences and, finally, a longer comment on these changes. The order of ideas is determined by Wicker's assumptions about his readers and by the guiding purpose of clear exposition. The essay is unified through its thesis and also its order of ideas—an order determined by what the reader needs to know in order to understand what follows.

QUESTIONS FOR STUDY AND DISCUSSION

1. How do the episode on the hot night in 1949 and the personality and actions of Tyson and Mike suggest the qualities of baseball as Wicker knew it and characterizes it later in the essay?

2. Does Wicker single out one essential change that came about, or is he concerned with many changes that together changed baseball?

3. Consider paragraphs 22–24 carefully. Is Wicker saying—and does he show—that the rules and "symmetry" of baseball have changed? What does he mean by "symmetry"?

4. Does Wicker consider the change in baseball typical of changes in American life? Is he commenting on American life generally? If you agree, do you think that his criticism of baseball today is also true of other sports?

5. Wicker informs us of unfamiliar details and experiences. What details and experiences does he assume we will understand or recognize?

6. Does Wicker want merely to inform us of his experiences and ideas, or is he trying also to persuade us of these ideas?

VOCABULARY STUDY

1. Consult your dictionary and also a dictionary of American slang, in the reference section of your library, on the meaning and currency of the following: *slap hitter, inside dope, batting cleanup, knuckle ball, billed caps, screwball.*

2. Discuss what images—visual or auditory—the following words and

phrases create: *zaniness, gobbler-like sound, thumped his telephone pole, showboated around the bases, the dust of skinned infields, jug-handle curve.*

SUGGESTIONS FOR WRITING

1. Discuss the changes you have witnessed in a favorite sport. In the course of your discussion, suggest an explanation and relate it to the changes you are describing.

2. Describe in detail an experience in playing a sport, or watching one. Use these details to make a point about the sport. Explain features of the sport that may be unfamiliar to the general reader of your essay.

3. The *setting* of the experience that Wicker describes is important to our understanding of his feelings. Explain what the setting contributes to this understanding.

4. Describe an unusual person that you associate with an experience in your life like Wicker's. Give enough details about this person so that your reader can see and know him or her as you did.

transitions

Formal connectives, or *transitions,* are often necessary to clarify the relation of ideas when natural transitions such as pronoun reference are absent or insufficient. If the steps of a process are presented chronologically and each requires much detail, we may introduce the words *first, second,* and *third* to keep the steps distinct. We may have to add *less important, just as important, more important* to show that the ideas are being presented in the order of their importance. The connectives *specifically* and *generally* show that we are proceeding from the specific to the general; *least of all* and *most of all,* from the least to the most frequent or common. Connectives like *thus, therefore, however, moreover,* and *furthermore* are sometimes used to show the logical relation of ideas. *Thus* and *therefore* show that the second idea is the consequence of the first, or that certain conclusions may be drawn from the evidence. *However* shows that the second idea qualifies the first or contradicts it. *Moreover* and *furthermore* show that something additional is to be said. Where connections can be shown through pronoun reference and sentence parallelism, formal transitions are best used sparingly to avoid too formal an effect or tone.

THE PLAYGROUND

John Updike

John Updike was born in Shillington, Pennsylvania, in 1932, and graduated from Harvard in 1954. He attended the Ruskin School of Drawing and Fine Art in Oxford, England, and later began writing for *The New Yorker,* where his sketches and stories have appeared regularly ever since. His novels include *The Poorhouse Fair* (1959), *The Centaur* (1963), *Rabbit, Run* (1964), *Couples* (1968), and *The Coup* (1978).

[1] The periphery I have traced; the center of my boyhood held a calm collection of kind places that are almost impossible to describe, because they are so fundamental to me, they enclosed so many of my hours, that they have the neutral color of my own soul, which I have always imagined as a pale oblong just under my ribs. In the town where I now live, and where I am writing this, seagulls weep overhead on a rainy day. No seagulls found their way inland to Shillington; there were sparrows, and starlings, and cowbirds, and robins, and occasionally a buzzard floating high overhead on immobile wings like a kite on a string too high to be seen.

[2] The playground: up from the hardball diamond, on a plateau bounded on three sides by cornfields, a pavilion contained some tables and a shed for equipment. I spent my summer weekdays there from the age when I was so small that the dust stirred by the feet of roof-ball players got into my eyes. Roof ball was the favorite game. It was played with a red rubber ball smaller than a basketball. The object was to hit it back up on the roof of the pavilion, the whole line of children in succession. Those who failed dropped out. When there was just one person left, a new game began with the cry *Noo*-oo *gay*-ame," and we lined up in the order in which we had gone out, so that the lines began with the strongest and tallest and ended with the weakest and youngest. But there was never any doubt that everybody could play; it was perfect democracy. Often the line contained as many as thirty pairs of legs, arranged chronologically. By the

time we moved away, I had become a regular front-runner; I knew how to flick the ball to give it spin, how to leap up and send the ball skimming the length of the roof edge, how to plump it with my knuckles when there was a high bounce. Somehow the game never palled. The sight of the ball bouncing along the tarpaper of the foreshortened roof was always important. Many days I was at the playground from nine o'clock, when they ran up the American flag, until four, when they called the equipment in, and played nothing else.

[3] If you hit the ball too hard, and it went over the peak of the roof, you were out, and you had to retrieve the ball, going down a steep bank into a field where the poorhouse men had stopped planting corn because it all got mashed down. If the person ahead of you hit the ball into the air without touching the roof, or missed it entirely, you had the option of "saving," by hitting the ball onto the roof before it struck the ground; this created complex opportunities for strategy and gallantry. I would always try to save the Nightingale, for instance, and there was a girl who came from Louisiana with a French name whom everybody wanted to save.* At twelve, she seemed already mature, and I can remember standing with a pack of other boys under the swings looking up at the undersides of her long tense dark-skinned legs as she kicked into the air to give herself more height, the tendons on the underside of her smooth knees jumping, her sneakered feet pointing like a ballerina's shoes.

[4] The walls of the pavilion shed were scribbled all over with dirty drawings and words and detailed slanders on the prettier girls. After hours, when the supervisors were gone, if you were tall enough you could grab hold of a crossbeam and get on top of the shed, where there was an intimate wedge of space under the slanting roof; here no adult ever bothered to scrub away the pencillings, and the wood fairly breathed of the forbidden. The very silence of the pavilion, after the daylong click of checkers and *pokabok* of ping-pong, was like a love-choked hush.

[5] Reality seemed more intense at the playground. There was a dust, a daring. It was a children's world; nowhere else did we gather in such numbers with so few adults over us. The playground occupied a platform of earth; we were exposed, it seems now, to the sun and sky. Looking up, one might see a buzzard or witness a portent.

---

*The Nightingale is a reference to one of the three groups in Updike's school music class—Nightingales, Robins, and Crows. Ed.

COMMENT

Updike has been describing the scenes and experiences of his childhood. In this section of his memoir, he makes his transition through a direct reference to the previous section: "The periphery I have traced." At the start of paragraph 2 he makes a transition through a short phrase: "The playground." Updike depends on key words like "playground" and "pavilion," and on personal reference. He also depends on parallel structure as a means of transition in the paragraph: "If you hit the ball too hard," "If the person ahead of you hit the ball into the air." Punctuation can be a means of transition: the colon shows that what follows is an explanation or amplification of what precedes, as in this sentence. One use of the semicolon is to join closely related details and ideas; this, too, is a kind of transition. Semicolons are more common in long paragraphs than in short ones that contain one or two ideas and few or no details. Updike uses the semicolon to connect closely related ideas: "But there was never any doubt that everybody could play; it was perfect democracy."

QUESTIONS FOR STUDY AND DISCUSSION

1. Where else in the essay does Updike use semicolons to join closely related ideas? What use does he make of the colon in paragraph 2?

2. How many formal transitions do you find in the essay? Where does Updike make transitions through reference to details or ideas of the preceding paragraph?

3. Updike evokes the playground through a few carefully chosen details—details evoked by the adult remembering his childhood. How different would these details be if Updike were showing the playground as the child sees it?

4. Does the essay have a controlling idea, or has Updike presented a series of random impressions?

5. Does Updike explain why the playground was a "more intense" reality? Is the answer merely that games are often intense?

6. What exactly were the special interests or appeals of "roof ball," and how does Updike illustrate these?

VOCABULARY STUDY

1. Many words have a wide range of meanings. This range is limited by the context of the word—by its use in a particular sentence or pas-

sage. State the general meaning of the italicized words in the following sentences. Then write a sentence of your own for each word, using it in the sense that Updike uses it:

a. "The *center* of my boyhood held a *calm* collection of *kind* places that are almost impossible to describe...."

b. "But there was never any doubt that everybody could play; it was perfect *democracy*."

c. "The playground occupied a *platform* of earth; we were exposed, it seems now, to the sun and sky."

d. "Somehow the game never *palled*."

2. Though he uses adjectives to help describe the games of the playground, Updike depends on exact details. Show how words like *skimming* and *bouncing* contribute to the exactness of the description.

SUGGESTIONS FOR WRITING

1. Develop the following statement from your own childhood experiences: "Reality seemed more intense at the playground."

2. Updike describes a childhood world in which adults are absent. Describe two childhood worlds from your own experience—one in which adults were absent from the play of children, and one in which they were present. Discuss the differences that emerge in your description—in the quality of the play, the feelings of the children, and the meaning of the games to them.

THE GO-ALONG ONES

Mari Sandoz

The American novelist and historian Mari Sandoz (1901–66) was born and raised in Sheridan County, Nebraska, and attended the University of Nebraska. Her novel, *Old Jules*, concerns her father and the Nebraska of her childhood. She wrote much about American Indian life and the American West. The essay printed here is both a personal account of her first experiences with the Sioux Indians and an informative discussion of their view of the world and one particular set of customs.

[1]The first Indian that I remember was far back in my child-hood, soon after I learned to walk. I was very shy with people but apparently I had the toddler's daring and fondness for exploration. I liked to slip back to something I had been shown, perhaps a bird's nest in a thistle or the first brush roses. This day it was the wild plum thicket down the slope, with the fruit ripe and sweet, that tolled me from my grandmother's side. I recall some uneasiness about the wasps buzzing over the rotting fruit on the ground. Then something startled me—a face peering through the fall leaves. It was a brown face with dark eyes, and although there were braids like my grandmother's, and no such beard as my father wore, I knew this was a man.

[2]The face was down at my level, the murmuring sounds of the man friendly and laughing, the hands reaching for me with no anger in them. I felt shy but I let myself be drawn out of the thicket, lifted high up on the man's shoulder, and given a braid for each hand, like reins. Then the man made the "Tchlch" sound that started horses, and prancing a little, but gently, he went up the slope toward our house, where there were more of these brown-faced people, a whole confusion of them, as I recall now—men, women with babies, some as large as I, on their backs, and many boys and girls running everywhere. Suddenly I became shy again, perhaps of all the people, and was clutching the man about the head with my arms so that everybody laughed. But my plump little old-country grandmother hurried up, as excited and alarmed as if I were being scalped. The man stooped so she could reach me. I cried, I am told, with fright, but as I was often reminded later, my fingers had to be pried out of the man's strong black braids—a little towheaded white girl clinging shamelessly to the hair of a bloodthirsty Sioux who had helped annihilate General Custer.

[3]Later I discovered that Bad Arm, as the man was called because real names of Indians were seldom spoken, had received his lumpy elbow from an injury in the fight on the Little Big Horn with Crazy Horse. In 1890 at Wounded Knee, South Dakota, Custer's Seventh Cavalry got its revenge. Bad Arm had to see his wife and

From *These Were the Sioux,* copyright © 1961 by Mari Sandoz. Reprinted by permission of Hastings House, Publishers.

children shot down by the Hotchkiss guns after he had surrendered his old pistol.

⁴ Yet somehow this man could still be so gentle and playful with a small girl of the whites. Later I saw much of this amused and playful way of the Sioux with small children as the Indians came and went from their old camping ground near our house. They liked to return to the place that they said was already smooth and warm from long living when the tribe first reached the Niobrara country almost two hundred years before. They liked to visit our father, too. He had hunted deer with them before the settlers came. He still repaired their guns, gave them salves to heal the many sores that came with the starvation diet of the reservation and he made silver-nitrate solution for their trachomatous eyes.

⁵ These old buffalo-hunting Sioux of my early childhood spoke very little English and I knew only the German-Swiss dialect of my grandmother. But young children learn the rudiments of sign talk more quickly than any spoken language, perhaps because it usually tells a story and is so descriptive, so amusing. The extended right hand held before the chest, palm inward, and moved to the left in a sinuous path was the simplified sign for *fish;* with only the index finger extended, like an inquiring head pushed forward, the curving motions made larger, it was a snake. To tell of the hunts the partly closed hands might be brought up to each side of the head and tilted forward a little, like curved horns, for *buffalo.* This, preceded by the thumb pointing back to the sign talker himself, and followed by the nearly closed right hand brought downward from the shoulder in the swift gesture of destruction said, all together, "I buffalo killed." Fingers held up added their numerical information: "I two buffalo killed," and so on.

⁶ The Indians made names for us children in their teasing way. Because our very busy mother kept my hair cut short, like my brothers', they called me Short Furred One, pointing to their hair and making the sign for short, the right hand with fingers pressed close together, held upward, back out, at the height intended. With me this was about two feet tall, the Indians laughing gently at my abashed face. I am told that I was given a pair of small moccasins that first time, to clear up my unhappiness at being picked out from the dusk behind the fire and my two unhappy shortcomings made conspicuous.

⁷ When I was about five or six I saw another kind of medicine,

a bit of magical Sioux rite. I was very much afraid of electrical storms, perhaps because our father, despite his training in science and his acknowledged fearlessness before a grizzly bear or a hired gunman, was terrified of lightning. In the violent summer storms of the Great Plains he ordered everybody under the feather ticks, considered lightning proof.

[8] One Sunday I sneaked away to watch the Indians spill out of several wagons and hurry to throw up their old canvas tipis before the great piling thunderhead that bent over us broke into rain from that flashing and roar. At an earth-shaking bolt of lightning and a shout from the house I turned to run home, but I was stopped by the sight of an old Indian coming out of one of the tipis walking on his moccasined hands, his bare toes gesturing in the air like blunt, appealing fingers above odd noises that seemed words spoken backward. Slowly he circled on the worn campground as though in stately ceremonial march while some of the Indians laughed and sang to him. Everything about the man seemed upside down and backward; even what had looked like his face was a mask of some sort, with the big nose pointing in the opposite direction from his toes. I think I laughed, too, my fear forgotten until I was yanked away by the collar of my dress and whipped soundly for disobedience.

[9] By the time I finished my short crying, the dry storm was gone, blown away. The Indian women had their blackened coffeepot on the fire for the man who, I discovered years later, was a *heyoka,* a Contrary. He was one of those who had dreamed of thunder in his puberty fasting and to avoid this threat of lightning for himself, and for those about him, he must do all things in an unexpected, backward and foolish way, like the walking upside down, with the false face behind. The *heyoka* often dipped his supper out of the boiling kettle with his bare hands (perhaps coated with a secret preparation from resinous plants) and rode his horse facing the tail, his bow or gun drawn against himself. And if a man giving himself pompous airs around the camp or village should hear laughing behind him he could guess that a Contrary was there, imitating him, but in reverse, turning all the sweetness of the man's self-importance to sand in the teeth.

[10] The Contrary not only tried to protect himself and those around him from lightning and other storm damage with his foolishness, he entertained the people as a clown entertains. With his

antics he lifted the hearts that were on the ground, perhaps from some great dying brought by the white man's diseases or in the sorrow of another great loss, as when many were killed in a buffalo stampede or in warring, and when the homes of the people, their beloved hunting grounds, were taken away. This double purpose of the Contrary's dream seems typically Sioux. To them all the destructive aspects of nature were matched by the good, the wholesome, the creative. Storms that scattered the camps, drowned the people and the earth's creatures, or froze them, also made the grasses grow, the buffalo fat, the people full and contented. The lightning that might kill a whole war party or a dozen people from a traveling village on a high ridge somewhere could also reveal enemies skulking in the night and save the camp. Since the reservation days there was danger from lightning in the wagons with iron tires. But the Contraries worked hard, and through their antics brought a feeling of safety, with a little laughter and gaiety even in these defeated times. And when the storm clouds broke away, there was sometimes a rainbow, and a cool, peaceful evening time, and songs and drumming around the night fires.

[11] The old Contrary, with his dancing in the thunderstorm, had lifted my frightened heart, too, yet although I think I grasped some of the meaning of his actions as I grew older, I was afraid of lightning until I was sixteen. That summer, while foolishly riding horseback between telephone lines in a dry electrical storm, an earthshaking violet bolt jumped from the high wires to my arm and down the reins to the horse's withers, burning a narrow strip down the foreleg to the ground. My left arm was numb and paralyzed for a day or so, but it recovered. Curiously, all my fear of lightning went in that one flash, almost as though the stupid ride between telephone lines had been my *heyoka* dance. One could wish that the special wisdom of the Contraries came as easily.

COMMENT

The more ideas contained in a paragraph, the more dependent a writer . is on transitions to focus the reader's attention. Sandoz achieves this focus through her opening words and phrases, as in the opening sentences of paragraph 2. The first sentence—"The face was down at my level . . ."—refers to the final sentence of paragraph 1: "Then something startled me—a *face* peering through the fall leaves. It was a brown *face* with dark eyes. . . ." Each succeeding sentence in paragraph 2 focuses attention simply and effectively:

> *Then* the man made the "Tchlch" sound that started horses . . .
> *Suddenly* I became shy again . . .
> *But* my plump little old-country grandmother hurried up. . . .

The initial position in sentences is one of prominence and therefore one of effective transition. The opening sentences of the succeeding paragraphs perform the same function—stating time relationships and focusing the subject of the paragraph. These transitions are used unobtrusively; they do not call attention to themselves.

QUESTIONS FOR STUDY AND DISCUSSION

1. How many other opening sentences in later paragraphs of the essay refer to immediately preceding ideas? How many sentences in paragraphs 4 and 5 make the same kind of transition—to a word or phrase in the preceding sentence?

2. What words in paragraph 8 express transitional ideas? How diverse are the ideas or experiences dealt with in this paragraph?

3. What is the order of ideas in the essay? Does Sandoz state her thesis directly? What do you think is her purpose in writing about the Sioux?

4. What is Sandoz saying or implying about the Sioux way of life, in contrast to that of the white American?

VOCABULARY STUDY

Compare the dictionary meaning of the italicized word with that of the word following it in brackets. Then write an explanation of how the bracketed word changes the meaning:

   a. Then something startled me—a face *peering* [staring] through the fall leaves.

   b. I cried, I am told, with fright, but as I was often reminded later, my fingers had to be *pried* [loosened] out of the man's strong black braids—a little towheaded white girl *clinging* [holding] shamelessly to the hair of a bloodthirsty Sioux who had helped *annihilate* [kill] General Custer.

   c. And if a man giving himself *pompous* [stately] airs around the camp or village should hear laughing behind him he could guess that a Contrary was there, imitating him, but in reverse. . . .

d. With his *antics* [gestures] he lifted the hearts that were on the ground. . . .

SUGGESTIONS FOR WRITING

1. Discuss a series of experiences that changed your ideas about people of a different race or religion. Decide on the order in which you present these experiences before you begin writing. State your thesis in the opening paragraph of your essay, or build to a statement of it in your concluding paragraph.

2. Sandoz writes that, to the Sioux, "all the destructive aspects of nature were matched by the good, the wholesome, the creative." Discuss what attitudes toward nature people in your world share. Consider what their feelings are about heavy rains or snowfalls.

3. Discuss what the *heyoka* shows about the values of the Sioux. Contrast these values with those of your world.

climax

In a sentence like the following the ideas are presented in the order of importance—the order of *climax:*

> The rudder might have been gone for all he knew, the fires out, the engines broken down, the ship ready to roll over like a corpse.—Joseph Conrad, *Typhoon*

Presenting ideas so that a less important idea follows an obviously more important one creates anticlimax:

> Convicted of murder at twenty, he had been arrested for jaywalking at fifteen.

Ideas do not always establish their relative importance so naturally. Indeed, we would not find Conrad's sentence strange if he had written:

> The ship was ready to roll over like a corpse, the rudder gone, the fires out, the engines broken down.

As in the following sentence, the writer may stress the weight of ideas through intensifiers:

> A furious gale attacks him like a personal enemy, tries to grasp his limbs, fastens upon his mind, seeks to rout his *very* spirit out of him.—Conrad, *Typhoon*

The same principle can apply to a paragraph or a whole essay. It is, of course, possible to arrange ideas in the order of importance without conveying a marked sense of climax. How much climax is conveyed depends on the force of the statements and the vividness of the details. The following paragraph describes Bushmen of the Kalahari Desert in southern Africa. The details build in importance to the final climactic idea:

The game was intoxicating. The boys danced so fast, so perfectly, and made their rhythm so vigorous and free, that Gai, who had been sitting quietly listening to Ukwane, could stand it no longer. Throwing his great cape around himself, he suddenly leaped to his feet and sprang among the little boys, scattering them like a hawk among sparrows, towering over their heads as he began to dance. He stamped, bent, straightened, and swung his long leg over the little boys' backs, dancing with far more abandon, not as precisely as they, but madly; he took our breath away.—Elizabeth Marshall Thomas, *The Harmless People*

TWO ESSAYS ON THE SEASONS

Hal Borland

"I am a fortunate man," wrote the American journalist and poet Hal Borland (1900–78). "I grew up on a frontier, escaped early success, had things to say when I matured. I have been able to make a living at work I wanted to do, to write what I believed and find an audience." Born in Sterling, Nebraska, Borland attended the University of Colorado, and afterward worked as a reporter and editor. For many years he was the outdoor editorial essayist for the *New York Times* and a columnist for other newspapers, receiving numerous awards for his journalism and conservation efforts. His books include *Country Editor's Boy* (1970), *Borland Country* (1971).

Big Thaw

February 21

[1] A big thaw, whether it marks the end of winter or only a break, has the drama of eons in it. One day the land lies white and silent under ice and snow; then a warm wind comes. Temperatures climb. The ice grip relaxes. Water, the concerted melt of all the hill-

sides, begins to flow. You hear it. You see it in a mist over the thinning snow. You feel it soggy underfoot. And you know you are witnessing, on a minor scale, what happened when the glaciers began to melt back. One Winter's ice age is beginning to go.

[2] A day passes, and a night, and great bare patches show in the pasture. The rocks on the hillside are in sight, black and wet, centers of warmth. Fence posts stand in deepening hollows in the snow. Beneath the ice in the gully you can hear the brook begin to talk; and if you follow the brook you will see it open to the sky in a few places, where it has eaten away the ice. Rivulets from the whole hillside have concentrated to clear the brook's channel. They talk in many voices.

[3] Another night of warmth and the hollows have become ponds. The brook leaps, now, its channel clear, and the big river comes to life. The ice in it begins to move, to break into floes and shards. Thus rivers came to life when the great ice sheets began to recede. The pasture shows faint green at the grass roots along the brook. The hillsides, by afternoon, are bare of snow.

[4] You watch the river and listen to the brook and feel the softness of the sodden earth with its icy solidity untouched a few inches down. But you forget the deeper ice and look at the trees, expecting to find fat buds. Expecting to see flocks of Spring birds, you look for fresh miracles, as if the big melt itself were not miracle enough.

The Urgency

June 24

[1] If man is ever going to admit that he belongs to the earth, not the other way round, it probably will be in late June. Then it is that life surpasses man's affairs with incredible urgency and outreaches him in every direction. Even the farmer, on whom we all depend for the substance of existence, knows then that the best he can do is cooperate with wind and weather, soil and seed. The incalculable energy of chlorophyll, the green leaf itself, dominates the earth, and the root in the soil is the inescapable fact. Even the roadside weed ignores man's legislation.

[2] The urgency is everywhere. Grass blankets the earth, reaching for the sun, spreads its roots, flowers and comes to seed. The

forest widens its canopy, strengthens its boles, nurtures its seedlings, ripens its perpetuating nuts. The birds nest and hatch their
fledglings. The beetle and the bee are busy at the grassroot and the
blossom, and the butterfly lays eggs that will hatch and crawl and
eat and pupate and take to the air once more. Fish spawn and
meadow voles harvest the wild meadows, and owls and foxes feed
their young. Dragonflies and swallows and nighthawks seine the air
where the minute winged creatures flit out their minute life spans.

[3] And man, who glibly calls the earth his own, neither powers
the leaf nor energizes the fragile wing. Man participates, but his
dominance is limited. It is the urgency of life, of growth, that rules.
Late June and early Summer are the ultimate, unarguable proof.

COMMENT

Both of Borland's essays build to a climax, but with a difference. "The
Urgency" builds to the climactic final paragraph, in which the idea is
given greater importance than what has gone before. The effect is promoted by the short emphatic sentences that contrast with the longer ones
of paragraph 2. Borland depends also on transitional words (in paragraphs 1 and 3) that create a sense of rising importance in ideas. "Big
Thaw," by contrast, presents details that suggest their own relative importance: "Another night of warmth and the hollows have become ponds.
The brook leaps, now, its channel clear, and the big river comes to life."
The whole essay builds to a climax through most of its sentences: the
thaw leads to the melting of the river, and Borland tells us that there are
even greater miracles to come.

QUESTIONS FOR STUDY AND DISCUSSION

1. What transitional words in paragraphs 1 and 3 of "The Urgency"
   indicate the greater importance of ideas?

2. What use does Borland make of short sentences in "Big Thaw" to
   create a sense of climax?

3. Which paragraphs in "Big Thaw" individually build to a climax?
   What do they contribute to the sense of climax in the whole essay?
   How does "The Urgency" build to a climax?

4. What view of nature and life do these essays express? What does this
   view suggest about Borland's values and personality?

VOCABULARY STUDY

1. Locate words in the two essays that intensify the experience—that express urgency or the potential energy of nature.

2. Explain the italicized words. Is the word used literally or metaphorically?
   a. Even the roadside weed ignores man's *legislation.*
   b. The forest widens its *canopy,* strengthens its *boles,* nurtures its seedlings, ripens its *perpetuating* nuts.
   c. The birds nest and hatch their *fledglings.*
   d. Fish spawn and meadow voles *harvest* the wild meadows. . . .
   e. Dragonflies and swallows and nighthawks *seine* the air. . . .
   f. A big thaw . . . has the drama of *eons* in it.
   g. The ice in it begins to move, to break into *floes* and *shards.*
   h. You watch the river and listen to the brook and feel the softness of the *sodden* earth with its icy *solidity* untouched a few inches down.

SUGGESTIONS FOR WRITING

1. Describe a day in your life, as Borland has done, building the events and feelings you experience to a climax. Build one of your paragraphs in the order of climax as Borland does in "Big Thaw."

2. Borland writes: "And man, who glibly calls the earth his own, neither powers the leaf nor energizes the fragile wing. Man participates, but his dominance is limited." Describe an experience that made you realize how small or helpless a person can be, under the assault of a violent storm or similar experience in nature.

THE DECLINE OF SPORT
(A Preposterous Parable)

E. B. White

E. B. White, the distinguished essayist, humorist, and editor, was born in Mount Vernon, New York, in 1899. He has long been associated with *The New Yorker* as writer and editor and has also written for *Harper's Magazine* and other publications. His books include *Charlotte's Web* (1952) and *Stuart Little* (1945), both for children, and *One Man's Meat* (1943), *The Second Tree from the Corner* (1954), and *The Points of My Compass* (1962), collections of his essays.

[1] In the third decade of the supersonic age, sport gripped the nation in an ever-tightening grip. The horse tracks, the ballparks, the fight rings, the gridirons, all drew crowds in steadily increasing numbers. Every time a game was played, an attendance record was broken. Usually some other sort of record was broken, too—such as the record for the number of consecutive doubles hit by left-handed batters in a Series game, or some such thing as that. Records fell like ripe apples on a windy day. Customs and manners changed, and the five-day business week was reduced to four days, then to three, to give everyone a better chance to memorize the scores.

[2] Not only did sport proliferate but the demands it made on the spectator became greater. Nobody was content to take in one event at a time, and thanks to the magic of radio and television nobody had to. A Yale alumnus, class of 1962, returning to the Bowl with 197,000 others to see the Yale-Cornell football game would take along his pocket radio and pick up the Yankee Stadium, so that while his eye might be following a fumble on the Cornell twenty-two-yard line, his ear would be following a man going down to second in the top of the fifth, seventy miles away. High in the blue sky above the Bowl, skywriters would be at work writing the scores of other major and minor sporting contests, weaving an interminable record of victory and defeat, and using the new high-visibility pink news-smoke perfected by Pepsi-Cola engineers. And in the frames of the giant video sets, just behind the goalposts, this same alumnus could watch Dejected win the Futurity before a record-breaking crowd of 349,872 at Belmont, each of whom was tuned to the Yale Bowl and following the World Series game in the video and searching the sky for further news of events either under way or just completed. The effect of this vast cyclorama of sport was to divide the spectator's attention, over-subtilize his appreciation, and deaden his passion. As the fourth supersonic decade was ushered in, the picture changed and sport began to wane.

[3] A good many factors contributed to the decline of sport. Sub-

stitutions in football had increased to such an extent that there were very few fans in the United States capable of holding the players in mind during play. Each play that was called saw two entirely new elevens lined up, and the players whose names and faces you had familiarized yourself with in the first period were seldom seen or heard of again. The spectacle became as diffuse as the main concourse in Grand Central at the commuting hour.

[4]Express motor highways leading to the parks and stadia had become so wide, so unobstructed, so devoid of all life except automobiles and trees that sport fans had got into the habit of travelling enormous distances to attend events. The normal driving speed had been stepped up to ninety-five miles an hour, and the distance between cars had been decreased to fifteen feet. This put an extraordinary strain on the sport lover's nervous system, and he arrived home from a Saturday game, after a road trip of three hundred and fifty miles, glassy-eyed, dazed, and spent. He hadn't really had any relaxation and he had failed to see Czlika (who had gone in for Trusky) take the pass from Bkeeo (who had gone in for Bjallo) in the third period, because at that moment a youngster named Lavagetto had been put in to pinch-hit for Art Gurlack in the bottom of the ninth with the tying run on second, and the skywriter who was attempting to write "Princeton 0–Lafayette 43" had banked the wrong way, muffed the "3," and distracted everyone's attention from the fact that Lavagetto had been whiffed.

[5]Cheering, of course, lost its stimulating effect on players, because cheers were no longer associated necessarily with the immediate scene but might as easily apply to something that was happening somewhere else. This was enough to infuriate even the steadiest performer. A football star, hearing the stands break into a roar before the ball was snapped, would realize that their minds were not on him, and would become dispirited and grumpy. Two or three of the big coaches worried so about this that they considered equipping all players with tiny ear sets, so that they, too, could keep abreast of other sporting events while playing, but the idea was abandoned as impractical, and the coaches put it aside in tickler files, to bring up again later.

[6]I think the event that marked the turning point in sport and started it downhill was the Midwest's classic Dust Bowl game of 1975, when Eastern Reserve's great right end, Ed Pistachio, was shot by a spectator. This man, the one who did the shooting, was seated well down in the stands near the forty-yard line on a bleak

October afternoon and was so saturated with sport and with the disappointments of sport that he had clearly become deranged. With a
minute and fifteen seconds to play and the score tied, the Eastern
Reserve quarterback had whipped a long pass over Army's heads
into Pistachio's waiting arms. There was no other player anywhere
near him, and all Pistachio had to do was catch the ball and run it
across the line. He dropped it. At exactly this moment, the spectator—a man named Homer T. Parkinson, of 35 Edgemere Drive,
Toledo, O.—suffered at least three other major disappointments in
the realm of sport. His horse, Hiccough, on which he had a five-
hundred-dollar bet, fell while getting away from the starting gate
at Pimlico and broke his leg (clearly visible in the video); his favorite shortstop, Lucky Frimstitch, struck out and let three men die on
base in the final game of the Series (to which Parkinson was tuned);
and the Governor Dummer soccer team, on which Parkinson's
youngest son played goalie, lost to Kent, 4–3, as recorded in the sky
overhead. Before anyone could stop him, he drew a gun and drilled
Pistachio, before 954,000 persons, the largest crowd that had ever
attended a football game and the *second*-largest crowd that had ever
assembled for any sporting event in any month except July.

[7]This tragedy, by itself, wouldn't have caused sport to decline,
I suppose, but it set in motion a chain of other tragedies, the cumu-
lative effect of which was terrific. Almost as soon as the shot was
fired, the news flash was picked up by one of the skywriters directly
above the field. He glanced down to see whether he could spot the
trouble below, and in doing so failed to see another skywriter
approaching. The two planes collided and fell, wings locked, leaving
a confusing trail of smoke, which some observers tried to interpret
as a late sports score. The planes struck in the middle of the nearby
east-bound coast-to-coast Sunlight Parkway, and a motorist driving
a convertible coupé stopped so short, to avoid hitting them, that he
was bumped from behind. The pileup of cars that ensued involved
1,482 vehicles, a record for eastbound parkways. A total of more
than three thousand persons lost their lives in the highway accident, including the two pilots, and when panic broke out in the stadium, it cost another 872 in dead and injured. News of the disaster
spread quickly to other sports arenas, and started other panics
among the crowds trying to get to the exits, where they could buy a
paper and study a list of the dead. All in all, the afternoon of sport
cost 20,003 lives, a record. And nobody had much to show for it
except one small Midwestern boy who hung around the smoking

wrecks of the planes, captured some aero news-smoke in a milk bottle, and took it home as a souvenir.

[8] From that day on, sport waned. Through long, noncompetitive Saturday afternoons, the stadia slumbered. Even the parkways fell into disuse as motorists rediscovered the charms of old, twisty roads that led through main streets and past barnyards, with their mild congestions and pleasant smells.

COMMENT

White depends on climax to make his satirical points. The opening sentence of paragraph 2 states that he is building to a more important idea: "*Not only* did sport proliferate *but* the demands it made on the spectator became greater." The transitional sentence that concludes paragraph 2 might suggest a turn to less important ideas; in fact, the following paragraphs present the reasons for the decline of sport in the order of their importance. White builds to the Dust Bowl game and the climactic accident on the Sunlight Parkway. At first glance, the brief concluding paragraph may seem anticlimactic; it is not, however, for the reader feels the importance to White of the old winding roads "that led through main streets and past barnyards, with their mild congestions and pleasant smells." The satirical force of the essay depends, then, on the sense of climax, achieved in many ways in the various paragraphs. That sense of climax is important to White's ironic comment on the American obsession with sports. We are being ironic when we imply more than we say; we do this sometimes through a smile or wink of the eye when we speak, or, in writing and in speech, through understatement or exaggeration.

QUESTIONS FOR STUDY AND DISCUSSION

1. What attitudes or habits is White satirizing in the America of late 1947, when this essay first appeared? Do you think he is on target about attitudes toward sport and the behavior of sports fans in the seventies?

2. Are the targets of White's satire limited to attitudes and habits relating to sport, or does he have general attitudes and habits in mind too?

3. What is a "parable"? And what does the subtitle "A Preposterous Parable" show about White's intention?

4. Names like *Dejected* and *Futurity* can be satirical as well as humor-

ous. Are they? Do you find other humorous names in the essay, and are they used satirically?

5. Where has White used overstatement for humor? Does he also use understatement?

6. White refers to the "high visibility pink news-smoke perfected by Pepsi-Cola engineers." Why "Pepsi-Cola" rather than "U.S. Steel" or "Dow Chemical"?

VOCABULARY STUDY

Write a paraphrase of paragraph 2 or paragraph 6—a sentence-for-sentence rendering in your own words. Be sure to find substitutes for *proliferate, interminable,* and *oversubtilize* (paragraph 2), and *deranged, whipped,* and *drilled* (paragraph 6). Try to retain the tone of White's original paragraph in your rendering.

SUGGESTIONS FOR WRITING

1. Discuss the extent to which White's predictions have come true. Cite events and attitudes in the seventies that support his predictions or show him to be mistaken.

2. Identify the targets of White's satire and explain how you discover them in the essay. Then compare his view of sport and ways of expressing it with Wicker's.

3. A writer sometimes can be characterized through his sense of humor. Discuss the qualities you believe the essay reveals about E. B. White. Comment also on his probable interests and attitudes.

THE PRINCESS AND THE TIN BOX

James Thurber

James Thurber (1894–1961) was born in Columbus, Ohio. He attended Ohio State University for three years, and later worked for the U.S. State Department as a code clerk. From 1920 to 1925 he worked as a journalist on the *Columbus Dispatch* and *Chicago Tribune*. His long association with *The New Yorker* began in 1925, the year it began publication, and most of his stories, sketches, and cartoons appeared in that magazine. Thurber was a humorist and a satirist of many aspects of American life, in particular the relations of the sexes. His many books include *My Life and Hard Times* (1933), *Fables for Our Time* (1943), *The Thurber Carnival* (1945), and *Thurber Country* (1953).

[1] Once upon a time, in a far country, there lived a king whose daughter was the prettiest princess in the world. Her eyes were like the cornflower, her hair was sweeter than the hyacinth, and her throat made the swan look dusty.

[2] From the time she was a year old, the princess had been showered with presents. Her nursery looked like Cartier's window. Her toys were all made of gold or platinum or diamonds or emeralds. She was not permitted to have wooden blocks or china dolls or rubber dogs or linen books, because such materials were considered cheap for the daughter of a king.

[3] When she was seven, she was allowed to attend the wedding of her brother and throw real pearls at the bride instead of rice. Only the nightingale, with his lyre of gold, was permitted to sing for the princess. The common blackbird, with his boxwood flute, was kept out of the palace grounds. She walked in silver-and-samite slippers to a sapphire-and-topaz bathroom and slept in an ivory bed inlaid with rubies.

[4] On the day the princess was eighteen, the king sent a royal ambassador to the courts of five neighboring kingdoms to announce that he would give his daughter's hand in marriage to the prince who brought her the gift she liked the most.

[5] The first prince to arrive at the palace rode a swift white stallion and laid at the feet of the princess an enormous apple made of solid gold which he had taken from a dragon who had guarded it for a thousand years. It was placed on a long ebony table set up to hold the gifts of the princess's suitors. The second prince, who came on a gray charger, brought her a nightingale made of a thousand diamonds, and it was placed beside the golden apple. The third prince, riding on a black horse, carried a great jewel box made of platinum and sapphires, and it was placed next to the diamond nightingale.

The fourth prince, astride a fiery yellow horse, gave the princess a gigantic heart made of rubies and pierced by an emerald arrow. It was placed next to the platinum-and-sapphire jewel box.

[6] Now the fifth prince was the strongest and handsomest of all the five suitors, but he was the son of a poor king whose realm had been overrun by mice and locusts and wizards and mining engineers so that there was nothing much of value left in it. He came plodding up to the palace of the princess on a plow horse and he brought her a small tin box filled with mica and feldspar and hornblende which he had picked up on the way.

[7] The other princes roared with disdainful laughter when they saw the tawdry gift the fifth prince had brought to the princess. But she examined it with great interest and squealed with delight, for all her life she had been glutted with precious stones and priceless metals, but she had never seen tin before or mica or feldspar or hornblende. The tin box was placed next to the ruby heart pierced with an emerald arrow.

[8] "Now," the king said to his daughter, "you must select the gift you like best and marry the prince that brought it."

[9] The princess smiled and walked up to the table and picked up the present she liked the most. It was the platinum-and-sapphire jewel box, the gift of the third prince.

[10] "The way I figure it," she said, "is this. It is a very large and expensive box, and when I am married, I will meet many admirers who will give me precious gems with which to fill it to the top. Therefore, it is the most valuable of all the gifts my suitors have brought me and I like it the best."

[11] The princess married the third prince that very day in the midst of great merriment and high revelry. More than a hundred thousand pearls were thrown at her and she loved it.

[12] *Moral: All those who thought the princess was going to select the tin box filled with worthless stones instead of one of the other gifts will kindly stay after class and write one hundred times on the blackboard "I would rather have a hunk of aluminum silicate than a diamond necklace."*

COMMENT

Thurber's humor derives through what for the reader will probably be anticlimax—but clearly is not anticlimax for the princess. This disparity between what we expect to happen and what does happen is at *our* expense, as the moral shows. Much of the humor also arises from incongruity—a kingdom that contains wizards and mining engineers—and from the disparity between the setting and the language of this very modern girl. Disparities of this sort are a major source of irony. Many authors allow the irony to make its point without commenting on it. One delight in reading Thurber is in the discovery of those little deceptions that keep us feeling confident and pleased with ourselves.

QUESTIONS FOR STUDY AND DISCUSSION

1. How do the details of the first six paragraphs lead us to believe that the princess will choose the fifth prince?

2. At what point does the reader discover the real character of the princess?

3. Thurber, in his moral, talks to us in a language different from that of the story. What exactly is this difference, and what humor arises from it?

4. What human frailties is Thurber satirizing? Is he satirizing the princess or the reader of the essay or possibly both?

5. Do you find Thurber's moral pertinent to the world today?

VOCABULARY STUDY

Look up the following words: *parable, fairy tale, fable, allegory.* How closely does "The Princess and the Tin Box" fit the definitions you found?

SUGGESTIONS FOR WRITING

1. Compare Thurber's ways of satirizing attitudes and values with E. B. White's. You might wish to compare the kinds of humor they use.

2. Write a fairy tale or fable or parable of your own that uses the order of climax.

point of view

In describing a person, a scene, or an event, we may specify the place of observation, the time we make it, or the angle of vision: the street window of an upstairs apartment at 8:00 in the morning. These comprise the *physical point of view*. Not all of them need be stated directly; how much information we provide depends on our purpose in writing and on the needs of the reader. If we are describing an event of the past, the physical point of view may be indefinite.

Usually our feelings and ideas about people and events color our description. One viewer will notice details that a second viewer will miss completely. Neither viewer may be aware of having mentioned certain details and ignored others. This stated or implied *psychological point of view* complements the first, as in these two passages from George Orwell's description of Marrakech, a city in Morocco:

> As the corpse went past the flies left the restaurant table in a cloud and rushed after it, but they came back a few minutes later.

> Most of Morocco is so desolate that no wild animal bigger than a hare can live on it. Huge areas which were once covered with forest have turned into a treeless waste where the soil is exactly like broken-up brick. Nevertheless a good deal of it is cultivated, with frightful labor.

The point of view of the first passage is limited to a particular time and place; the point of view of the second is indefinite about both. Orwell saw the flies leave the table at the moment the corpse passed the restaurant; he observed most of the country over a period of time that need not be specified. In both passages attitudes are implied: the foreign visitor may notice and report the swarm of flies because he is not used to seeing them in his own country; a native of Marrakech might take no notice of them at all. Most of Morocco is desolate in comparison with southern England. To a person not used to hard manual labor, the work required to cultivate the rocky Moroccan ground is "frightful." Whether we realize it or not, we identify with a point of view as we read and perhaps absorb the attitudes of the writer revealed in his description.

ON THE A TRAIN

Maeve Brennan

Since 1953 the short-story writer and essayist Maeve Brennan has written in the guise of "The Long-Winded Lady" for *The New Yorker*. Her sketches and commentaries on New York City life appear in "The Talk of the Town," a collection of unsigned editorials, commentaries, personal essays, and sketches at the beginning of the magazine. "The long-winded lady" reports her experiences and observations in a rambling but engaging style, which conveys a special point of view and humor.

There were no seats to be had on the A train last night, but I had a good grip on the pole at the end of one of the seats and I was reading the beauty column of the *Journal-American,* which the man next to me was holding up in front of him. All of a sudden I felt a tap on my arm, and I looked down and there was a man beginning to stand up from the seat where he was sitting. "Would you like to sit down?" he said. Well, I said the first thing that came into my head, I was so surprised and pleased to be offered a seat in the subway. "Oh, thank you very much," I said, "but I am getting out at the

From *The Long-Winded Lady* (William Morrow & Co.). Reprinted by permission; © 1969 Maeve Brennan.

next station." He sat back and that was that, but I felt all set up and I thought what a nice man he must be and I wondered what his wife was like and I thought how lucky she was to have such a polite husband, and then all of a sudden I realized that I wasn't getting out at the next station at all but the one after that, and I felt perfectly terrible. I decided to get out at the next station anyway, but then I thought, If I get out at the next station and wait around for the next train I'll miss my bus and they only go every hour and that will be silly. So I decided to brazen it out as best I could, and when the train was slowing up at the next station I stared at the man until I caught his eye and then I said, "I just remembered this isn't my station after all." Then I thought he would think I was asking him to stand up and give me his seat, so I said, "But I still don't want to sit down, because I'm getting off at the next station." I showed him by my expression that I thought it was all rather funny, and he smiled, more or less, and nodded, and lifted his hat and put it back on his head again and looked away. He was one of those small, rather glum or sad men who always look off into the distance after they have finished what they are saying, when they speak. I felt quite proud of my strong-mindedness at not getting off the train and missing my bus simply because of the fear of a little embarrassment, but just as the train was shutting its doors I peered out and there it was 168th Street. "Oh, dear!" I said. "That was my station and now I have missed the bus!" I was fit to be tied, and I had spoken quite loudly, and I felt extremely foolish, and I looked down, and the man who had offered me his seat was partly looking at me, and I said, "Now, isn't that silly? That was my station. A Hundred and Sixty-eighth Street is where I'm supposed to get off." I couldn't help laughing, it was all so awful, and he looked away, and the train fidgeted along to the next station, and I got off as quickly as I possibly could and tore over to the downtown platform and got a local to 168th, but of course I had missed my bus by a minute, or maybe two minutes. I felt very much at a loose end wandering around 168th Street, and I finally went into a rudely appointed but friendly bar and had a Martini, warm but very soothing, which only cost me fifty cents. While I was sipping it, trying to make it last to exactly the moment that would get me a good place in the bus queue without having to stand too long in the cold, I wondered what I should have done about that man in the subway. After all, if I had taken his seat I probably would have got out at 168th Street, which would have meant that I would hardly have been sitting down before I would have been getting up again, and that would have seemed odd. And rather grasping of me. And he wouldn't have got his seat back, because some other grasping person would have slipped into it ahead of him when I got up. He seemed a retiring sort of man, not pushy at all. I hesitate to think of how he must have regretted offering me his seat. Sometimes it is very hard to know the right thing to do.

COMMENT

The long single paragraph suggests the speech of this "long-winded lady," who relates the episode in a breathless tone—excited and at the same time dismayed. We see the episode from the author's point of view, not from that of the man on the train. *His* might be entirely different; he might, in fact, not have noticed her confusion and embarrassment. The point of view heightens the truth of the final sentence: "Sometimes it is very hard to know the right thing to do." Brennan's thesis is not a fully developed idea but rather an afterthought—a momentary reflection on her amusing experience.

QUESTIONS FOR STUDY AND DISCUSSION

1. If the man who offered his seat had not seemed shy, how would the author's response to the situation have been different?

2. What personal qualities does Brennan reveal to us in her telling of the episode, and how do these contribute to our understanding of her concluding statement? What do her long rambling sentences show?

3. What is gained by developing the episode in a single paragraph?

4. Brennan has developed her idea humorously. What experiences of city life could be used to develop the idea seriously? Could you draw upon your experiences at home or at school in the same way?

VOCABULARY STUDY

1. Identify words in the essay that have negative connotations and be ready to discuss how they reveal the feelings of the author.

2. How do the details of the essay explain the italicized words in this sentence?
   He seemed a *retiring* sort of man, not *pushy* at all.

3. Find synonyms for the following words and phrases: *brazen it out; glum; peered out; fidgeted along; rudely appointed; queue.*

SUGGESTIONS FOR WRITING

1. Develop in a single, well-developed paragraph the final sentence of Brennan's essay. Use a similar experience of your own, and be careful to select only those details that clearly illustrate it.

2. Use another experience to illustrate an idea of your own. But this time omit any statement of it, so that your point or thesis is implied. Remember that you will succeed in communicating the thesis to your reader only if your details directly illustrate it.

3. Rewrite the subway episode from the point of view of the man, or from that of another passenger seated nearby. Create new details and commentary on the episode.

I'LL MEET YOU AT THE Y

John Craig

John Craig was born in Peterborough, Canada, in 1921. He attended the University of Manitoba and the University of Toronto, served in the Canadian Navy, and worked for twenty years in public opinion and marketing research. In addition to writing for Canadian television, he is the author of a number of books, including *Wagons West* (1955), *The Pro* (1966), *No Word for Good-bye* (1969), and *Zach* (1972).

[1] The Y.M.C.A. in our town, like Y.M.C.A.s of that period the world over, was a red brick, military-looking building, with Gothic towers at the corners. You had the feeling that, with a moat around its stone base, it could have repelled legions of infidels almost indefinitely. It stood on the main street, just on the northern fringe of the business section, and immediately south of the park where the World War I memorial stood.

[2] During the '30s the Y was a combined community center, soup kitchen, rest home, and meeting place as well as the hang-out for most of the town's athletes. The baseball and football teams used to dress there, walking back and forth over the hill and across the cement bridge to the ball park in their uniforms.

[3] It's hard to understand now how the place managed to keep open through those lean years, but it must have been subsidized through some central organization, no doubt supported by the churches. There was a businessmen's group, mostly fat, older guys in knee-length white shorts, who did calisthenics on Tuesday evenings and played volleyball Saturday afternoons, and presumably they paid their annual fees. Hardly any of the rest of us did, though, even if it *was* the best bargain in the world at fifteen dollars a year.

[4] The Y was managed by a man who emerges in retrospect as a somewhat unlikely, and at the time completely unsung, hero of the long, bitter fight against the Depression. "G. H.", as we called him— among ourselves, though not to his face—was a fairly tall, slim man with trim whitish-gray hair. To us, at the time, he seemed to have a somewhat stern countenance and a cold manner, but in reality he was undoubtedly a very kind man of substantial understanding and almost infinite patience.

[5] Every year the pattern was the same. Each September we would scrape up a dollar or two with which to make a token payment on that year's membership. It never occurred to us to be grateful that the balance of the previous year's fees was waived at that point; after all, that was ancient history. The initial installment would be enough to get you your membership card for the up-coming season. As of that moment, you were a member in good standing (no matter how much you might owe in back dues), entitled to use the gym and the shower room, the bowling alley and the pool table, and all the other facilities the Y had to offer. From then on, it became a matter of stretching that first, token payment as far as possible; the man who eventually had to adjudicate its elasticity was, of course, G. H.

[6] He presided behind a circular desk off the lobby to the right. That desk was the nerve center of the Y; it was there that you took out the snooker balls for the pool table, picked up your towels for the pool or the shower room, had your card stamped if you wanted to take part in any of the hobby classes, and so on. And it was from there that the buzzer was controlled which unlocked the door giving you access to the downstairs locker rooms, showers, pool, and gym.

That all-important door was about twenty feet to the left of G. H.'s desk and it was as critical, in its way, as the Khyber Pass or the Franco-German frontier. Each time it remained locked to you, you knew that you were finally due again for a little chat with G. H.

[7] You could cross that lobby a dozen times, or thirty or fifty times, and always the buzzer would sound as you approached the door so that you knew it would open when you got to it. And then one day, without warning, you would saunter in for a shower, or, worse still, for an important basketball game, and as you moved towards the door the ominous silence would continue. As you drew nearer, step by increasingly resigned step, you would carefully avoid any glance towards the desk. Finally there would remain no recourse but to reach out and try the door, which, of course, would not open. And then you would hear the quiet voice of reckoning from behind the desk.

[8] "Hmmmm, hmmmm ... Pete [or John, or Sam, or Jimmy] ... hmmmm ... hmmmm ... can I see you a minute?"

[9] You would go over to the desk with your head down, conscious of the snooker players watching you as you walked towards your confrontation. G. H. would fidget with the blotter on the desk, straighten and restraighten the towels on the shelf under the counter, and do everything he could to avoid looking at you. We didn't realize then how much he must have hated having to do it, and he would always speak in a low voice so that nobody else around the lobby could hear.

[10] "Hmmmm ... hmmmm ... haven't had a chance to talk with you in a while, Pete. How's it going?"

[11] "Not bad."

[12] "Well, hmmmm ... the year's getting on, Pete. What would you think about making a small payment on your fees?"

[13] You'd study your shoelaces and mutter something about "bringing in something next week," and both you and G. H. would know that there was no way in the world you were going to pay any more until the initial installment the following September.

[14] "That's fine, Pete ... hmmmm ... appreciate that. Nice talking to you, Pete."

[15] And then he'd press the button and let you go down for your shower or basketball game, and you would know that you were a member in good standing, and that the sound of the ever-loving buzzer was assured, for another few weeks.

[16] The Y was like a home away from home. You could play table

tennis there, shoot pool, bowl, have a swim, play volleyball or basketball, read the papers and magazines in the reading room, go to the dances on Saturday nights. Even on Sunday nights, when it was officially closed, there was a way to get in and make use of some of the facilities. The Y had a few boarders, more or less impoverished bachelors, who used to come and go by a side door to which each of them had a key. You could hide in the shadows in the lane, slip out after a boarder entered, and quickly insert a foot so that the door wouldn't close. Then you waited until the boarder's footsteps receded up the stairs, opened the door and went in.

[17] There was a ghostly atmosphere about the place on Sunday nights. You couldn't turn on any lights, of course, and the faint glow from the street lights outside the windows would transform the familiar shapes in subtle and mysterious ways. Sometimes, if the snooker balls had been left out, you could shoot a game of pool in the pale, bluish light, wincing with each click of the ivory balls for fear somebody might hear. We didn't dare bowl because of the noise. There were always some lights left on in the gym and sometimes we would go in and shoot some baskets, but dribbling was strictly forbidden.

[18] There was a cafeteria on the second floor where they served meals to the boarders, and provided occasional banquets for various Y groups. The door to the kitchen led off a back hall, and the bolt could be slipped quite easily with a piece of cardboard. Once inside, it was often possible to pilfer a pie or a plate of doughnuts, which could do a lot to brighten up a cold, dark winter night. The trouble was that, if the caretaker happened to come by while you were in the kitchen, the only way out was through a window and onto a ledge which ran around one of the corner towers. It was a pretty precarious perch, if you had to outwait the caretaker for any length of time on a bitter-cold Sunday night in January. Once Gus Gunsolus was out there for almost an hour and when we finally got him in, he looked like a survivor (just barely) from a seal-hunting disaster on the Labrador ice floes. There were icicles hanging from his hair, eyebrows and nose, and he was shaking like the last, dried maple leaf in a November gale. It was a long time before he came around enough to talk coherently.

[19] The worst part of it was that all the kitchen staff had left out that Sunday night was a big pot full of tired old carrots, soaking in water.

COMMENT

The physical point of view is stated immediately; we are seeing the Y as Craig saw it in the thirties, and as he remembers it in later years. His memories reveal an attitude, a controlling impression, composed of many feelings—ranging from security to mystery and excitement. The view we are given of the Y would be incomplete without a statement of these feelings. And so Craig shows us the Y at various times and on various days. The proportion of details in the whole essay is important to the impression we receive: we are told more about G. H. than we are about the businessmen who used the Y. That is because we are seeing the Y mainly as Craig the boy saw it, and G. H. was more important to his experience than the businessmen. The description would be different in many ways if we were seeing the Y through the eyes of one of these people or of an impoverished boarder.

QUESTIONS FOR STUDY AND DISCUSSION

1. What is the controlling impression of the Y in the whole essay? Is Craig developing a thesis through it?

2. What do the details about G. H. contribute to our impression of the Y? How does Craig indicate that we are seeing G. H. from the point of view of a boy rather than of a businessman or boarder?

3. What features of life at the Y might have been stressed by the businessman or boarder?

4. In what order are the various impressions presented? Is Craig moving from morning to evening, or through the days of the week, or from less to more exciting experiences? Is he possibly employing two or more principles of order?

5. What feelings or attitudes are implied in Craig's details and impressions?

6. Do you know people like G. H. who reveal one self on the job and another self off? What do you think explains this difference in these instances?

VOCABULARY STUDY

Use reference books like *The Columbia Encyclopedia, Facts on File, New York Times Index,* and *Encyclopedia of World History* to gain information

on the following. Then write an explanation of the allusion to each in the essay:
  a. Khyber Pass
  b. the Franco-German frontier in the thirties (Maginot Line)
  c. Gothic towers

SUGGESTIONS FOR WRITING

1. Describe the Y in your hometown, or the gymnasium of your high school, or a general recreation area in your town or city—at various times and on various days. You need not specify your feelings about the place: carefully chosen details will reveal these to your reader.

2. Describe a room in your house in the same way. In the course of your description, contrast your view of the room with that of a stranger in the house.

3. Describe the main street of your hometown or city in the same way— from the point of view of an inhabitant and that of a visitor.

A WHOLE SOCIETY OF LONERS AND DREAMERS

William Allen

William Allen was born in 1940 in Dallas. He teaches creative writing at Ohio State University and is the editor of *The Ohio Journal*. His fiction and nonfiction have appeared in numerous periodicals including *The Antioch Review, Saturday Review,* and the *New York Times*. His book *Starkweather: The Story of a Mass Murderer* was published in 1976; his novel *To Tojo from Billy-Bob,* in 1977.

[1] On Sunday afternoons here, if you're tired of taking walks in the country and fighting off the green-bellied hogflies, your next best choice is thumbing magazines at the downtown drugstore. One Sunday not long ago, when I ran out of anything else to thumb, I

started looking through one of those magazines geared toward helping new writers achieve success. I used to pore over them a lot when
I was a teenager, and the first thing I noticed now was that the ads
haven't changed much over the past fifteen years:

²"IMAGINE MAKING $5,000 A YEAR WRITING IN YOUR
SPARE TIME! Fantastic? Not at all. . . . Hundreds of People Make
That Much or More Every Year—and Have Fun Doing It!"

³"TO PEOPLE WHO WANT TO WRITE FOR PROFIT BUT
CAN'T GET STARTED. Have You Natural Writing Ability? Now a
Chance to Test Yourself—FREE!"

⁴"I FIRE WRITERS . . . with enthusiasm for developing God-
given talent. You'll 'get fired' too with my 48-lesson home study
course. Over-the-shoulder coaching . . . personalized critiques!
Amazing sales opportunity the first week. Write for my FREE
STARTER KIT."

⁵The ad that struck me the most showed a picture of a hand-
some and darkly serious young man sitting on a hill, picking his
teeth with a weed, and gazing out over the countryside. The caption
read: DO YOU HAVE THE "FAULTS" THAT COULD MEAN YOU
WERE MEANT TO BE A WRITER? The ad went on to list the outstanding characteristics of writers. They are dreamers, loners, bookworms. They are too impractical, too intense, too idealistic.

⁶When I was fourteen and had just started trying to write, I
saw an ad much like this and was overwhelmed by it. That fellow on
the hill was just like me, I thought. It was a tremendous feeling to
discover that I might not be alone—that there was a whole society
of loners and dreamers, that they were called writers, and that by
sending off for a free writing IQ test I could find out by return mail
if I qualified to climb the hill and chew straw with them.

⁷I took that test and blew the top off it. The writing school said
I demonstrated a rare creative potential unlike anything they had
seen in years. They did wonder, though, if I had what it took to stick
with them through long months of arduous training to develop my
raw talent. If I really did have that kind of fortitude, the next step
would be to send in some actual samples of my writing.

⁸Spurred, I sent off everything I had ever written—two stories
of about 200 words each. One was about some unidentified creatures
who lived in dread of an unidentified monster who came around
every week or so to slaughter as many of them as he could. Some of
the persecuted creatures had the option of running, hopping, scur-
rying, or crawling to safety, but the others, for some unexplained

reason, couldn't move and had just to stand there and take it. There was a description of the monster's roaring approach. Then the last line hit the reader like a left hook: "The lawn mower ran swiftly over. . . ."

[9] The other story I have preserved these many years:

THE RACE

Two gleaming hot rods stand side by side, poised and tensed—eager to scream down the hot asphalt track, each secretly confident that he will be the supreme victor. The time is drawing close now; in just a few minutes the race will be on.

There is a last minute check of both cars . . . everything is ready. A yell rings out for everyone to clear the track. The flagman raises the starting flag above his head, pauses for a second, and with a downward thrust of the flag, he sends the cars leaping forward with frightening speed.

They fly down the track, side by side, neither able to take the lead. They are gaining speed with every second. Faster and faster they go, approaching the half-way mark with incredible momentum. . . .

Wait! Something is wrong—one of the cars is going out of control and skidding toward the other car! The rending sound of ripping metal and sliding tires cuts through the air as the two autos collide and spin crazily off the track.

For a moment the tragic panorama is hidden by a self-made curtain of dust, but it isn't a second before the curtain is pulled away by the wind, revealing the horrible sight. There are the two hot rods, one turned over, both broken and smashed. All is quiet. . . .

Two small children, a boy and a girl, get up from the curb where they have been sitting. They eye each other accusingly as they walk slowly across the street where the two broken toy cars lay silent. . . . "Woman driver," grumbles the little boy.

THE END

[10] The correspondence school's copy desk quickly replied that the writing samples confirmed my aptitude test results and that they looked forward to working with me to the point of publication and

beyond. I couldn't imagine what could be beyond publication but finally figured out they meant to handle my work later as agent-representative. They praised my choice of subject matter, sense of drama, and powerful surprise endings—all of which they said indicated I could sell to the sci-fi market. This made sense, because science fiction was all I had ever read voluntarily except for *Comic Classics* and, as a child, *Uncle Wiggily*. The school was particularly impressed by my style, which they said was practically poetry, in places. They made references to my use of alliteration ("rending sound of ripping metal") and of metaphor ("self-made curtain of dust . . . pulled away by the wind").

[11] They were quick to make clear, however, that what I had here were only germs of stories. They needed to be expanded to publishable lengths and had to have better character development—particularly the one about the bugs and grass being slaughtered by the lawn mower. They said a good writer could give even an insect an interesting personality.

[12] The next step was to send them $10 for each of the two stories—the standard fee for detailed, over-the-shoulder copy-desk criticism. Then after these stories had been redone and rushed off for publication, I should enroll in their thirty-six-lesson course, in which I would be taught the ins and outs of plotting, characterization, point of view, theme, tone, and setting. The fee was $10 a lesson, and after my successful completion of the course they would then handle my literary properties, protect my legal rights, etc., for the regular 10 per cent.

[13] At this point I began to wonder if I might be going in over my head. I was getting only a dollar a week from my folks and didn't understand half of what the writing school was talking about. In English class I had heard of such terms as "alliteration," "tone," and "point of view" but had no clear idea what they meant. Also I felt like an imposter. I had given my age as twenty-one. Of course, I was strutting because at fourteen I was doing better than anybody they had worked with in years, but I wondered if I could keep it up. "Rending sound of ripping metal" was genius, but could I crank out lines like that on a daily basis? I decided to try.

[14] First I wrote them that I was a little short of cash this month and asked if just to get started, it would be all right to work on one story for $10 instead of two for $20. They replied that that would be fine—just send in the ten bucks so they could get rolling.

¹⁵Meanwhile I hadn't been able to get even that much money together. I approached my family and was turned down flat because my father thought there was something unhealthy about people who wanted to write. He was bothered by the school's remark that my writing was like poetry. "If you were a girl, it might be different," he said, and showed me a copy of *Men's Adventure*. "Look here, why don't you get one of these two ninety-eight worm ranches? Or one of these small-game boomerangs?"

¹⁶After a few days of trying to drum up work around the neighborhood, I realized I wasn't going to be able to pull it off and decided just not to write back. But in a week I got a curt note saying they wanted to help me, were trying to be patient, but I was going to have to be more responsible. They said that writing was 1 per cent inspiration and 99 per cent perspiration and wondered if in my case the figures might be reversed.

¹⁷This both goaded and scared me. I wrote back that on account of unexpected medical expenses I could afford to give them only $5 at first. Could they possibly let me have a cut rate? They replied that it was strictly against their policy, but in view of my undeniably vast potential the copy-desk team had voted to go along with me just this once—send the $5.

¹⁸By mowing lawns and selling bottles, I had by this time scraped together $3, but there my earning potential dropped sharply. Another week went by, and I made only 48 cents more. Then a letter arrived stamped in red, front and back: URGENT! IMPORTANT! DO NOT DISCARD! It said I had violated an agreement based on mutual trust and had exactly twenty-four hours to send in the $5. Without exactly spelling it out, they gave the impression that legal action might be taken. The letter ended: "Frankly, Mr. Allen, we're about at our wits' end with you."

¹⁹I was hurt as well as shaken. I felt that I just didn't have what it takes. If there ever had been a chance of my climbing that hill and sitting with that elite group of loners and dreamers, it was gone now. I had my mother write them that I had suddenly been struck down with polio and was unable even to write my name, much less take their course. I hung onto the little money I had in case I had to give it to them to avoid a lawsuit, but I didn't hear from them after that. In a few weeks I relaxed and mailed off for the $2.98 worm ranch.

COMMENT

Allen implies more than he actually states. That "whole society of loners and dreamers" probably includes all adolescents. But everyone has been intimidated by clerks and salesmen and dunning letters. The point of view, in other words, is one shared by adolescent and adult, as Allen's opening paragraphs show. The point of view also shapes the reader's response in one important way. Allen is not developing a thesis, and therefore we need not be on our intellectual guard, as we are in active if silent debate with a writer. We give more of ourselves imaginatively to the essay, maybe identifying with the experience through one of our own. One of the important means to this identification is the lively detail. We are not merely told about the stories Allen wrote: we are given passages from them, and also his responses to the ad and to the letters that followed, and the response of his father to his interest in writing. Another important means to identification is the careful focus and consistent point of view. Once he has introduced himself and mentioned his experience in the drugstore, Allen does not stray from the point of view he establishes.

QUESTIONS FOR STUDY AND DISCUSSION

1. What qualities does Allen reveal about himself as a boy and a man? What are the qualities of "dreamers, loners, bookworms"?

2. What personal qualities do Allen's stories reveal?

3. What information about or view of himself as a boy—information or a view that the boy could not have possessed—does Allen share with the reader? What humor arises through this information or view?

4. What does Allen show about adolescence in general? What in your experience illustrates these same qualities? Do you find his comments generally true of people you know?

VOCABULARY STUDY

1. Study current advertisements in magazines for writers and compare their language with that cited by Allen. How similar are the vocabulary and the appeals? Do you find exaggerated claims? Take notes on your findings for class discussion.

2. Look up *metaphor* and *alliteration* and write sentences containing both that could be added to one of the stories Allen wrote.

SUGGESTIONS FOR WRITING

1. Develop the topic "A Whole Society of Loners and Dreamers," from your own point of view and experience. Contrast your awareness of the world today with your awareness of it as a boy or girl.

2. Develop the topic "Magazine Advertisements" from your point of view and experience. You might contrast advertisements for different products and for the same product. Use your discussion to reach a conclusion about the use of language and the appeals you found.

THE REVOLT OF THE EVIL FAIRIES

Ted Poston

Ted Poston (1907–1974) was born and raised in Hopkinsville, Kentucky, and graduated from Tennessee Agricultural and Industrial College in 1928. He worked in politics, then as a free-lance journalist, and later as a reporter for the *New York Amsterdam News* and the *New York Post*. Poston was one of the first black journalists to work for a major New York newspaper. The essay printed here is one of many that he wrote about his Kentucky boyhood.

[1] The grand dramatic offering of the Booker T. Washington Colored Grammar School was the biggest event of the year in our social life in Hopkinsville, Kentucky. It was the one occasion on which they let us use the old Cooper Opera House, and even some of the white folks came out yearly to applaud our presentation. The first two rows of the orchestra were always reserved for our white friends, and our leading colored citizens sat right behind them—with an empty row intervening, of course.

[2] Mr. Ed Smith, our local undertaker, invariably occupied a box to the left of the house and wore his cutaway coat and striped breeches. This distinctive garb was usually reserved for those rare occasions when he officiated at the funerals of our most prominent colored citizens. Mr. Thaddeus Long, our colored mailman, once rented a tuxedo and bought a box too. But nobody paid him much mind. We knew he was just showing off.

[3] The title of our play never varied. It was always "Prince Charming and the Sleeping Beauty," but no two presentations were ever the same. Miss H. Belle LaPrade, our sixth-grade teacher, rewrote the script every season, and it was never like anything you read in the story books.

[4] Miss LaPrade called it "a modern morality play of conflict between the forces of good and evil." And the forces of evil, of course, always came off second best.

[5] The Booker T. Washington Colored Grammar School was in a state of ferment from Christmas until February, for this was the period when parts were assigned. First there was the selection of the Good Fairies and the Evil Fairies. This was very important, because the Good Fairies wore white costumes and the Evil Fairies black. And strangely enough most of the Good Fairies usually turned out to be extremely light in complexion, with straight hair and white folks' features. On rare occasions a dark-skinned girl might be lucky enough to be a Good Fairy, but not one with a speaking part.

[6] There never was any doubt about Prince Charming and the Sleeping Beauty. They were *always* light-skinned. And though nobody ever discussed those things openly, it was an accepted fact that a lack of pigmentation was a decided advantage in the Prince Charming and Sleeping Beauty sweepstakes.

[7] And therein lay my personal tragedy. I made the best grades in my class, I was the leading debater, and the scion of a respected family in the community. But I could never be Prince Charming, because I was black.

[8] In fact, every year when they started casting our grand dramatic offering my family started pricing black cheesecloth at Franklin's Department Store. For they knew that I would be leading the forces of darkness and skulking back in the shadows—waiting to be vanquished in the third act. Mamma had experience with this sort of thing. All my brothers had finished Booker T. before me.

[9] Not that I was alone in my disappointment. Many of my class-mates felt it too. I probably just took it more to heart. Rat Joiner, for instance, could rationalize the situation. Rat was not only black; he lived on Billy Goat Hill. But Rat summed it up like this:

[10] "If you black, you black."

[11] I should have been able to regard the matter calmly too. For our grand dramatic offering was only a reflection of our daily community life in Hopkinsville. The yallers had the best of everything. They held most of the teaching jobs in Booker T. Washington Colored Grammar School. They were the Negro doctors, the lawyers, the insurance men. They even had a "Blue Vein Society," and if your dark skin obscured your throbbing pulse you were hardly a member of the élite.

[12] Yet I was inconsolable the first time they turned me down for Prince Charming. That was the year they picked Roger Jackson. Roger was not only dumb; he stuttered. But he was light enough to pass for white, and that was apparently sufficient.

[13] In all fairness, however, it must be admitted that Roger had other qualifications. His father owned the only colored saloon in town and was quite a power in local politics. In fact, Mr. Clinton Jackson had a lot to say about just who taught in the Booker T. Washington Colored Grammar School. So it was understandable that Roger should have been picked for Prince Charming.

[14] My real heartbreak, however, came the year they picked Sarah Williams for Sleeping Beauty. I had been in love with Sarah since kindergarten. She had soft light hair, bluish gray eyes, and a dimple which stayed in her left cheek whether she was smiling or not.

[15] Of course Sarah never encouraged me much. She never answered any of my fervent love letters and Rat was very scornful of my one-sided love affair. "As long as she don't call you a black baboon," he sneered, "you'll keep on hanging around."

[16] After Sarah was chosen for Sleeping Beauty, I went out for the Prince Charming role with all my heart. If I had declaimed boldly in previous contests, I was matchless now. If I had bothered Mamma with rehearsals at home before, I pestered her to death this time. Yes, and I purloined my sister's can of Palmer's Skin Success.

[17] I knew the Prince's role from start to finish, having played the Head Evil Fairy opposite it for two seasons. And Prince Charming

was one character whose lines Miss LaPrade never varied much in her many versions. But although I never admitted it, even to myself, I knew I was doomed from the start. They gave the part to Leonardius Wright. Leonardius, of course, was yaller.

[18] The teachers sensed my resentment. They were almost apologetic. They pointed out that I had been such a splendid Head Evil Fairy for two seasons that it would be a crime to let anybody else try the role. They reminded me that Mamma wouldn't have to buy any more cheesecloth because I could use my same old costume. They insisted that the Head Evil Fairy was even more important than Prince Charming because he was the one who cast the spell on Sleeping Beauty. So what could I do but accept?

[19] I had never liked Leonardius Wright. He was a goody-goody, and even Mamma was always throwing him up to me. But above all, he too was in love with Sarah Williams. And now he got a chance to kiss Sarah every day in rehearsing the awakening scene.

[20] Well, the show must go on, even for little black boys. So I threw my soul into my part and made the Head Evil Fairy a character to be remembered. When I drew back from the couch of Sleeping Beauty and slunk away into the shadows at the approach of Prince Charming, my facial expression was indeed something to behold. When I was vanquished by the shining sword of Prince Charming in the last act, I was a little hammy perhaps—but terrific!

[21] The attendance at our grand dramatic offering that year was the best in its history. Even the white folks overflowed the two rows reserved for them and a few were forced to sit in the intervening one. This created a delicate situation, but everybody tactfully ignored it.

[22] When the curtain went up on the last act, the audience was in fine fettle. Everything had gone well for me too—except for one spot in the second act. That was where Leonardius unexpectedly rapped me over the head with his sword as I slunk off into the shadows. That was not in the script, but Miss LaPrade quieted me down by saying it made a nice touch anyway. Rat said Leonardius did it on purpose.

[23] The third act went on smoothly though until we came to the vanquishing scene. That was where I slunk from the shadows for the last time and challenged Prince Charming to mortal combat.

The hero reached for his shining sword—a bit unsportsmanlike I always thought, since Miss LaPrade consistently left the Head Evil Fairy unarmed—and then it happened!

[24] Later, I protested loudly—but in vain—that it was a case of self-defense. I pointed out that Leonardius had a mean look in his eye. I cited the impromptu rapping he had given my head in the second act. But nobody would listen. They just wouldn't believe that Leonardius really intended to brain me when he reached for his sword.

[25] Anyway he didn't succeed. For the minute I saw that evil gleam in his eye—or was it my own?—I cut loose with a right to the chin, and Prince Charming dropped his shining sword and staggered back. His astonishment lasted only a minute though, for he lowered his head and came charging in, fists flailing. There was nothing yellow about Leonardius but his skin.

[26] The audience thought the scrap was something new Miss LaPrade had written in. They might have kept on thinking so if Miss LaPrade hadn't been screaming so hysterically from the sidelines. And if Rat Joiner hadn't decided that this was as good a time as any to settle old scores. So he turned around and took a sock at the male Good Fairy nearest him.

[27] When the curtain rang down, the forces of Good and Evil were locked in combat. And Sleeping Beauty was wide awake, and streaking for the wings.

[28] They rang the curtain back up fifteen minutes later, and we finished the play. I lay down and expired according to specifications, but Prince Charming will probably remember my sneering corpse to his dying day. They wouldn't let me appear in the grand dramatic offering at all the next year. But I didn't care. I couldn't have been Prince Charming anyway.

COMMENT

Like William Allen, Ted Poston does not argue a thesis, and the response of his reader to the experience would be different if he had. The humor of the essay is to be enjoyed for its own sake. It is humor, however, that arises from keen observation of a world whose attitudes and contradictions are still with us. We laugh at what we see to be true; knowing this, Poston presses the implied similarities between the world he is describing and his present world. As in Allen, it is the careful selection of details that makes the writing successful. Poston is not satisfied to report the outlines of the experience: he allows us to see and feel the black world of Hopkinsville, Kentucky. Superimposed on the point of view of the black boy destined to play the Head Evil Fairy is that of the adult remembering and savoring the revolt—and revealing the frustrations and pain of a black boy in a black world.

QUESTIONS FOR STUDY AND DISCUSSION

1. How do the details of the adult black world of Hopkinsville help the reader to understand the attitude of the black boys toward the lighter-skinned children in the grammar school?

2. Poston finds irony in the conception of the play—"a modern morality play of conflict between the forces of good and evil"—and the circumstances of its performance. The irony arises from the contradiction, the disparity between what should be and what is—between how adults should behave and set an example and how they do. How does Poston explore that irony?

3. The attitudes that made it impossible for Poston to play Prince Charming are not shown to be vicious. What exactly is the attitude Poston expresses toward them?

4. If Poston had wished to comment on contemporary social values directly, how might the organization and selection of details have been different?

5. What examples would you use to comment on the same social values?

VOCABULARY STUDY

1. Decide how the connotations of the following words are determined by their use in the essay: skulking, yallers, hammy, slunk off. Then write sentences of your own, using these words to reveal these meanings.

2. Find synonyms for the following words: pigmentation (paragraph 6); rationalize (paragraph 9); obscured, elite (paragraph 11); declaimed, purloined (paragraph 16); tactfully (paragraph 21); fettle (paragraph 22); impromptu (paragraph 24); sneering (paragraph 28).

SUGGESTIONS FOR WRITING

1. Write a characterization of the author on the basis of what he reveals about himself—through his choice of incident and the details he selects to narrate it.

2. Narrate a similar incident in your school experience that reveals the effect of social values on the feelings and attitudes of children and grownups. Let the details reveal the effect. Don't state it directly.

3. Rewrite a paragraph of the essay from the point of view of Leonardius Wright. Change the details or the presentation of the original details of the paragraph to accord with how you think he may have felt about the Head Evil Fairy and the play itself.

tone

We know the meaning of a statement when we know the attitude or feeling it expresses—its *tone*. The statement

What a tragedy!

expresses pain—but the speaker may also be expressing anger or sarcasm. The statement

What a lucky boy!

can express wonder, delight, amazement, or even jealousy or sarcasm. Hearing a statement rather than reading it on a page, we usually discover this attitude from the speaker's face or inflection of voice. When we read the statement, however, we may have to look for details or other statements that clarify it. Dickens is usually plain in his anger and sarcasm, as in this comment on the birth of Oliver Twist in an early nineteenth-century workhouse:

Oliver cried lustily. If he could have known that he was an orphan, left to the tender mercies of churchwardens and overseers, perhaps he would have cried the louder.

We cannot be quite sure of the tone of Jane Austen, in her opening statement in *Pride and Prejudice:*

It is a truth universally acknowledged, that a single man in possession of a good fortune must be in want of a wife.

Jane Austen is certainly not angry, but is she serious? Does she believe the statement herself? Her next statement clarifies her attitude and therefore the tone of her opening statement:

However little known the feelings or views of such a man may be on his first entering a neighborhood, this truth is so well fixed in the minds of the surrounding families, that he is considered as the rightful property of some one or other of their daughters.

We now know what Austen means: it is a truth generally believed by families with marriageable daughters. She is being ironic, and her irony expresses amusement over small-town attitudes and values. An ironic statement, in general, *implies* more than is actually said. Compare Austen's opening sentences with her plain description of Mrs. Bennet, who has five marriageable daughters:

> She was a woman of mean understanding, little information, and uncertain temper. When she was discontented, she fancied herself nervous. The business of her life was to get her daughters married; its solace was visiting and news.

The tone of a statement like the above may express several feelings and attitudes simultaneously. And so may an essay. The longer the essay, the greater the opportunity for changes in and development of tone. Because statements can express so many feelings and attitudes, we must look carefully at what we write, and revise statements that may say more than we intend or that are not consistent with the general tone we have in mind.

WORKING OUT A DEAL

Calvin Trillin

Calvin Trillin was born in Kansas City, Missouri, in 1935 and lives in New York City. He has been a staff member of *The New Yorker* since 1963. His books include *An Education in Georgia* (1964) and three collections of essays on life and food in the United States: *U.S. Journal* (1970), *American Fried: The Adventures of a Happy Eater* (1975), and *Let's Eat, Alice* (1978).

[1]The merchandising method of Reedman's, the world's largest car dealer, seems to be based on the theory that a lot of Americans have bought so many new cars that they consider themselves experts at the art. Respecting the fact that a man of experience will have gone beyond loyalty to any one make of car, Reedman salesmen are equally helpful about selling him a new Chevrolet or a new

Plymouth or a new almost anything else; Reedman's has fourteen new-car franchises. Reedman salesmen will reassure a customer that the small Plymouth station wagon and the small Dodge station wagon, both of which Reedman's handles, are virtually the same car—the slight difference in headlights and the different names being merely a way to make one car do for two different dealers. Good hard shoptalk is expected among experts. Included in the Reedman display of the Plymouth Duster and the American Motors' Hornet is the competing car not handled by Reedman's, the Ford Maverick—its roof decorated with a sign drawing attention to the relative puniness of its wheelbase, its trunk open to reveal a sign that says "The Exposed Gas Tank Is in the Trunk Floor." Since the customer will be sophisticated enough to know precisely what he wants in a car—whether, for example, he can do without air-conditioning but must have vinyl bucket seats—Reedman's has an inventory of some five thousand cars, and a computer that will instantly find out if a particular model is available and will then type out a precise description of it before the customer's eyes. An enormous selection being a great advantage in dealing with expert car purchasers, some people in the trade say that Reedman's sells so many cars because it has so many to sell—a merchandising adaptation of Mies van der Rohe's "Less is More" dictum that comes out "More is More."

[2] The Reedman newspaper advertisement invites customers to a hundred-and-fifty-acre, one-stop car center that has a ten-million-dollar selection of cars—and then, adding the note of exclusivity that is considered necessary in advertising even the world's largest, it says, "Private Sale Now Going On." The premises on which the private sale is held look like the average citizen's vision of the supply depot at Cam Ranh Bay. Behind a series of showrooms on Route 1, just down the road from the Greenwood Dairies, the five thousand cars are lined up on acres and acres of asphalt—the neat rows interrupted by occasional watchtowers and the entire area surrounded by a heavy, iron, electronically monitored fence. On a busy Saturday, attendants direct streams of traffic in and out of the customer's parking lot. Hostesses with the dress and manner of airline stewardesses circulate in the showrooms offering to call a salesman for anybody who feels the need of one. Muzak, which reaches the most remote line of hardtops, is interrupted every two or three bars by calls for salesmen.

[3] The opportunity to perfect a veteran car buyer's style is so

great at Reedman's—the opportunity to shrug off a computer's offer of a Dodge Coronet with fourteen extras, to exchange jargon about engines and wheelbases, to take a new model for a few spins around the Reedman test track and make some observations to the family about how she handles on the curves—that some people seem to make Saturday at Reedman's a kind of outing. A lot of them, of course, find themselves buying a car, with vinyl bucket seats and air-conditioning. The route back to the customers' parking lot leads through a small building where the customer is greeted by a man even more helpful than the hostesses. "How'd you make out, sir?" the man asks. "What kind of car were you looking at? What was your trade-in? Who was your salesman? Of course you want to think about it, but why wait?" There is no reason for an experienced car buyer to concern himself with the fact that his most recent experience was so recent that he has yet to pay for the car he has; the first sign on the Reedman lot begins, "If you still have payments on your present car, truck, etc., we will pay off the balance and work out a deal."

[4] Although selling at Reedman's is based on working out a deal rather than on glamour or showmanship, a car dealer cannot afford to create an atmosphere of pure, unglamorous functionalism. If anyone is going to be totally practical, why should he spend his money on an overlarge, gas-eating, non-functional, instantly depreciating new car? Although the Chevrolet section of the Reedman showrooms is crowded with as many models as can be crammed in, the decor includes huge crystal chandeliers and wallpaper of raised-velvet fleur-de-lis patterns on ersatz gold leaf. On one wall of the showroom, a picture display of Reedman service facilities describes one of the three waiting rooms available for service customers as having "fifteen stereophonic speakers mounted in the acoustical ceiling," as well as "embossed vinyl covered walls, plus carpeting, velvet draperies, a crystal chandelier, and living-room type furniture." Any car buyer of experience recognizes that as a description of something that, with the addition of some heavy-duty whitewall tires, could provide great transportation until next year's models come out.

COMMENT

Since tone expresses the writer's attitude toward reader as well as subject, we must ask what Trillin is assuming about his reader's preference in cars and in ways they are sold. The reader may agree that "Good hard shop-talk is expected among experts," and at the same time be amused or disgusted or, instead, admiring of people who know how to work out a deal. The answer to this question depends on what we hear as we read Trillin's words. In writing, we can substitute turns of phrase for the inflections of voice that convey tone in speech. We can also reveal our attitude implicitly through our selection of details and the emphasis we give them.

QUESTIONS FOR STUDY AND DISCUSSION

1. Is Trillin merely reporting in paragraph 2 what the first sign on the car lot says, or is he expressing approval or disapproval through this detail?

2. What details in the essay reveal the attitude at Reedman's toward buying and selling cars? What interests Trillin most about Reedman's, and how do you know?

3. Examine paragraph 4 carefully. Is Trillin stating his own preference for cars in the opening sentences? Does he seem to assume that these sentences express the preference of his reader?

4. Would you describe the overall tone of the essay as sarcastic, amused, passionate, serious, objective, or perhaps a combination of these? What is the chief way Trillin establishes his tone?

5. Has Trillin described your preference in cars in paragraph 4? What is your preference in ways of buying and selling them? If you were describing the scene at Reedman's, would you describe it in the same tone and emphasize the same details?

VOCABULARY STUDY

1. State how the italicized words convey tone through their connotative meanings:
   a. "the relative *puniness* of its wheelbase"
   b. "to make Saturday at Reedman's a kind of *outing*"
   c. "*ersatz* gold leaf"

2. Find other words and phrases in the essay that contribute to the overall tone through their connotative meaning and descriptive power.

3. Rewrite one of the paragraphs in a different tone. Select new words and phrases appropriate to this tone.

1. Analyze the structure and details of the final paragraph to specify its tone. Then discuss what the paragraph contributes to the overall tone of the essay.

2. Describe a place of business—a grocery store, a clothing store, a motorcycle shop—and through your selection of details show the attitude of the proprietor toward his or her customers. Do not specify this attitude: let your details establish it.

BEAUTY AND EVERLASTING FAITH— LOCAL LEVEL

Frank Deford

Frank Deford was born in Baltimore in 1938, and was educated at Princeton, where he edited *The Daily Princetonian* and the humor magazine *The Tiger*. A senior writer for *Sports Illustrated,* he has written on tennis, basketball, roller derbies, and the Miss America pageant. His books include *Cut 'n' Run* (1973) and *The Owner* (1976). In the essay printed here a section from a chapter of his book *There She Is* (1971), he is describing the preliminary contest in Wilson, North Carolina, for the state title.

[1]The judging formally begins with the Saturday luncheon at the Heart of Wilson Motel. Dr. Vincent Thomas, the head of the judges' committee, welcomes all the judges, and is himself thereafter always introduced as "Dr. Vincent," by Jerry Ball, the well-known "dean of beauty-pageant judges." Jerry has sent two state queens on to become Miss America, and judged in states as far away as Alaska. Jerry is joined on the jury by Mrs. Judy Cross, who was

Most Photogenic at Miss North Carolina a few years ago, and by Mrs. Marilyn Hull, a former Miss New Jersey. She is married, as so many beauty queens are, to an athlete. Her husband is Bill Hull, a former Kansas City Chief. The other two judges are Jim Church, chairman of the board of the North Carolina Jaycees, and Bob Logan, Charlotte sales manager for Fabergé, the beauty products concern. It is a hot-shot panel for any local Pageant.

[2] The eight contestants keep a wary eye out as they sit down to lunch and make sure to reach for the correct implements. The judges, however, show no interest whatsoever in what eating tools are being utilized. They are genial and pleasant; the girls could be dispensing peas with a knife for all they seem to care about such formalities.

[3] Doris's hat tumbles off. She does not realize it has gone, which is not surprising, since hats are as foreign to these girls as bustles or U.S. Army fatigues would be. Judi has a hat on for exactly the second time in her life. The first time was when she was in another beauty pageant. There are speeches and everyone in attendance is introduced. Then the room is cleared, and a table set up for the judges at the far end. It is time for the serious interviewing. Officially, the girls in any *Miss America* Pageant are not graded on their interviews. Actually, it is the underside of the iceberg that determines the winner.

[4] The girls are directed to another room where, one by one, they will be funneled toward the judges. Following an interview, the contestant will proceed on to another room for a sort of debriefing. The judges arrange themselves and pour coffee. The men must concentrate to do their best, for the South Carolina-Duke basketball game is just starting on TV, and their hearts all lie there. Jerry Ball presides in the middle, like a Chief Justice, a leader among equals, and everyone agrees that there will be no set order to the questioning, just "catch as catch can."

[5] Dr. Thomas sits at the other end of the room with a stop watch. Jerry says, "All right, Dr. Vincent, bring in the first young lady." The girls have been assigned an order in which they will present their talents in the show; they visit the judges in the same order. Rita Deans is first. Like all the others, she has her little hat on and carries a handbag, and she walks, as she has been taught, in the proper manner. This is an unfamiliar gait for all the girls and makes them resemble the little dogs on the Ed Sullivan Show, who

have outfits on, are balanced precariously on their hind feet, and take desperate little steps to keep from pitching forward.

[6] Rita, seated, is straightforward and demure. She assures the panel that her fourteen-year Sunday School record is not in any danger of being jeopardized by a victory tonight. The judges spring what is considered as a controversial question: what does Rita think of coed college dormitories? Rita thinks awhile. "Well, I haven't formed an opinion about that," she finally says. Mrs. Butner has instructed the girls to answer that way whenever they feel that they are unsure of an answer. The judges nod and agree that Rita would be unwise, indeed, to venture into unknown philosophical territory.

[7] Sharon Shackleford is next. Talkative anyway, she seems especially garrulous when juxtaposed to Rita. "You've got to pull the plug on her," a judge says upon her departure. Wendy Formo, the third contestant, makes the best approach of all. Over six feet tall, she cannot help walking like a normal person. Also, she shuffles a question about Vice President Agnew beautifully, and the panel is obviously impressed. "It reminds you," Jim Church says. "I always liked that Jeanne Swanner."

[8] Bob Logan asks, "What time is it?"

[9] Jerry answers, "About the end of the first quarter."

[10] Peggy Murphy, recovered from the flu, is next, and for her, the judges reach back for a classic old standard of a question: what kind of person do you think you are yourself? There is one stock answer to this question, which every girl ever in a beauty pageant has always provided. In so many words, it is: that I am naturally a shy, thoughtful person, but I love a good time on occasion. Also, I am nuts about people. Peggy is close enough.

[11] The interviewing is now halfway through, so the judges stand and reach for some coffee. Doris comes in. She is in yellow, with a matching handbag that she sets on the rug by the side of her chair. She banters back the usual polite preliminaries, and then one of the judges asks her if she believes there is a generation gap. "Yes, I definitely believe there is one," Doris replies firmly. All the judges sit up and cock their heads. The regular answer to this question is that there certainly isn't one around my house, where everyone works to understand each other better. Doris proceeds. "Ours is the first generation brought up with the threat of the hydrogen and atom bombs, and the first generation to have grown up with television as a major force in our lives. I really don't even believe it is

surprising that there is a gap. Maybe we should only be surprised that there is not more of one."

[12] The judges nod sagely, and to test her further, pull another old chestnut out of the fire. All right, what about coed dorms? Doris backs down here; she comes out with the company line. "It may be fine for other people," she says, "but I can certainly see enough of the opposite sex on dates and other things." Doris has inserted a proper amount of righteous indignation in her voice by the end of her speech. The judges draw a breath, relieved not to have a genuine revolutionary on their hands. They are spent, though, so they ask her if she has any questions for them.

[13] Gay Butner has informed the girls that they may be faced with this request, and to have a question on stand-by. "Yes," Doris says, "I'd like to know why you're still interested in judging. Does it keep you closer to our generation and help close the gap for you?" Yes, the judges agree, yes, it certainly works that way for them.

[14] Time is up; the panel smiles and thanks her; and Doris is hardly out of the door when Jerry slams his hand down. "She came through like 'Gangbusters,'" he exclaims. "She took everything we threw at her and came right back."

[15] "A live cookie," Jim Church says.

[16] Vince Thomas goes to fetch Judi. She comes in, smiling broadly, wearing her aunt's bright orange sleeveless dress. She talks enthusiastically, almost conversationally, from the moment she deposits herself in the chair before the judges. It is as if she has been doing this all her life. Judi is restrained only by what she keeps reminding herself, to keep her hands anchored in her lap and not to say "you know." She is bright and cheery and carries the judges along with her. "Learn to gain control over the interview," Gay has told all the girls. "Give a brief answer, then lead into another area that you particularly like to talk about."

[17] That advice was like giving Judi a license to steal. She and all the other modern Southern belles are born and bred in this briar patch. In Atlantic City a few months later, Phyllis George, Judi's temperamental and verbal kin, babbled on with such dazzle about her pet crab and her dog that the most serious thing that the judges found time to ask her was whether or not she liked beer—and Phyllis even side-stepped that one, and went rambling right on, absolutely stunning the judges from start to finish of the interview. Judi's footwork is proportionately as good at the Heart of Wilson

Motel, but she slows down and twice permits the judges time to reach into their portfolio of controversial questions.

[18] First, they want to know if Judi endorses drugs. Well, she doesn't. Then Marilyn Hull remembers Doris. "Do you think there is a generation gap?" she asks. Judi pauses but for a second, then replies: "I don't think there's any more gap now than there's ever been." The judges nod, and then they want to know if she might have a question for them.

[19] Judi has come loaded for that bear. "What is your idea of a Miss Wilson?" she rips back at them.

[20] A girl with poise, the judges solemnly agree.

[21] "Now, do you have any other question you would like to ask us?" Jerry asks. This is a formality, like drop-over-some-time-and-see-us, but Judi tears into it at face value. "Do you think there is a generation gap?" she asks. Marilyn fields the answer, uneasily, and this time Jerry does not ask Judi if she has another question to ask. "I'm afraid Dr. Vincent is signaling that our time is up," he informs her. Judi thanks everyone and leaves. As soon as she is out of the room, the judges start marveling about her performance. "Imagine," one says, "we asked if she had another question, and she did." There is a first time for everything.

[22] They are still chuckling at Judi's effervescence as Rose Thorne comes in. She expresses a solid opposition to coed dorms, and then Connie Whisenant finishes up by voicing displeasure at those college students who had participated in the Vietnam Moratorium.

[23] Outside the room Doris and Judi are already comparing notes. It is immediately obvious to each that her rival was not disappointed; at the least, neither felt she had done poorly. Judi is stunned to learn, though, that Doris has actually said that there is a generation gap. Was she right? Was that the correct answer that the judges were fishing for? Anyway, it only reinforces Judi's growing opinion. By the time she goes home to put her hair up in curlers, and to affix false eyelashes for the first time in her life, Judi Brewer is absolutely convinced that Doris Smith is the only thing that stands between her and Miss Wilson 1970.

COMMENT

In this early section of his book on Miss America, Frank Deford describes the preliminary interview in the local Miss America contest in Wilson,

North Carolina. In succeeding sections he describes the events that followed. The judges of the local contest are old hands and have long memories; one of them mentions Jeanne Swanner, Miss North Carolina of 1963, who sometimes emcees local contests. The chapter from which this section is taken focuses on Doris Smith and Judi Brewer, who became finalists for first and second place.

Deford's attitude toward Miss America is suggested by his opening comment in the book: "Maligned by one segment of America, adored by another, misunderstood by about all of it, Miss America still flows like the Mississippi, drifts like amber waves of grain, sounds like the crack of a bat on a baseball, tastes like Mom's apple pie, and smells like dollar bills." He is obviously concerned with the values the contest represents. In the section printed here, he is direct about how the contest affects the participants. "Over six feet tall," he says about Wendy Formo, "she cannot help walking like a normal person." And he has similar things to say about how the girls act on the advice of Mrs. Butner, a woman from Rocky Mount who has been tutoring them. Another important indication of tone is the incongruity he stresses: the girls are forced to walk and sit in uncomfortable ways; their answers to questions are also forced. Deford need not comment directly on their situations. His sympathy for them shapes his attitude and therefore his tone; so does his complex attitude toward the contest and the idea of "Miss America." Tone is revealed unmistakably in exaggeration as in understatement—if the author prefers not to state his or her attitude directly. The details selected for emphasis can be equally revealing.

QUESTIONS FOR STUDY AND DISCUSSION

1. How does Deford's choice of details stress the incongruous? How do his comparisons to Army fatigues, bustles, and little dogs make the incongruities vivid to us?

2. Does he express or imply the same attitude toward all the girls in the contest? To what extent is his sympathy toward them qualified by his attitude toward the values represented by or implied in the contest?

3. What are those values, and what details best reveal them?

4. How sympathetic is Deford toward the judges? Is it his view that the panel is "hot-shot," or is he giving someone's opinion of it?

5. What does Deford mean by the statement that "it is the underside of the iceberg that determines the winner"? How does he illustrate the statement?

6. Does Deford resort to understatement or irony, or does he depend solely on the details to create tone?

7. How does he establish and maintain a consistent point of view in the whole essay? What is the order of ideas?

8. What are your feelings toward the contestants and the judges? How much were they shaped for you by Deford?

VOCABULARY STUDY

Identify words and phrases that you would classify as slang (such as "hotshot") and determine their use in the essay, in particular their contribution to the overall tone. If this slang is no longer current, suggest how the statements might be reworded to convey the same tone.

SUGGESTIONS FOR WRITING

1. Describe a contest in which you participated. Focus on the behavior and attitude of the judges or the participants, and use your discussion to reveal your attitude toward the contest. Choose vivid details that best reveal the values represented by or implied in the contest.

2. Discuss what you think Deford is saying or implying about the contest. Consider his details about the judges as well as about the contestants.

3. Rewrite a part of this essay from the point of view of one of the contestants. Allow her attitude toward the judges and the contest itself to emerge in the details she selects and the feelings she expresses.

definition

There are many ways to define a word, each depending on our purpose in writing and on the knowledge of our readers. In talking to a child, it may be enough to define a cow by pointing to one in a pasture or picture book. To an older child we may point to a cow through words: first by relating it to the class *animal,* then stating the *specific differences* between the cow and all other animals: "the mature female of domestic cattle (genus *Bos*)" (*Webster's New World Dictionary*). Also, we could explain that *cow* can refer to the female elephant or whale and other female animals.

These definitions are called *denotative* because they point to the object or single it out from all others. *Connotative* definitions by contrast refer to ideas and feelings associated to the word. Denotative definitions are the same for everyone; connotative definitions are not. To some people *cow* suggests laziness, or stupidity—connotations that explain phrases like "dumb as an ox"; others may associate a cow with feelings of nourishment and contentment. These connotations are sometimes called *subjective.* Connotations may, however, express intrinsic, *objective* properties: the cow is a passive animal, compared to the bull.

If we want to explain the origin or derivation of a word, perhaps for the purpose of explaining current meanings, we may state its etymology. The word *coward* derives from the idea of an animal whose tail hangs between its legs. The etymology illuminates one or more connotations of the word. We may, if we wish, propose or stipulate a new word for an idea or discovery. In the thirties Congressman Maury Maverick proposed the word *gobbledygook* as a description for pretentious, involved official writing. Such definitions may gain general acceptance. Some definitions remain in use for years, only to fall into disuse as new discoveries are made and new ideas appear, and better terms are invented to describe them.

How full our definition is depends on its purpose in the essay, as well as on the reader. For one kind of reader it may not be necessary to point to or single out an object: the writer will assume that the reader knows what the object is, and needs only to be told how it works. Parts of the object (the blade casing of a manual lawn mower) may be defined fully in the course of describing how to care for or fix it; other parts may not be defined because they are unimportant to the process. It may be enough to tell readers of novels written about the twenties that the Pierce-Arrow is an expensive automobile, or we may give one or two distinctive qualities of the Pierce-Arrow to explain an allusion to it.

THE WOOLEN SARAPE

Robert Ramirez

Robert Ramirez was born in Edinburg, Texas, in 1950. He graduated from Pan American College, where he later taught freshman composition. He also taught elementary school and he is now a photographer, reporter, and announcer for a television news department in Texas.

[1]The train, its metal wheels squealing as they spin along the silvery tracks, rolls slower now. Through the gaps between the cars blinks a streetlamp, and this pulsing light on a barrio streetcorner beats slower, like a weary heartbeat, until the train shudders to a halt, the light goes out, and the barrio is deep asleep.

[2]Throughout Aztlán (the Nahuatl term meaning "land to the north"), trains grumble along the edges of a sleeping people. From Lower California, through the blistering Southwest, down the Rio Grande to the muddy Gulf, the darkness and mystery of dreams

Reprinted by permission of Robert Ramirez.

engulf communities fenced off by railroads, canals, and express-ways. Paradoxical communities, isolated from the rest of the town by concrete columned monuments of progress, and yet stranded in the past. They are surrounded by change. It eludes their reach, in their own backyards, and the people, unable and unwilling to see the future, or even touch the present, perpetuate the past.

[3] Leaning from the expressway or jolting across the tracks, one enters a different physical world permeated by a different attitude. The physical dimensions are impressive. It is a large section of town which extends for fifteen blocks north and south along the tracks, and then advances eastward, thinning into nothingness beyond the city limits. Within the invisible (yet sensible) walls of the barrio, are many, many people living in too few houses. The homes, how-ever, are much more numerous than on the outside.

[4] Members of the barrio describe the entire area as their home. It is a home, but it is more than this. The barrio is a refuge from the harshness and the coldness of the Anglo world. It is a forced refuge. The leprous people are isolated from the rest of the community and contained in their section of town. The stoical pariahs of the barrio accept their fate, and from the angry seeds of rejection grow the flowers of closeness between outcasts, not the thorns of bitterness and the mad desire to flee. There is no want to escape, for the feeling of the barrio is known only to its inhabitants, and the material needs of life can also be found here.

[5] The *tortillería* fires up its machinery three times a day, pro-ducing steaming, round, flat slices of barrio bread. In the winter, the warmth of the tortilla factory is a wool *sarape* in the chilly morning hours, but in the summer, it unbearably toasts every noontime customer.

[6] The *panadería* sends its sweet messenger aroma down the dimly lit street, announcing the arrival of fresh, hot sugary *pan dulce*.

[7] The small corner grocery serves the meal-to-meal needs of customers, and the owner, a part of the neighborhood, willingly gives credit to people unable to pay cash for foodstuffs.

[8] The barbershop is a living room with hydraulic chairs, radio, and television, where old friends meet and speak of life as their salted hair falls aimlessly about them.

[9] The pool hall is a junior level country club where 'chucos, strangers in their own land, get together to shoot pool and rap, while

veterans, unaware of the cracking, popping balls on the green felt, complacently play dominoes beneath rudely hung *Playboy* foldouts.

[10] The *cantina* is the night spot of the barrio. It is the country club and the den where the rites of puberty are enacted. Here the young become men. It is in the taverns that a young dude shows his *machismo* through the quantity of beer he can hold, the stories of *rucas* he has had, and his willingness and ability to defend his image against hardened and scarred old lions.

[11] No, there is no frantic wish to flee. It would be absurd to leave the familiar and nervously step into the strange and cold Anglo community when the needs of the Chicano can be met in the barrio.

[12] The barrio is closeness. From the family living unit, familial relationships stretch out to immediate neighbors, down the block, around the corner, and to all parts of the barrio. The feeling of family, a rare and treasurable sentiment, pervades and accounts for the inability of the people to leave. The barrio is this attitude manifested on the countenances of the people, on the faces of their homes, and in the gaiety of their gardens.

[13] The color-splashed homes arrest your eyes, arouse your curiosity, and make you wonder what life scenes are being played out in them. The flimsy, brightly colored, wood-frame houses ignore no neon-brilliant color. Houses trimmed in orange, chartreuse, lime-green, yellow, and mixtures of these and other hues beckon the beholder to reflect on the peculiarity of each home. Passing through this land is refreshing like Brubeck, not narcoticizing like revolting rows of similar houses, which neither offend nor please.

[14] In the evenings, the porches and front yards are occupied with men calmly talking over the noise of children playing baseball in the unpaved extension of the living room, while the women cook supper or gossip with female neighbors as they water the *jardines*. The gardens mutely echo the expressive verses of the colorful houses. The denseness of multicolored plants and trees gives the house the appearance of an oasis or a tropical island hideaway, sheltered from the rest of the world.

[15] Fences are common in the barrio, but they are fences and not the walls of the Anglo community. On the western side of town, the high wooden fences between houses are thick, impenetrable walls, built to keep the neighbors at bay. In the barrio, the fences may be rusty, wire contraptions or thick green shrubs. In either case you

can see through them and feel no sense of intrusion when you cross them.

[16] Many lower-income families of the barrio manage to maintain a comfortable standard of living through the communal action of family members who contribute their wages to the head of the family. Economic need creates interdependence and closeness. Small barefooted boys sell papers on cool, dark Sunday mornings, deny themselves pleasantries, and give their earnings to *mamá.* The older the child, the greater the responsibility to help the head of the household provide for the rest of the family.

[17] There are those, too, who for a number of reasons have not achieved a relative sense of financial security. Perhaps it results from too many children too soon, but it is the homes of these people and their situation that numbs rather than charms. Their houses, aged and bent, oozing children, are fissures in the horn of plenty. Their wooden homes may have brick-pattern asbestos tile on the outer walls, but the tile is not convincing.

[18] Unable to pay city taxes or incapable of influencing the city to live up to its duty to serve all the citizens, the poorer barrio families remain trapped in the nineteenth century and survive as best they can. The backyards have well-worn paths to the outhouses, which sit near the alley. Running water is considered a luxury in some parts of the barrio. Decent drainage is usually unknown, and when it rains, the water stands for days, an incubator of health hazards and an avoidable nuisance. Streets, costly to pave, remain rough, rocky trails. Tires do not last long, and the constant rattling and shaking grind away a car's life and spread dust through screen windows.

[19] The houses and their *jardines,* the jollity of the people in an adverse world, the brightly feathered alarm clock pecking away at supper and cautiously eyeing the children playing nearby, produce a mystifying sensation at finding the noble savage alive in the twentieth century. It is easy to look at the positive qualities of life in the barrio, and look at them with a distantly envious feeling. One wishes to experience the feelings of the barrio and not the hardships. Remembering the illness, the hunger, the feeling of time running out on you, the walls, both real and imagined, reflecting on living in the past, one finds his envy becoming more elusive, until it has vanished altogether.

[20] Back now beyond the tracks, the train creaks and groans, the cars jostle each other down the track, and as the light begins its pulsing, the barrio, with all its meanings, greets a new dawn with yawns and restless stretchings.

COMMENT

The word *barrio* is Spanish in origin; in Spanish-speaking countries it refers to a neighborhood, district, or suburb. Ramirez goes beyond this simple denotative definition to objective connotations of the word—the associations the barrio has for its inhabitants. We know that Ramirez considers these connotations objective, for he states that he is describing barrios in the southwestern United States. The word also has subjective connotations for him; he suggests these toward the beginning and at the end of the essay. Through his definition Ramirez defines not only a place but a culture. His details reveal the quality of life that distinguishes the barrio from other cultural worlds in the United States.

QUESTIONS FOR STUDY AND DISCUSSION

1. What statements and details show that Ramirez is writing to an audience unfamiliar with the barrio?

2. What qualities do the people of the barrio share? Does Ramirez show qualities or attitudes that mark them as individuals—as separate people living in the same neighborhood?

3. Is Ramirez saying that the barrio culture is a protest against the "Anglo" world outside the barrio?

4. What are the objective connotations of the barrio for Ramirez? What subjective connotations does the barrio hold for him?

5. In what order are the details of the barrio presented? What is the physical and personal point of view of the essay?

6. Do you find an overall tone in the essay—or several tones?

7. What details of barrio life do you recognize in your own neighborhood or town or city? In general, what similarities and differences are there between the barrio and your own world?

VOCABULARY STUDY

1. Look up the following words in a Spanish-English dictionary and state their use in the essay: *tortillería, sarape, panadería, pan dulce, cantina, machismo, jardines, rucas.*

2. Write sentences of your own, using the following words to reveal their dictionary meanings: *paradoxical, permeated, stoical, pariahs, mutely, adverse.*

SUGGESTIONS FOR WRITING

1. Discuss how the title of the essay contributes to the overall tone and point of view. Then analyze the order of ideas and development of the thesis.

2. Describe the prevailing culture, or variety of cultures, in a neighborhood or community you know well. Include the extent to which people of the neighborhood share a common language, perhaps a slang that protects them from the world outside. Give particular attention to their feelings and attitudes toward that outside world. Note that you will be defining through a listing of properties.

THE WOOD STOVE

The Foxfire Book

Eliot Wigginton was born in Wheeling, West Virginia, in 1942. In 1966 he came to Rabun Gap, Georgia, a small town in the Appalachians, to teach English and journalism at Rabun Gap-Nacoochee School. In the following year, with his help, the students of the school began publication of *Foxfire,* a magazine that described their world and ways of doing things. The contents of the magazine—and of *The Foxfire Book* (1972)—is the work of these students. This book and its sequels preserve the crafts, lore, and folkways of the older rural communities in the Appalachian mountains—much of this knowledge transmitted orally from generation to generation, rather than written down. In preserving this knowledge, the students who put together the *Foxfire* books have come to understand better important traditions and ways of life.

[1] Wood stoves were considered to be an improvement over fireplaces for cooking, but they still required a lot of attention. As with the fireplace, dry kindling and green wood had to be cut to fit the firebox and kept on hand, and the fire had to be watched so that it didn't go out or get too hot.

[2] The fire was built in the firebox located on the left-hand side of the stove right under the cooking surface. To save time, people often used coals right from the fireplace to start the fire.

[3] At the bottom of the firebox is a coarse iron grate through which the ashes fall into the ash box. The soot which rises into the flue later falls back down into the soot tray which is directly underneath the oven. Both the ash box and soot tray are drawers that must be cleaned out once a week if the stove is used regularly.

[4] The cooking surface of a wood stove usually has six eyes (round openings with iron lids). Sometimes they are all the same size, sometimes of varying sizes. The one at the center in the back of the stove is the hottest, the two over the woodbox are middling, and the other three are the cooler ones. The heat under the eyes cannot be regulated individually, so pots have to be moved from one to the other according to how much heat is required. Sometimes, when people wanted to heat something in a hurry, they would remove an eye and place the pot directly over the flames in the firebox.

[5] Most of the stoves were fairly simple, though some of them got quite elaborate. One larger variety even had a flat griddle on top for frying things like pancakes, eggs, and bacon.

[6] The oven is usually located on the right-hand side of the stove and is heated from the left and top by the circulation of heat from the firebox. The heat flows from the firebox through a four-inch high air space directly under the cooking surface to the other side. It heats more evenly than one might imagine, but if something tends to cook more on one side than the other, it has to be turned around

at regular intervals. The main problem with the oven is that it is difficult to keep the temperature constant. Many varieties have a temperature gauge on the door, but this acts as a warning signal rather than as a regulator. If the oven gets too cool, more wood has to be added; and if it gets too hot, the only thing that can be done is to open the door slightly or put a pan of cold water on one of the racks. For something that takes an hour to bake, the fire has to be tended three or four times to maintain the temperature.

[7]When cooking biscuits and cornbread, early cooks often started them on the lower rack of the oven to brown the bottom and then placed them on the higher rack to brown the top. Cakes, pies and roasts were usually kept on the bottom rack all the time. When broiling meat or toasting bread, the top rack was used.

[8]About two feet above the cooking surface, most wood stoves have two warming closets. These are metal boxes about six inches deep with a door on each, and they are used to keep food warm until it is ready to be served. The stoves also have a damper that seals off the right side of the firebox and greatly cuts the circulation of heat. It doesn't put out the fire, but it cools the rest of the stove so that it can be left unattended fairly safely. When the damper is closed, the coals will remain hot for several hours. It has to be left open when the stove is in use.

[9]We asked Margaret Norton, a real chef on a wood stove, what some of the advantages and disadvantages of using one are. Here's what she told us—

[10]"I've always used a wood stove because we live up here in the woods and there's always plenty of wood. They're good in the wintertime because they sure do warm up the kitchen. In the summer it gets uncomfortable hot in here; 'course we can go out on the porch every few minutes. But we're used to it. With this you have to build a fire and wait till it's ready, but by the time you make up your cornbread or peel your potatoes, it's hot.

[11]"Sometimes wind'll blow down the pipe hard and smoke the house, and the soot flies out all over the place and you have to wipe off everything. And you have to clean it out every so often and watch that sparks don't fall out on the floor.

[12]"And of course you have to gather your wood, and that's a disadvantage when you're out of it. But if the electricity goes off or the gas gives out, you're alright if you've got wood."

COMMENT

If the object under discussion is well known, the writer may dispense with a formal definition of it, or may provide only the specific difference between it and other objects in the same class. The author here dispenses with part of the definition, assuming that the reader has a general idea of the wood stove, and states only a few of its specific differences from fireplaces and other stoves. The purpose of the essay is to explain the use of wood stoves, and the author accordingly discusses those properties basic to cooking.

QUESTIONS FOR STUDY AND DISCUSSION

1. In what order are the properties of the wood stove presented? Would you present these in the same order in teaching a person how to cook on a wood stove?

2. What are the disadvantages mentioned? Would you mention them in the order the author does in teaching a person how to avoid them?

3. What does the description suggest about the life and values of people who cook on wood stoves?

4. Can you think of advantages and disadvantages of the wood stove not mentioned by the author but implied in the description?

VOCABULARY STUDY

1. Write a formal definition of *wood stove* on the basis of the information provided in the essay and your knowledge of other stoves, including the fireplace.

2. The class of a denotative dictionary definition may be exceedingly broad (*tool*) or relatively narrow (*saw*). A saw might be defined as a tool or cutting instrument that is different from other tools or cutting instruments in specific ways; a hacksaw would be defined as a saw that is different from all other saws in specific ways. Examine the class in the dictionary definitions of the following objects, and decide how broad or narrow you think it is: *woodbox, griddle, temperature gauge, pan, damper, rack.*

3. The following words are mainly connotative in their meanings. Write definitions for two of them, distinguishing their objective from their subjective connotations—that is, the general associations everyone

makes and the special associations you make to the words: *cute, cool, flip, crazy, silly.*

SUGGESTIONS FOR WRITING

1. Define an object in the kitchen or workshop by listing its properties and various uses. Decide on a principle of order for your details before you begin writing.

2. Describe the advantages and disadvantages of an automobile or other vehicle that you drive or use. You may wish to compare the vehicle with another of the same kind.

THE GOOD, THE BAD, AND THE CUTE

Ben Yagoda

Ben Yagoda, a 1975 Yale graduate, was born and grew up in New York City, where he now lives and works as a free-lance writer. His articles have been published in *American Heritage, Sports Illustrated, New Republic, Dissent,* and *Newsweek,* and his film criticism appears regularly in *The American Spectator.* Besides the movies, another special interest of Yagoda's, as this essay makes clear, is words—their origin and meaning, and their effect as a social force.

[1] What do Tony Manero, Rocky Balboa, R2D2 and C3PO, the aliens in "Close Encounters," Annie Hall, Peter Frampton, my 3-year-old cousin and Jimmy Carter have in common? They're cute, that's what.

[2] You'll have to take my word about my cousin, and that of a Portland, Ore., woman about the President (she made him blush by telling him recently, "I think you're really cute, I really do"). As for Frampton, a rock writer recently reported: "An editor sent me to a Peter Frampton concert with orders to 'talk to those girls and find

out why they like him.' I came back with a notebook in which the word 'cute' was scrawled 452 times."

[3] And it seems undeniable that the appeal of the cinematic examples springs from a common source. They are good-hearted, not too bright and, in various ways, ineffectual. Tony and Rocky are tongue-tied, Annie is scatterbrained and the robots and aliens have a hard time getting around. They all represent, it seems to me, a standard of attractiveness that has gained a lamentable ascendancy in America today: the esthetics of cute.

[4] Although in nineteenth-century America cute was a synonym for shrewd or clever, it now means, according to my dictionary, "pleasingly pretty or dainty." The first thing to be called cute in this sense, I'd be willing to bet, was a baby. I don't know why we find babies so adorable. Perhaps the attraction evolved so we wouldn't kick them in the head when they bawled at 3 in the morning and thereby finish off the species. Whatever the reason, babies definitely represent the platonic ideal of cute. Other things—dogs, older humans, knickknacks, hats, hair-dos—are called cute insofar as they are babylike and possess those qualities of softness and inadvertent charm that knock us out in 2-year-olds.

[5] Cute is not so terrible in itself; it represents, after all, another kind of beauty in the world. But to call someone cute is, in a way, to insult him: it puts him in the class of toddlers and domestic animals. Valuing cuteness also means giving short shrift to more honorable virtues, like intelligence and moral courage, that are self-conscious, complex, ethically relevant and risky. Esthetically, cute leads us to overlook the grand in favor of the easily digestible, to prefer Donny and Marie to Mahler. In general, it reduces the scale of our sensibilities.

[6] But worst of all is cute's habit of expanding its influence, until it is not merely an esthetic standard, but a principle of behavior. Some people, in other words, *try* to be cute, feigning innocence or helplessness in order to be appealing. They make intentionally silly jokes, speak in outdated slang, perpetually play the bumpkin. This preciousness is certainly the low point of cute: it may offer some momentary charm, but it is really a selling out of the self.

[7] The esthetics of cute have been put to their most widespread use in romantic love. It is a venerable Hollywood dictum that screen lovers must "meet cute," and so they have—in stalled elevators, upending each other's cafeteria trays, wearing embarrassing costumes, and so forth, ad infinitum. The population at large eagerly

participates in this conception of romance, in the idea of love as coincidence and caprice; after all, cute is America's most popular adjective for sexual prospects.

[8] Behavior has been affected, too. Men chat up women they are interested in with "lines" that could have been lifted straight from a '30s comedy, and women respond in kind, with a coquettishness they have been taught is their chief weapon. The reason for this playacting, as the geniuses of Hollywood shrewdly realized, is that being cute lets us manage what makes us uncomfortable without really confronting it; it defuses the dangers of love.

[9] Looking to Hollywood again, it's easy to see that more than just love is involved. I am convinced that a major reason for the success of "One Flew Over the Cuckoo's Nest" was the portrayal of the victims of mental illness as cuddly and harmless. Cute old people, spry and feisty, are a cinematic convention that takes the sting out of aging and sells the elderly short. Remember all those comically simple brown-skinned servants? The exotic location films where entire countries were rendered cute?

[10] Viewing foreigners (or anyone) as picturesque robs them of the respect we accord individuals. It leads to travesties like Bloomingdale's theme show, "India: The Ultimate Fantasy," which ignored the dominant characteristic of the fantasized country, horrible poverty. It can be argued, too, that our country's readiness to intervene in Southeast Asia a decade and a half ago was conditioned by our habit of seeing natives as nothing more than lovable and/or inscrutable features of a landscape.

[11] The esthetics of cute can be applied to things as well as people. Consider, for example, the design of franchised fast-food restaurants. When these establishments were first constructed, they resembled tacky spaceships or futuristic factories and thus paid homage to the car culture that spawned them. Today the trend is to make the structures look like suburban homes. Now one can stop for a burger or a pizza in a mock-colonial, mock-Tudor, mock-ranch or mock-Cape Cod joint. This form of cuteness not only plays hooky from the form-reflects-function school of architecture, it also substitutes fraudulent good taste for truthful kitsch.

[12] I sometimes imagine what it would be like if the esthetics of cute took over the whole country. All lettering would be soft and rounded, like a Burger King sign. All men would blush like John Travolta and stumble over words of more than two syllables. All women would wear the Annie Hall look. All advertisements would

be self-consciously "wacky." Knickknacks and pets, would proliferate. Everybody would dot their i's with circles—or, worse yet, with hearts. Everybody would be a character. And I would move to the Khyber Pass.

COMMENT

Yagoda defines *cute* in a number of ways—through its uses today, through its uses in the past, through comparison with other words like *beauty*. Some of these kinds of definition are denotative, some connotative; together they give us what is sometimes called a *theoretical* definition that proposes a general idea or theory. Yagoda's theory occurs in his statement about contemporary American attitudes and values: "Valuing cuteness also means giving short shrift to more honorable virtues, like intelligence and moral courage, that are self-conscious, complex, ethically relevant and risky." The first ten paragraphs concern cuteness in people; the concluding two paragraphs, cuteness in things. Yagoda draws on contemporary as well as past experiences and attitudes to make his points. Writing for a different audience, perhaps people of another country who have never eaten at a Burger King and have never seen American movies like *Saturday Night Fever* and *Rocky,* he would have explained some of his examples and described particular situations.

QUESTIONS FOR STUDY AND DISCUSSION

1. What is the "common source" from which the appeal of the movies cited in paragraph 1 derives? Do you understand why Yagoda considers these examples of cuteness? What examples would you cite?

2. Yagoda tells us that cuteness reduces "the scale of our sensibilities," that is, it reduces our feelings to those of a baby and infantilizes everything around us. What are the feelings Yagoda has in mind? Does this meaning of cuteness accord with your understanding of the word?

3. What is the difference between cuteness as "an esthetic standard" and as "a principle of behavior"?

4. What is the "idea of love" implied in the behavior of screen lovers described in paragraph 7?

5. What are the serious consequences of cuteness, according to Yagoda? What consequences does he not consider serious?

6. How does the "mock-colonial" or "mock-ranch" burger or pizza place depart from "the form-reflects-function school of architecture," the idea that the design of a building should serve its chief purpose and nothing else?

7. What use does Yagoda make of denotative definition in the course of the essay? What parts of his definition of cuteness are connotative?

8. Do you agree with the theory that Yagoda proposes in the essay?

VOCABULARY STUDY

1. How do the details of paragraph 3 explain why the movie examples cited are "ineffectual"?

2. Yagoda refers to "a standard of attractiveness that has gained a lamentable ascendancy in America today." Does the word *ascendancy* suggest that the change in standards of beauty occurred overnight? What does his statement in paragraph 4 that "perhaps the attraction evolved "suggest about the speed of the change?

3. What is a *knickknack* denotatively? What is it connotatively?

4. What does the word *toddler* connote that the word *baby* does not?

5. Look up Gustav Mahler in an encyclopedia or reference book on music. What qualities are usually associated with his music? Why does Yagoda contrast him with Donny and Marie?

6. What is a *psychosis,* and why is it not "cuddly and harmless"?

7. Look up *esthetics.* Which of its meanings does Yagoda use in the course of the essay?

SUGGESTIONS FOR WRITING

1. Find advertisements in a recent issue of a popular magazine that Yagoda would consider cute. Write on three or four of them, explaining why you think he would consider them cute. State whether you agree with his definition and the application he makes of it.

2. Provide your own examples of cuteness from current movies and television shows. Explain why they illustrate Yagoda's definition.

3. Discuss the various meanings the word *cute* has for you. Distinguish the areas of use for this word—from people to things.

division

To *divide* is to arrange in constituent groups or parts. The grouping depends on the basis or principle of division. For example, apples can be divided in a number of ways:

> *by color:* red apples, green apples, yellow apples, etc.
> *by use:* eating apples, cooking apples, etc.
> *by variety:* Winesap, Jonathan, Golden Delicious, etc.
> *by taste:* sweet, tart, winy, etc.

The principle of division depends on the purpose of the analysis. In instructing people what apples to buy for eating raw, cooking, or canning, we would group or divide apples according to use, variety, and taste at least. Color would not be important. The division need be only as complete as our purpose requires, but we should state whether the division is an exhaustive one—that is, whether we have listed all the uses or varieties or tastes. If more than one division is made in the course of an essay (that is, a division according to color, use, and variety), each should be distinguished for the reader. Division is, like definition, an important method of analysis in exposition and argument.

THE VIOLENT GANG

Lewis Yablonsky

Lewis Yablonsky was born in 1924 in Irvington, New Jersey and studied at Rutgers and New York University, where he received his Ph.D. in 1957. He has taught at several universities, including the University of Massachusetts and the University of California at Los Angeles, and he is now professor of sociology at

California State University in Northridge. He has written much about juvenile crime. This essay was first published in 1960.

[1] It is a truism that criminal organizations and criminal activities tend to reflect social conditions. Just as surely as the Bowery gang mirrored aspects of the 1900's, the Capone mob aspects of the twenties, and the youth gangs of the depression elements of the thirties, so do the delinquent gangs that have developed since the 1940's in the United States reflect certain patterns of our own society.

[2] The following quotations indicate the tone and ethos of a representative gang of today, the so-called Egyptian Kings, whose members beat and stabbed to death a fifteen-year-old boy named Michael Farmer in a New York City park not long ago. Michael Farmer, who had been crippled by polio, was not known to the Kings before the killing, nor had he been acquainted with any members of the gang.

> He couldn't run any way, 'cause we were all around him. So then I said, "You're a Jester," and he said "Yeah," and I punched him in the face. And then somebody hit him with a bat over the head. And then I kept punchin' him. Some of them were too scared to do anything. They were just standin' there, lookin'.

> I was watchin' him. I didn't wanna hit him, at first. Then I kicked him twice. He was layin' on the ground, lookin' up at us. I kicked him on the jaw, or some place; then I kicked him in the stomach. That was the least I could do, was kick 'im.

> I was aimin' to hit him, but I didn't get a chance to hit him. There was so many guys on him—I got scared when I saw the knife go into the guy, and I ran right there. After everybody ran, this guy stayed, and started hittin' him with a machete.

> Somebody yelled out, "Grab him. He's a Jester." So then they grabbed him. Magician grabbed him, he turned around and stabbed him in the back. I was . . . I was stunned. I couldn't do nuthin'. And then Magician—he went like that and he pulled . . . he had a switch blade and he said, "You're gonna hit him with the bat or I'll stab you." So I just hit him lightly with the bat.

> Magician stabbed him and the guy he . . . like hunched over. He's standin' up and I knock him down. Then he was down on the ground,

everybody was kickin' him, stompin' him, punchin' him, stabbin' him so he tried to get back up and I knock him down again. Then the guy stabbed him in the back with a bread knife.

The attitudes toward homicide and violence that emerge from these statements led to eleven gang killings last summer and can be expected to produce an even greater number from now on.

[3] One important difference between the gangs of the past and those that now operate on our city streets is the prevalence of the psychopathic element in the latter. The violent gangs of the twenties contained psychopaths, but they were used to further the profitmaking goal of the gang, and were themselves paid for their violence. Here, for example, is how Abe "Kid Twist" Reles—who informed on Murder, Inc., and confessed to having committed over eighteen murders himself—described the activities of the Crime Trust to a writer in the *Nation:*

The Crime Trust, Reles insists, never commits murders out of passion, excitement, jealousy, personal revenge, or any of the usual motives which prompt private unorganized murders. It kills impersonally and solely for business considerations. No gangster may kill on his own initiative; every murder must be ordered by the leaders at the top, and it must serve the welfare of the organization. . . . Any member of the mob who would dare kill on his own initiative or for his own profit would be executed. . . . The Crime Trust insists that murder must be a business matter organized by the chiefs in conference and carried out in a disciplined way.

[4] Frederic Thrasher's famous analysis of Chicago gangs in the mid-twenties describes another group that bears only a limited resemblance to the violent gangs of today. Thrasher's gangs

. . . broke into box cars and "robbed" bacon and other merchandise. They cut out wire cables to sell as junk. They broke open telephone boxes. They took autos for joy-riding. They purloined several quarts of whiskey from a brewery to drink in their shack. . . .

[5] Nor do the gangs of the thirties and early forties described by W. F. Whyte in *Street Corner Society* bear much resemblance to the violent gang of today. The difference becomes strikingly evident

when we compare the following comments by two Egyptian Kings with those of Doc, the leader of Whyte's Norton Street gang.

> I just went like that, and I stabbed him with the bread knife. You know I was drunk so I stabbed him. [*Laughs*] He was screamin' like a dog. He was screamin' there. And then I took the knife out and told the other guys to run. . . .

> The guy that stabbed him in the back with the bread knife, he told me that when he took the knife out o' his back, he said, "Thank you."

Now Doc, leader of the Norton Street gang:

> Nutsy was a cocky kid before I beat him up. . . . After that, he seemed to lose his pride. I would talk to him and try to get him to buck up. . . . I walloped every kid in my gang at some time. We had one Sicilian kid on my street. When I walloped him, he told his father and the father came out looking for me. I hid up on a roof, and Nutsy told me when the father had gone. When I saw the kid next, I walloped him again—for telling his father on me. . . . But I wasn't such a tough kid, Bill. I was always sorry after I walloped him.

[6] Doc's comments about beating up Nutsy—"I would talk to him and try to buck him up"—or about fighting the other kids—"I was always sorry after I walloped them"—are in sharp contrast to the post-assault comments of the Egyptian Kings. Here is how one of the Kings who stabbed Farmer replied to my questions about his part in the homicide. The interview took place in a reformatory.

> KING: "I stab him with the butcher—I mean the bread-knife and then I took it out."
> QUESTION: "What were you thinking about at the time, right then?"
> KING: "What was I thinking? [*Laughs*] I was thinking whether to do it again."
> QUESTION: "Are you sorry about what happened?"
> KING: "Am I sorry? Are you nuts; of course, I'm sorry. You think I like being locked up?"

The element of friendship and camaraderie—one might almost call it cooperativeness—that was central to the Norton Street gang and others like it during the depression is entirely absent from the violent gang of today. To be sure, "candy store" or corner hang-out groups similar to those described by Whyte still exist, but it is not such groups who are responsible for the killings and assaults that have caused so much concern in our major cities in recent years.

[7] Today's violent gang is, above all, characterized by flux. It lacks all the features of an organized group, having neither a definite number of members, nor specific membership roles, nor a consensus of expected norms, nor a leader who supplies directive for action. It is a moblike collectivity which forms around violence in a spontaneous fashion, moving into action—often on the spur of an evening's boredom—in search of "kicks." Violence ranks extremely high in the loose scheme of values on which such gangs are based. To some boys it acts as a kind of existential validation, proving (since they are not sure) that they are alive. Others, clinging to membership in this marginal and amorphous organization, employ violence to demonstrate they are "somebody." But most members of the gang use violence to acquire prestige or to raise their "rep."

> I didn't want to be like ... you know, different from the other guys. Like they hit him, I hit him. In other words, I didn't want to show myself as a punk. You know, ya always talkin', "Oh, man, when I catch a guy, I'll beat him up," and all of that, you know. And after you go out and you catch a guy, and you don't do nothin' they say, "Oh, man, he can't belong to no gang, because he ain't gonna do nothin'."

> Momentarily I started to thinking about it inside: I have my mind made up I'm not going to be in no gang. Then I go on inside. Something comes up, den here come all my friends coming to me. Like I said before, I'm intelligent and so forth. They be coming to me—then they talk to me about what they gonna do. Like, "Man, we'll go out here and kill this cat." I say, "Yeah." They kept on talkin'. I said, "Man, I just gotta go with you." Myself, I don't want to go, but when they start talkin' about what they gonna do, I say, "So, he isn't gonna take over my rep. I ain't gonna let him be known more than me." And I go ahead just for selfishness.

> If I would of got the knife, I would have stabbed him. That would have gave me more of a build-up. People would have respected me for what I've done and things like that. They would say, "There goes a cold killer."

> It makes you feel like a big shot. You know some guys think they're big shots and all that. They think, like you know, they got

the power to do everything they feel like doing. They say, like, "I wanna stab a guy," and then the other guy says, "Oh, I wouldn't dare to do that." You know, he thinks I'm acting like a big shot. That's the way he feels. He probably thinks in his mind, "Oh, he probably won't do that." Then, when we go to fight, you know, he finds out what I do.

[8] The structure of the violent gang can be analyzed into three different levels. At the center, on the first level, are the leaders, who—contrary to the popular idea that they could become "captains of industry if only their energies were redirected"—are the most psychologically disturbed of all the members. These youths (who are usually between eighteen and twenty-five years old) need the gang more than anyone else, and it is they who provide it with whatever cohesive force it has. In a gang of some thirty boys there may be five or six such leaders who desperately rely on the gang to build and maintain a "rep," and they are always working to keep the gang together and in action. They enlist new members (by force), plot, and talk gang warfare most of their waking hours.

[9] At the second level, there are youths who claim affiliation to the gang but only participate in it sporadically. For example, one of the Egyptian Kings told me that if his father had not given him a "bad time" and kicked him out of the house the night of the homicide, he would not have gone to the corner and become involved in the Michael Farmer killing. The gang was for this boy, on that night, a vehicle for acting out aggressions related to another area of his life. Such a "temporal" gang need, however, is a common phenomenon.

[10] At the third level are boys who occasionally join in with gang activity but seldom identify themselves as members of the gang at any other time. One boy, for instance, went along with the Egyptian Kings and participated in the Farmer killing, as he put it, "for old time's sake." He never really "belonged" to the gang: he just happened to be around that night and had nothing else to do.

[11] The "size" of violent gangs is often impossible to determine. If a leader feels particularly hemmed in at a given moment, he will say—and believe—that his gang is very large. But when he is feeling more secure, he will include in his account of the gang's size only those members he actually knows personally. In the course of a one-hour interview, for example, a gang leader variously esti-

mated the size, affiliations, and territory of his gang as follows: membership jumped from one hundred to four thousand, affiliation from five brother gangs or alliances to sixty, and territorial control from about ten square blocks to jurisdiction over the boroughs of New York City, New Jersey, and part of Philadelphia. To be sure, gangs will often contact one another to discuss alliances, and during the street-corner "negotiations," the leaders will brag of their ability to mobilize vast forces in case of a fight. On a rare occasion, these forces will actually be produced, but they generally appear quite spontaneously—the youths who participate in such alliances have very little understanding of what they are doing.

[12] The meaning of gang membership also changes according to a boy's needs of the moment. A youth will belong one day and quit the next without necessarily telling any other member. To ask certain gang boys from day to day whether they are Dragons or Kings is comparable to asking them, "How do you feel today?" So, too, with the question of role. Some boys say that the gang is organized for protection and that one role of a gang member is to fight—how, when, whom, and for what reason he is to fight are seldom clear, and answers vary from member to member. One gang boy may define himself more specifically as a protector of the younger boys in the neighborhood. Another will define his role in the gang by the statement, "We are going to get all those guys who call us Spics." Still others say their participation in the gang was forced upon them against their will.

[13] Despite these differences, however, all gang members believe that through their participation they will acquire prestige and status; and it is quite clear, furthermore, that the vagueness which surrounds various aspects of gang life and organization only enables the gang to stimulate such expectations and, in some respects, actually helps it to fulfill them. Similarly, if qualifications for membership were more exact, then most gang members would not be able to participate, for they lack the ability to assume the responsibilities of more structured organizations.

[14] The background out of which the violent gang has emerged is fairly easy to sketch. In contemporary American society, youth is constantly bombarded by images—from the media, schools, and parents—of a life of ownership and consumption, but for the great majority of young people in this country, and especially for those

from depressed social and economic backgrounds, the means of acquiring such objectives are slim. Yet something more definite than class position or the inadequate relation between means and ends disturbs young people. It is the very fact of their youth which places them at an immediate disadvantage; objects and goals that adults take for granted are, for them, clearly unattainable. As a consequence, many young people step beyond the accepted social boundaries in an attempt to find through deviant means a dramatic short-cut to an immediate feeling of success.*

[15] Drugs and alcohol are two possible short cuts; another characteristic deviant path is the search for thrills or "kicks." The violent gang, especially because it is both flexibly organized and amenable to the distortions of fantasy, is an obvious vehicle for acting out the desire for ownership and status. In the gang, a youth can be "president" and control vast domains, while the members can reinforce one another's fantasies of power—"Don't call my bluff and I won't call yours." In the gang, it is only necessary to talk big and support the talk with some violent action in order to become a "success," the possessor of power and status: "We would talk a lot and like that, but I never thought it would be like this. Me here in jail. It was just like fun and kidding around and acting big."

[16] The choice of violence as a means toward achieving "social" success seems to be the result in part of the past two decades of war as well as the international unrest that filters down to the gang boy and gives him the same feelings of uneasiness that the average citizen experiences. At this level of analysis, direct casual relations are by *no means* precise; yet a number of connections do seem apparent.

[17] A considerable amount of explicit data indicates that recent wars and current international machinations serve as models for gang warfare. For example, one form of gang battle is called a "Jap": "a quick stomp where a group of guys go into an enemy's territory, beat up some of their guys and get out fast. The thing is not to get caught." "Drafting" members is another common gang practice. The boys themselves freely use such terms as "drafting," "allies" (brother gangs), "war counselor," "peace treaty," etc., and they often refer, both directly and indirectly, to more complex patterns of con-

---

*This statement is a gross oversimplification of conceptual developments of Emile Durkheim, Robert Merton, and others, who have examined the means-goal dislocation.

flict and structure. Here is one Egyptian King talking about a territorial dispute:

> You have a certain piece of land, so another club wants to take over your land, in order to have more space, and so forth. They'll fight you for it. If you win, you got your land; if you don't win, then they get your land. The person that loses is gonna get up another group, to help out, and then it starts all over again. Fight for the land again.

Here is another discussing gang organization:

> First, there's the president. He got the whole gang; then there comes the vice president, he's second in command; then there's the war counselor, war lord, whatever you're gonna call it—that's the one that starts the fights; then there's the prime minister— you know, he goes along with the war counselor to see when they're gonna fight, where they're gonna fight. And after that, just club members.

Murder, Inc., Thrasher's gangs, and Whyte's Norton Street gang did not have the "divisions," "war lords," and "allies" typical of the contemporary violent gang.

[18] In addition to this international model, it is important to note that many weapons now used by gangs were brought to this country by veterans of recent wars. Where in former years, gang wars were more likely to be fought with sticks, stones, and fists, today abandoned World War II weapons such as machetes (one was used in the Michael Farmer killing) and Lugers consistently turn up. The returning soldiers also brought back stories of violence to accompany the weapons. War and violence dominated not only the front pages of the press, but everyday family discussion, and often it was a father, an uncle, or an older brother whose violent exploits were extolled.

[19] Another aspect of international events which gang youths may have absorbed, and which they certainly now emulate, is the authoritarian-dictatorial concept of leadership. Earlier gangs sometimes utilized democratic processes in appointing leaders. But, today, in the violent gang, the leader is usually supreme and gang members tend to follow him slavishly. In recent years, in fact, there have been many abortive attempts—several on the Upper West Side of New York City—to pattern gangs specifically upon the model of Hitler and the Nazi party.

[20] What finally confronts the youth of today is the possibility of total destruction by atomic power—everyone is aware of this on some level of consciousness—and the possibility of induction into the army at a point when he might be establishing himself in the labor force. In short, the recent history of international violence, the consequences of the past war, and the chance of total annihilation, establish a framework which may not only stimulate the formation of gangs but in some respects may determine its mode of behavior—in other words, its violence.

[21] But such background factors, however much they create an atmosphere that gives implicit social approval to the use of violence, cannot actually explain how violence functions for the gang boy. As I have already indicated, gang youths feel extremely helpless in their relations to the "outside" world. The gang boy considers himself incapable of functioning in any group other than the gang, and is afraid to attempt anything beyond the minimal demands of gang life. One interesting indication of this is the way gang boys respond to flattery. They invariably become flustered and confused if they are complimented, for the suggestion that they are capable of more constructive activity upsets their conviction of being unfit for the hazards of a life outside the protective circle of the gang.

[22] Given this low self-estimate, the gang boy has carved out a world and a system of values which entail only the kind of demands he can easily meet. Inverting society's norms to suit himself and the limits of his partly imagined and partly real potential, he has made lying, assault, theft, and unprovoked violence—and especially violence—the major activities of his life.

[23] The very fact that it is *senseless* rather than premeditated violence which is more highly prized by the gang, tells us a great deal about the role violence plays for the gang boy. He is looking for a quick, almost magical way of achieving power and prestige, and in a single act of unpremeditated intensity he at once establishes a sense of his own existence and impresses this existence on others. No special ability is required—not even a plan— and the anxiety attendant upon executing a premeditated (or "rational") act of violence is minimized in the ideal of a swift, sudden, and "meaningless" outbreak. (To some extent, the public's reaction to this violence, a reaction, most obviously of horror, also expresses a sort of covert aggrandizement—and this the gang boy instinctively understands.)

[24] Thus the violent gang provides an alternative world for the

disturbed young who are ill-equipped for success in a society which in any case blocks their upward mobility. The irony is that this world with its nightmare inversion of the official values of our society is nevertheless constructed out of elements that are implicitly (or unconsciously) approved—especially in the mass media—and that its purpose is to help the gang boy achieve the major value of respectable society: success. "I'm not going to let anybody be better than me and steal my 'rep' . . . when I go to a gang fight, I punch, stomp, and stab harder than anyone."

COMMENT

Yablonsky uses division in two ways in the course of the essay. First he divides gangs of the past from gangs of the present; then he defines their purpose and structure. Second, he divides gangs of the present—the violent street gangs—according to their "levels." This division is, in fact, a more detailed analysis of the structure of the gang, for Yablonsky's earlier discussion of that structure is concerned only with its general features. Characterized by constant change or "flux," and existing to express spontaneous violence, the violent gang "lacks all the features of an organized group." The three levels reveal the various motives of the gang members. Reflecting the values of the fifties, the violent gang shows how people are directed by forces beyond their control. Yablonsky's concern over the death of Michael Farmer is in part a concern over wanton acts by boys who did not know their victim or themselves. He returns to this point at the end. His essay shows how an episode (the murder of Michael Farmer) can be used to say much about a society—its values, its structure, the motives of acts that seem "senseless."

QUESTIONS FOR STUDY AND DISCUSSION

1. How does Yablonsky explain the difference between gangs of the past and the violent gang of the fifties?

2. By what other principles might the violent gang be divided? To what use could these divisions be put in another essay?

3. Yablonsky states: "In contemporary American society, youth is constantly bombarded by images—from the media, schools, and parents," and he identifies those images and their effect. Yablonsky was

writing in 1960. Do you believe youth in the late seventies is bombarded by the same images? Are the effects of images the same today?

4. What does Yablonsky mean in paragraph 14 by "the inadequate relation between means and ends"? How does the context of the statement help to explain it?

5. Yablonsky cites the Second World War and the atomic bomb as causes of certain attitudes and behavior in youth of the fifties. Do you believe war and fear of destruction are a major cause of juvenile crime today? Do you believe the pressures to conform are as strong today as they were in the fifties?

6. The phrase "society's norms" (paragraph 22) refers to the values or standards by which people live. How does Yablonsky show that not all of these "norms" are admitted or recognized by the people who live by them?

7. What is Yablonsky's thesis and where is it first stated? How does he restate it in the course of the essay?

8. To what extent does Yablonsky depend on formal transitions?

VOCABULARY STUDY

Complete the following sentences, using the italicized word according to one of its dictionary meanings:
    a. It is a *truism* of life that
    b. One *aspect* of the energy crisis is
    c. There was no *consensus*
    d. The *phenomenon* of flying saucer reports
    e. The teacher was *amenable* to
    f. She could distinguish between *fantasy* and
    g. They could not *emulate*
    h. The contract *entails*
    i. There was a *covert* recognition

SUGGESTIONS FOR WRITING

1. Analyze the "levels" of a group you belong to, or divide the group by another principle. Use your analysis to develop a thesis or to support or argue against one of Yablonsky's conclusions.

2. Make a list of principles of division for each of the following. Then write an essay on one of them, employing a single principle of division:
   a. recreational vehicles
   b. health fads
   c. exercise enthusiasts
   d. animal lovers

THE MEN OUT HUNTING

Vance Bourjaily

Born in Cleveland in 1922, the American novelist Vance Bourjaily has worked as a newspaperman, television dramatist, and playwright, and has taught for many years in the Writers Workshop at the University of Iowa. His novels include *Confessions of a Spent Youth* (1960) and *The Man Who Knew Kennedy* (1967). In the essay reprinted here Bourjaily writes about the various reasons for which people hunt animals.

[1] The man in the duck blind is cold. He snagged his hip boot on barbed wire, walking here in the dark of 5 A.M. It is not much of a snag, but enough to let some water in as he waded around, setting out his decoys. His hands are mittened, his ears muffed, and his body cased with thermal underwear, but the damp sock chilling his right foot is really uncomfortable; armor needs only one chink to fail.

[2] The man out pheasant hunting is footsore. There has been a lot of walking already today, and he is not in shape for it. Four miles of fields and borders, carrying a gun which no longer seems light and with heavy boots to which he is unaccustomed, are too much.

When he gets in the car to go to the next field, the next border, he fights down the impulse to say to his companions: "Let's quit. I've had enough for today."

³The man with the quail dog is hot and itchy. He wore only a shell vest over his short-sleeved shirt, but the vest makes him sweat. The sweat irritates a long briar scratch on his bare right arm, on this warm Southern morning, and mosquitos have started to find him.

⁴The man with the beagles has four rabbits, and is missing a dog; it is almost intolerable to think of carrying the rabbits—seven or eight pounds hanging from his shoulder in a hip-level game pocket—all the way back to the car, let alone haul them around in the woods, whistling and shouting for the errant pup. The man with the magnum goose gun is cross, because people in neighboring pits have been shooting at high birds, spoiling his chances. The man hunting deer is frustrated and half-lost; he has not seen a deer yet, in two days' hunting, and this ridge seems much steeper than the one he climbed yesterday and planned to be on again. The dove hunter's fingertips are full of sandbur spines. The grouse hunter's eye still stings from having an alder branch poked into it, and on a log in the hardwood timber sits a bored man with a squirrel rifle and a crick in his neck from looking up so long and so unavailingly . . .

⁵Hunting, while seldom a dangerous sport in this country, is often an uncomfortable one. It is also often a tedious one, with game quite scarce in most localities—a long time between shots. It is quite frequently an irritating sport, with the commercializers making a pitch to lure more and more of the inexperienced into it, men who innocently or sometimes deliberately so conduct themselves as to spoil things for others. And success, in our democratic hunting, is always crowned with unregal exertions: it is not really much fun to pluck four ducks properly, or drag a hundred-odd pounds of deer carcass through the brush. Constantly one meets men who, having hunted all their lives, up to a couple of years ago, now have second-hand guns for sale and, instead of knowing this year's canvasback limit, can name you all the middle linebackers in professional football. Nevertheless there are many more, several million, who are still hunters, and the question becomes, *why?* What do they get out of it?

⁶Though anti-hunters will, as they always do, pick up their

jolly pens to reply that the enjoyment of hunting lies in the expression by brutal men of their most hideous traits of character, I am not, this time, going to formulate the general defense against this kind of attack. To do so would be to lose the opportunity for making some tentative distinctions among hunters in which there may be more illumination.

⁷Hunters are various sorts of men, and from the sport they take various sorts of pleasure; in a rough way, to which there will be infinite exceptions, they can be divided and understood according to the particular game pursued.

⁸That duck hunter with the cold right foot, for example, is a romantic aesthete, though he might knock you down for saying so. He likes the hush of the world at dawn, the whisper of wings, the gray water lightening and the shadows of birds plunging through mist. He will drive miles, out of season, to watch ducks fly their marvelous patterns. He will take great pleasure in a well-tuned call, a well-made decoy, and perhaps in winter he will himself carve duck figures from walnut or wild cherry. It is no accident that most of the sporting prints and paintings we see are of waterfowl; there is enormous beauty in these birds and in their setting, and in this the duck hunter participates. There is even a moment of painful beauty when a duck falls through the air, displaced from its element by an accurate shot—the hunter catches his breath not in triumph but in wonder at what he has done.

⁹The pheasant hunter is apt to be more gregarious. Pheasant hunting, for most men, is a sociable sort of sport, often involving groups of five or more, walking and hunting together. There are trips from one place to the next, with joshing about shots made or missed and perhaps the passing of a jug. The general heartiness takes the form of quasi-military organization when a new field is reached, with some of the party stationed as blockers at one end, others assigned to walk through driving up birds from the other. The pheasant is not the world's most difficult bird to hit, and a feeling of mutual competitiveness often prevails as to who will get off his shot first, or account for the most birds. Curiously enough, this down-the-middle, regular-fellow aspect of pheasant hunting has an analogy in the quality of the pheasant as a table bird: unlike the exotic wild duck, the pheasant is a perfectly familiar bird to eat. It is a chicken, especially if it has been feeding in cornfields, and while

it can be cooked elegantly if one likes, one generally sees it fried or roasted quite straightforwardly.

[10] Quail hunting is a sport involving decorum. While I would not insist that all quail hunters are fastidious men who enjoy rules and procedures, it seems to me that the best of them are (and I should explain that I am trying to categorize each of these sorts of hunter at his best; there are boors, louts and brutes hunting each kind of game, too, but let us avoid them on the page as we try to in the field, searching for the coverts they do not use). The quail-hunting ritual begins with the training of highly specialized dogs, and a great deal of the pleasure comes in watching the dogs perform correctly. There are other refinements attached to quail shooting, as for example what percentage of a covey may properly be taken (never more than half); and who shall walk in on a point, once the covey is broken up and the singles are being hunted (it is done in turn). The double-barreled shotgun and the unhurried pace are correct in quail shooting—one may proceed differently, of course, just as one may catch trout with worms or lose one's temper publicly in a racket game.

[11] Coming to rabbits, we are again concerned with eating, for the rabbit hunter, more than any other, deserves (and even finds unobjectionable) the epithet of meat hunter. He is a man troubled by empty spaces in his freezer. He would probably not be hunting rabbits for the sport alone, with perhaps an exception to be made for jackrabbit hunters in the West—the jacks are much faster and more difficult to hit than cottontails. The proof that rabbit hunters work for meat might lie, for you, in the matter of donations: in a good year you may occasionally, if you are highly deserving, be offered a duck, or a pheasant or even a brace of quail. But you will not be offered a rabbit. It is not a princely gift, to begin with, and the man who shot it intended to get it home for supper. I don't mean that he is necessarily gluttonous, or that there is no fun in shooting rabbits: but it is essentially a harvester's fun, the pleasure of providing.

[12] Squirrels are quite a different thing. The squirrel hunter, at his best, is an American traditionalist. Unlike the quail man, whose hunting manners come, like his shotgun design, from Europe, the squirrel hunter is a rifleman. His exemplars are Boone and Crockett; he moves well and quietly through the woods, or waits with great patience for the chance to place a difficult, well-calculated shot. Ideally, though the practice could hardly be called widespread,

the squirrel hunter will use a muzzle-loading rifle—there is considerable trade in them among enthusiasts. And with it he will shoot as the frontiersman did, not to hit the squirrel directly but to bark him—that is, to strike the limb just under the squirrel's head, so that the animal is killed instantly, by concussion, from the impact of the heavy lead ball against wood, with no visible wound. There is another sort of dedicated rifleman around, it should be added, whose weapon is the most technologically advanced—scoped and custom-fitted, embodying esoteric ballistic principles in the way its ammunition is loaded. But these riflemen are not generally after squirrels; their engineering natures require open shots at long ranges for fulfillment, and it is the groundhog by a distant burrow, the crow on a far limb, which most engages them.

[13] Goose hunting, as it is done in many of the major centers like Cairo, Illinois, or Swan Lake, Missouri, seems to me so poor and distasteful a sport that I must exclude the customers of these highly organized places from my discussion of hunting pleasures. Geese are entirely too susceptible of being managed, with the result that great concentrations can be held at a given place, and men shuttled in and out to shoot at them in a way which has nothing to do with hunting. If there is pleasure in it, it is a pleasure I do not understand. But there are states which geese cross in their fall migration whose game managers have held out, so far, against the pressure to develop such areas. Through these states the geese still pass in smaller bunches, spending a day or two at isolated sandbars or potholes spread over a whole region. With luck, the waterfowler will take a goose every second or third season. Where hunting conditions have been left natural, the pleasure of taking a goose is a gambler's pleasure, the pleasure of being by chance at the right place to win a magnificent prize.

[14] Deer hunting is subject to a great deal of sectional variation, and I am no authority even locally. But the deer hunter is, of course, a big-game man, finding pleasure in matching himself against the size and wariness of the creature, and not indifferent to the trophy he may acquire. This must of course be true of hunting other American big game as well—bear and moose, elk, buffalo, antelope and big horn sheep. The deer hunter must be a good woodsman, in the East at any rate, and must learn a good deal of lore and technique. A good deer hunter—I know a few, though they are in smaller proportion to the clowns than in other sorts of hunting—is a good man

physically, needing more strength and endurance than do those who hunt birds and small game. Men with this sort of strength, men who have learned hunting skills and woodsmanship to a high degree, quite naturally enjoy entering situations which require their use. It is the pleasure of exercising training and endowment, of learning that one measures up. (In my own region, which is Iowa, where deer are more often found in fields than in deep woods, it is the fox and coon hunters who employ this complex of virtues and aspirations.)

[15] The dove hunter (and in a less widespread way, the snipe hunter) is a man who enjoys shooting. Doves and snipe are small, fast birds, with extraordinarily tricky flight patterns. Even the finest shot may have difficulty in shooting a limit of doves (ten) with a single box of shells (twenty-five), and many of the dove hunters I know are trap and skeet enthusiasts as well. It is a somewhat lazy sport, as far as walking and general exertion go, but pleasantly so—one sits under a tree, or by a fence, perhaps, on a warm day, making or trying pass shots of extreme difficulty. As in deer hunting, the pleasure lies in the exercise of skill, though of quite a different kind.

[16] Though I am newly come to grouse and woodcock shooting, a few days' experience convinces me that here again we have an appeal to a particular sort of hunter personality. Success here is in the excitement, sometimes almost continuous, of contending with innumerable unexpected obstacles. It is a kind of hunting which moves in and out of thick brush and deep woods, with every branch a barrier. Birds are flushing quite constantly, but there are chances to shoot at no more than perhaps 25 per cent of them. Even these are opportunities which exist only for an instant—the bird is there (where?), in the clear for just an instant, and then gone, perhaps before the gun is raised. One needs to love the woods, and the birds themselves, to take a kind of wild pleasure in being eluded. Yet when the woodcock are around in good number, to supplement the resident but scarcer grouse, there is, it seems to me, more continuous adventure in this kind of hunting than in any other. Though it may be less productive, it will satisfy certain natures abundantly.

[17] There are, of course, other sorts of game, some of them outside my experience, but my purpose is not to detail them all. Rather, I am interested in making the point that the term *hunter* covers a considerable variety of men, seeking a considerable variety of values. Often one meets a man who, having begun by hunting everything more or less at random, comes gradually to specialize on the

particular sort of game and hunting situation which best suits his nature. And while my suggestions as to what traits of character are reflected in the choice are, as I have said, tentative, it is possible that something could be added to our understanding of ourselves if these beginning notions could be refined and studied further.

COMMENT

Bourjaily first *classifies* hunters as a way of introducing his readers to the subject; that is, he singles out hunters as a class and shows what experiences they share. He states his principle of division in paragraph 7: he will divide "according to the particular game pursued"—not according to the "various sorts of pleasure" hunters enjoy, or the discomforts mentioned in the opening of the essay. He then builds gradually to his thesis through his observations and experiences. Bourjaily is writing to a wide audience, not to an audience solely of hunters who probably do not have to be convinced that people hunt for various reasons. People who know little or nothing about hunting, and hold various opinions about it, perhaps think of hunters as single in their motive and attitude. The gradual build to the thesis is an effective way of exposing mistaken ideas.

QUESTIONS FOR STUDY AND DISCUSSION

1. How early in the essay does Bourjaily introduce his thesis? Where does he state it fully?

2. Why do you think Bourjaily describes various hunters in the order he does? Could this order be changed without affecting the thesis?

3. Does Bourjaily state or imply an attitude toward hunting in general? Does he state or imply a preference for one kind of hunting? Can you tell what kind he enjoys most, or would like to do?

4. In what other ways could hunters be divided? What purpose would these new divisions serve?

5. Could Bourjaily's division be applied to other classes of people—for example, fishermen or football players or sports fans?

VOCABULARY STUDY

1. Find synonyms for the following words, and decide whether the word is positive or negative in its connotations: *errant* (paragraph 4); *tedi-*

ous, unregal (paragraph 5); aesthete (paragraph 8); gregarious, joshing (paragraph 9); boors, louts, brutes (paragraph 10); traditionalist,
exemplars (paragraph 12).

2. Give the meaning of the following words, in the context of the sentence in which each appears: decorum (paragraph 10); susceptible
(paragraph 13); wariness (paragraph 14).

SUGGESTIONS FOR WRITING

1. Divide another group of sportsmen according to a principle of your
own choosing. Build your analysis to a thesis, as Bourjaily does. Be
specific in your detail.

2. Write two paragraphs on one of the following topics. Divide the subject according to one principle in the first paragraph, and according
to another principle in the second. Use your division to make a different point in each paragraph:
a. high-school textbooks
b. toothpaste ads
c. automobile commercials on television
d. college freshmen
e. excuses made to teachers for class absence

comparison and contrast

Like definition and division, comparison and contrast is an important method of analysis in exposition. *Comparison* deals with similarities, *contrast* with differences. In comparing, we show what two or more people or objects or places have in common; in contrasting, how they are unlike. There are many ways of organizing paragraphs of comparison or contrast. One way is to list the qualities of the first person or place, then to list the qualities of the second—in the same order:

> Chicago, at the southern tip of Lake Michigan, is a port city and an important commercial and industrial center of the Middle West. It is also an important educational, cultural, and recreational center, drawing thousands to its concert halls, art museum, and sports arenas. Cleveland, on the south shore of Lake Erie, is similarly a port city and a commercial and industrial center important to its area. Like Chicago, it has several important colleges and universities, a distinguished symphony orchestra, one of the fine art museums of the world, and many recreational centers. The location of the two cities undoubtedly contributed to their growth, but this similarity is not sufficient to explain their wide cultural diversity. (paragraph of comparison)

A second way is to make the comparison or contrast point by point:

> Chicago is at the southern tip of Lake Michigan; Cleveland, on the south shore of Lake Erie. Both are important commercial and

industrial centers of the Middle West, and both offer a wide range of educational, cultural, and recreational activities.

In developing such paragraphs, transitions like *similarly, likewise, by comparison,* and *by contrast* may be needed to clarify the organization. The purpose of comparison and contrast is sometimes to provide a relative estimate: we discover the qualities of the first person or object or place *through* the qualities of the second (or third). If Cleveland and Chicago share these characteristics and have the same history of growth, we are better able to understand the causes that shape cities. A contrast with Atlanta or Omaha—large inland cities—would clarify these causes further through a similar relative estimate.

ON FRIENDSHIP

Margaret Mead and Rhoda Metraux

Margaret Mead (1901–78), one of America's most distinguished anthropologists, was a curator of ethnology at the Museum of Natural History in New York City from 1926 to 1969. She also taught at Columbia and other universities, and participated in the work of numerous United States and United Nations agencies. She traveled widely and wrote about many cultures, including her own, in such widely read books as *Growing Up in New Guinea* (1930), *And Keep Your Powder Dry* (1942), and *Male and Female* (1949).

Rhoda Metraux was educated at Vassar, Yale, and Columbia, and has done field work in anthropology in many countries including Haiti, Mexico, Argentina, and New Guinea. She has been on the staff of various government agencies, and has also been a research associate at the Museum of Natural History. She and Margaret Mead worked together for many years, collaborating in the writing of *The Study of Culture at a Distance* (1953) and *Themes in French Culture* (1954).

[1] Few Americans stay put for a lifetime. We move from town to city to suburb, from high school to college in a different state, from a job in one region to a better job elsewhere, from the home where we raise our children to the home where we plan to live in retirement. With each move we are forever making new friends, who become part of our new life at that time.

[2] For many of us the summer is a special time for forming new friendships. Today millions of Americans vacation abroad, and they go not only to see new sights but also—in those places where they do not feel too strange—with the hope of meeting new people. No one really expects a vacation trip to produce a close friend. But surely the beginning of a friendship is possible? Surely in every country people value friendship?

[3] They do. The difficulty when strangers from two countries meet is not a lack of appreciation of friendship, but different expectations about what constitutes friendship and how it comes into being. In those European countries that Americans are most likely to visit, friendship is quite sharply distinguished from other, more casual relations, and is differently related to family life. For a Frenchman, a German or an Englishman friendship is usually more particularized and carries a heavier burden of commitment.

[4] But as we use the word, "friend" can be applied to a wide range of relationships—to someone one has known for a few weeks in a new place, to a close business associate, to a childhood playmate, to a man or woman, to a trusted confidant. There are real differences among these relations for Americans—a friendship may be superficial, casual, situational or deep and enduring. But to a European, who sees only our surface behavior, the differences are not clear.

[5] As they see it, people known and accepted temporarily, casually, flow in and out of Americans' homes with little ceremony and often with little personal commitment. They may be parents of the children's friends, house guests of neighbors, members of a committee, business associates from another town or even another country. Coming as a guest into an American home, the European visitor finds no visible landmarks. The atmosphere is relaxed. Most people, old and young, are called by first names.

From *A Way of Seeing* by Margaret Mead and Rhoda Metraux. Copyright © 1970, 1969, 1968, 1967, 1966, 1965, 1964, 1963, 1962, 1961 by Margaret Mead and Rhoda Metraux. Reprinted by permission of the publishers, Saturday Review Press/E. P. Dutton & Co., Inc.

[6] Who, then, is a friend?

[7] Even simple translation from one language to another is difficult. "You see," a Frenchman explains, "if I were to say to you in France, 'This is my good friend,' that person would not be as close to me as someone about whom I said only, 'This is my friend.' Anyone about whom I have to say *more* is really less."

[8] In France, as in many European countries, friends generally are of the same sex, and friendship is seen as basically a relationship between men. Frenchwomen laugh at the idea that "women can't be friends," but they also admit sometimes that for women "it's a different thing." And many French people doubt the possibility of a friendship between a man and a woman. There is also the kind of relationship within a group—men and women who have worked together for a long time, who may be very close, sharing great loyalty and warmth of feeling. They may call one another *copains*— a word that in English becomes "friends" but has more the feeling of "pals" or "buddies." In French eyes this is not friendship, although two members of such a group may well be friends.

[9] For the French, friendship is a one-to-one relationship that demands a keen awareness of the other person's intellect, temperament and particular interests. A friend is someone who draws out your own best qualities, with whom you sparkle and become more of whatever the friendship draws upon. Your political philosophy assumes more depth, appreciation of a play becomes sharper, taste in food or wine is accentuated, enjoyment of a sport is intensified.

[10] And French friendships are compartmentalized. A man may play chess with a friend for thirty years without knowing his political opinions, or he may talk politics with him for as long a time without knowing about his personal life. Different friends fill different niches in each person's life. These friendships are not made part of family life. A friend is not expected to spend evenings being nice to children or courteous to a deaf grandmother. These duties, also serious and enjoined, are primarily for relatives. Men who are friends may meet in a café. Intellectual friends may meet in larger groups for evenings of conversation. Working people may meet at the little *bistro* where they drink and talk, far from the family. Marriage does not affect such friendships; wives do not have to be taken into account.

[11] In the past in France, friendships of this kind seldom were open to any but intellectual women. Since most women's lives centered on their homes, their warmest relations with other women

often went back to their girlhood. The special relationship of friendship is based on what the French value most—on the mind, on compatibility of outlook, on vivid awareness of some chosen area of life.

[12] Friendship heightens the sense of each person's individuality. Other relationships commanding as great loyalty and devotion have a different meaning. In World War II the first resistance groups formed in Paris were built on the foundation of *les copains*. But significantly, as time went on these little groups, whose lives rested in one another's hands, called themselves "families." Where each had a total responsibility for all, it was kinship ties that provided the model. And even today such ties, crossing every line of class and personal interest, remain binding on the survivors of these small, secret bands.

[13] In Germany, in contrast with France, friendship is much more articulately a matter of feeling. Adolescents, boys and girls, form deeply sentimental attachments, walk and talk together—not so much to polish their wits as to share their hopes and fears and dreams, to form a common front against the world of school and family and to join in a kind of mutual discovery of each other's and their own inner life. Within the family, the closest relationship over a lifetime is between brothers and sisters. Outside the family, men and women find in their closest friends of the same sex the devotion of a sister, the loyalty of a brother. Appropriately, in Germany friends usually are brought into the family. Children call their father's and their mother's friends "uncle" and "aunt." Between French friends, who have chosen each other for the congeniality of their point of view, lively disagreement and sharpness of argument are the breath of life. But for Germans, whose friendships are based on mutuality of feeling, deep disagreement on any subject that matters to both is regarded as a tragedy. Like ties of kinship, ties of friendship are meant to be irrevocably binding. Young Germans who come to the United States have great difficulty in establishing such friendships with Americans. We view friendship more tentatively, subject to changes in intensity as people move, change their jobs, marry, or discover new interests.

[14] English friendships follow still a different pattern. Their basis is shared activity. Activities at different stages of life may be of very different kinds—discovering a common interest in school, serving together in the armed forces, taking part in a foreign mission, staying in the same country house during a crisis. In the midst of the activity, whatever it may be, people fall into step—sometimes two

men or two women, sometimes two couples, sometimes three people—and find that they walk or play a game or tell stories or serve
on a tiresome and exacting committee with the same easy anticipation of what each will do day by day or in some critical situation.
Americans who have made English friends comment that, even
years later, "you can take up just where you left off." Meeting after
a long interval, friends are like a couple who began to dance again
when the orchestra strikes up after a pause. English friendships are
formed outside the family circle, but they are not, as in Germany,
contrapuntal to the family nor are they, as in France, separated
from the family. And a break in an English friendship comes not
necessarily as a result of some irreconcilable difference of viewpoint
or feeling but instead as a result of misjudgment, where one friend
seriously misjudges how the other will think or feel or act, so that
suddenly they are out of step.

[15] What, then, is friendship? Looking at these different styles,
including our own, each of which is related to a whole way of life,
are there common elements? There is the recognition that friendship, in contrast with kinship, invokes freedom of choice. A friend is
someone who chooses and is chosen. Related to this is the sense each
friend gives the other of being a special individual, on whatever
grounds this recognition is based. And between friends there is inevitably a kind of equality of give-and-take. These similarities make
the bridge between societies possible, and the American's characteristic openness to different styles of relationship makes it possible for
him to find new friends abroad with whom he feels at home.

COMMENT

The essay is developed mainly through contrast, beginning with the initial
one between the American idea of friendship and the European. The
European styles of friendship are described one by one: first the French,
then the German, finally the English. The authors do, however, return to
earlier styles for contrast:

> Between French friends, who have chosen each other for the conge-
> niality of their point of view, lively disagreement and sharpness of
> argument are the breath of life. But for Germans, whose friendships are
> based on mutuality of feeling, deep disagreement on any subject that
> matters to both is regarded as a tragedy.

The essay closes with comparison, for the authors state the similarities between Americans and Europeans. This careful ordering of ideas allows the authors to present many different ones without confusing the reader about the central purpose of the analysis. Comparison and contrast are fitted to a thesis—anticipated in the opening paragraphs and stated fully in the concluding one.

QUESTIONS FOR STUDY AND DISCUSSION

1. What is the thesis of the essay? How is it anticipated in the opening paragraphs?

2. What kind of definition do Mead and Metraux use in defining friendship toward the beginning, and later in the essay? What is the purpose of this definition?

3. How is the American style of friendship different from the European? Which of the three European styles does the American most and least resemble? Are these resemblances important to the thesis?

4. Why do the authors begin with the French and end with the English, before proceeding to the final comparison? Could the essay just as well have begun with the English and ended with the French?

5. The authors are describing the world of 1966, when the essay first appeared in print. Do you believe styles of American friendships—as you have experienced them—have changed in the seventies?

VOCABULARY STUDY

Examine the dictionary meanings of the following words. Then write a sentence for each, making the content reveal the meaning of the word: *affection, love, acquaintance, pal, buddy, confidante.*

SUGGESTIONS FOR WRITING

1. Illustrate the following statement from your own experience, and use comparison and contrast to develop it: "There are real differences among these relations for Americans—a friendship may be superficial, casual, situational or deep and enduring." Define each of the adjectives in the course of your discussion.

2. Compare or contrast two of your friendships to show how they resemble or differ from one of the styles described in the essay.

3. Discuss the extent to which the gang relationships described by Lewis

Yablonsky fit one or more of the styles of friendships described in the essay.

ARE CHILDREN PEOPLE?

Phyllis McGinley

Phyllis McGinley (1905–78) was born in Ontario, Oregon. She worked as a schoolteacher, an advertising copywriter, a poetry editor, and a writer of many articles and children's books. Best known for her light verse, she won numerous literary prizes, including the 1961 Pulitzer Prize for poetry.

[1] The problem of how to live with children isn't as new as you might think. Centuries before the advent of Dr. Spock or the PTA, philosophers debated the juvenile question, not always with compassion. There's a quotation from one of the antique sages floating around in what passes for my mind which, for pure cynicism, could set a Montaigne or a Mort Sahl back on his heels.

[2] "Why," asks a disciple, "are we so devoted to our grandchildren?"

[3] And the graybeard answers, "Because it is easy to love the enemies of one's enemies."

[4] Philosopher he may have been but I doubt his parental certification. Any parent with a spark of natural feeling knows that children aren't our enemies. On the other hand, if we're sensible we are aware that they aren't really our friends, either. How can they be, when they belong to a totally different race?

[5] Children admittedly are human beings, equipped with such human paraphernalia as appetites, whims, intelligence, and even hearts, but any resemblance between them and people is purely coincidental. The two nations, child and grown-up, don't behave alike or think alike or even see with the same eyes.

⁶Take that matter of seeing, for example. An adult looks in the mirror and notices what? A familiar face, a figure currently over-weight, maybe, but well-known and resignedly accepted; two arms, two legs, an entity. A child can stare into the looking glass for min-utes at a time and see only the bone buttons on a snowsuit or a pair of red shoes.

⁷Shoes, in fact, are the first personal belongings a child really looks at in an objective sense. There they are to adore—visible, shiny, round-toed ornamental extensions of himself. He can observe them in that mirror or he can look down from his small height to admire them. They are real to him, unlike his eyes or his elbows. That is why, for a child, getting a pair of new shoes is like having a birthday. When my daughters were little they invariably took just-acquired slippers to bed with them for a few nights, the way they'd take a cuddle toy or smuggle in a puppy.

⁸Do people sleep with their shoes? Of course not. Nor do they lift them up reverently to be fondled, a gesture children offer even to perfect strangers in department stores. I used to think that a child's life was lived from new shoe to new shoe, as an adult lives for love or payday or a vacation.

⁹Children, though, aren't consistent about their fetish. By the time they have learned to tie their own laces, they have lapsed into an opposite phase. They start to discard shoes entirely. Boys, being natural reactionaries, cling longer than girls to their first loves, but girls begin the discalced stage at twelve or thirteen—and it goes on interminably. Their closets may bulge with footwear, with every-thing from dubious sneakers to wisps of silver kid, while most of the time the girls themselves go unshod. I am in error, too, when I speak of shoes as reposing in closets. They don't. They lie abandoned under sofas, upside down beside the television set, rain-drenched on ver-andas. Guests in formal drawing rooms are confronted by them and climbers on stairways imperiled. When the phase ends, I can't tell you, but I think only with premature senescence.

¹⁰My younger daughter, then a withered crone of almost twenty, once held the odd distinction of being the only girl on record to get her foot stabbed by a rusty nail at a Yale prom. She was, of course, doing the Twist barefoot, but even so the accident seems unlikely. You can't convince me it could happen to an adult.

¹¹No, children don't look at things in the same light as people. Nor do they hear with our ears, either. Ask a child a question and

he has an invariable answer: "What?" (Though now and then he alters it to "Why?")

¹²Or send one on a household errand and you will know that he—or she—is incapable of taking in a simple adult remark. I once asked an otherwise normal little girl to bring me the scissors from the kitchen drawer, and she returned, after a mysterious absence of fifteen minutes, lugging the extension hose out of the garage. Yet the young can hear brownies baking in the oven two blocks away from home or the faintest whisper of parents attempting to tell each other secrets behind closed doors.

¹³They can also understand the language of babies, the most esoteric on earth. Our younger child babbled steadily from the age of nine months on, although not for a long while in an intelligible tongue. Yet her sister, two years older, could translate for us every time.

¹⁴"That lady's bracelet—Patsy wishes she could have it," the interpreter would tell me; and I had the wit hastily to lift my visitor's arm out of danger.

¹⁵Or I would be instructed, "She'd like to pat the kitten now."

¹⁶We used occasionally to regret their sibling fluency of communication. Once we entertained at Sunday dinner a portrait painter known rather widely for his frequent and publicized love affairs. He quite looked the part, too, being so tall and lean and rakish, with such a predatory moustache and so formidable a smile, that my husband suggested it was a case of art imitating nature.

¹⁷The two small girls had never met him, and when the baby saw him for the first time she turned tail and fled upstairs.

¹⁸The older, a gracious four, came back into the living room after a short consultation, to apologize for her sister's behavior. "You see," she told him winningly, "Patsy thinks you're a wolf."

¹⁹It was impossible to explain that they had somehow confused the moustache and the smile with a description of Little Red Riding Hood's arch foe and were not referring to his private life. We let it pass. I often thought, however, that it was a pity the older girl's pentecostal gifts did not outlast kindergarten. She would have been a great help to the United Nations.

²⁰Young mothers have to study such talents and revise their methods of child rearing accordingly. To attempt to treat the young like grown-ups is always a mistake.

²¹Do people, at least those outside of institutions, drop lighted

matches into wastebaskets just to see what will happen? Do they tramp through puddles on purpose? Or prefer hot dogs or jelly-and-mashed-banana sandwiches to lobster Thermidor? Or, far from gagging on the abysmal inanities of *Raggedy Ann,* beg to have it read to them every evening for three months?

[22] Indeed, the reading habits alone of the younger generation mark them off from their betters. What does an adult do when he feels like having a go at a detective story or the evening paper? Why, he picks out a convenient chair or props himself up on his pillows, arranges the light correctly for good vision, turns down the radio, and reaches for a cigarette or a piece of chocolate fudge.

[23] Children, however, when the literary urge seizes them, take their comic books to the darkest corner of the room or else put their heads under the bedcovers. Nor do they sit *down* to read. They wander. They lie on the floor with their legs draped over the coffee table, or, alternatively, they sit on the coffee table and put the book on the floor. Or else they lean against the refrigerator, usually with the refrigerator door wide open. Sometimes I have seen them retire to closets.

[24] Children in comfortable positions are uncomfortable—just as they are miserable if they can't also have the phonograph, the radio, the television and sometimes the telephone awake and lively while they pore on *The Monster of Kalliwan* or *The Jungle Book.*

[25] But then, children don't walk like people, either—sensibly, staidly, in a definite direction. I am not sure they ever acquire our grown-up gaits. They canter, they bounce, they slither, slide, crawl, leap into the air, saunter, stand on their heads, swing from branch to branch, limp like cripples, or trot like ostriches. But I seldom recall seeing a child just plain walk. They can, however, dawdle. The longest period of recorded time is the interval between telling children to undress for bed and the ultimate moment when they have brushed their teeth, said their prayers, eaten a piece of bread and catsup, brushed their teeth all over again, asked four times for another glass of milk, checked the safety of their water pistols or their tropical fish, remembered there was something vital they had to confide to you, which they have forgotten by the time you reach their side, switched from a panda to a giraffe and back to the panda for the night's sleeping companion, begged to have the light left on in the hall, and finally, being satisfied that your screaming voice is in working order, fallen angelically into slumber.

[26]Apprentice parents are warned to disregard at least nine-tenths of all such requests as pure subterfuge but to remember that maybe one of the ten is right and reasonable, like the night-light or the value of a panda when one is in a panda mood.

[27]Not that reason weighs much with children. It is the great mistake we make with a child, to think progeny operate by our logic. The reasoning of children, although it is often subtle, differs from an adult's. At base there is usually a core of sanity, but one must disentangle what the lispers mean from what they say.

[28]"I believe in Santa Claus," a daughter told me years ago, when she was five or six. "And I believe in the Easter Rabbit, too. But I just can't believe in Shirley Temple."

[29]Until I worked out a solution for this enigmatic statement, I feared for the girl's mind. Then I realized that she had been watching the twenty-one-inch screen. After all, if you are six years old and see a grown-up Shirley Temple acting as mistress of ceremonies for a TV special one evening and the next day observe her, dimpled and brief-skirted, in an old movie, you are apt to find the transformation hard to credit.

[30]I managed to unravel that utterance, but I never did pierce through to the heart of a gnomic pronouncement made by a young friend of hers. He meandered into the backyard one summer day when the whole family was preparing for a funeral. Our garden is thickly clustered with memorials to defunct wildlife, and on this particular afternoon we were intent on burying another robin.

[31]John looked at the hole.

[32]"What are you doing?" he asked, as if it weren't perfectly apparent to the most uninformed.

[33]"Why, John," said my husband, "I'm digging a grave."

[34]John considered the matter a while. Then he inquired again, with all the solemnity of David Susskind querying a senator, "Why don't you make it a double-decker?"

[35]Not even Echo answered that one, but I kept my sense of proportion and went on with the ceremonies. You need a sense of proportion when dealing with children, as you also need a sense of humor. Yet you must never expect the very young to have a sense of humor of their own. Children are acutely risible, stirred to laughter by dozens of human mishaps, preferably fatal. They can understand the points of jokes, too, so long as the joke is not on them. Their egos are too new, they have not existed long enough in the world to

have learned to laugh at themselves. What they love most in the way of humor are riddles, elementary puns, nonsense, and catastrophe. An elderly fat lady slipping on the ice in real life or a man in a movie falling from a fifteen-foot ladder equally transports them. They laugh at fistfights, clowns, people kissing each other, and buildings blowing up. They don't, however, enjoy seeing their parents in difficulties. Parents, they feel, were put on earth solely for their protection, and they cannot bear to have the fortress endangered.

[36] Their peace of mind, their safety, rests on grown-up authority; and it is that childish reliance which invalidates the worth of reasoning too much with them. The longer I lived in a house with children, the less importance I put on cooperatively threshing out matters of conduct or explaining to them our theories of discipline. If I had it to do over again I wouldn't reason with them at all until they arrived at an *age* of reason—approximately twenty-one. I would give them rules to follow. I would try to be just, and I would try even harder to be strict. I would do no arguing. Children, in their hearts, like laws. Authority implies an ordered world, which is what they— and, in the long run, most of the human race—yearn to inhabit. In law there is freedom. Be too permissive and they feel lost and alone. Children are forced to live very rapidly in order to live at all. They are given only a few years in which to learn hundreds of thousands of things about life and the planet and themselves. They haven't time to spend analyzing the logic behind every command or taboo, and they resent being pulled away by it from their proper business of discovery.

[37] When our younger and more conversational daughter turned twelve, we found she was monopolizing the family telephone. She would reach home after school at 3:14 and at 3:15 the instrument would begin to shrill, its peal endless till bedtime. For once we had the good sense neither to scold nor to expostulate. We merely told her she could make and receive calls only between five and six o'clock in the afternoon. For the rest of the day, the telephone was ours. We expected tears. We were braced for hysterics. What we got was a calm acceptance of a Rule. Indeed, we found out later, she boasted about the prohibition—it made her feel both sheltered and popular.

[38] But, then, children are seldom resentful, which is another difference between them and people. They hold grudges no better than

a lapdog. They are too inexperienced to expect favors from the world. What happens to them happens to them, like an illness; and if it is not too extravagantly unfair, they forget about it. Parents learn that a child's angry glare or floods of tears after a punishment or a scolding may send the grown-up away feeling like a despotic brute; but that half an hour later, with adult feelings still in tatters, the child is likely as not to come flying into the room, fling both carefree arms about the beastly grown-up's neck, and shout, "I love you," into her ear.

[39] The ability to forget a sorrow is childhood's most enchanting feature. It can also be exasperating to the pitch of frenzy. Little girls return from school with their hearts broken in two by a friend's treachery or a teacher's injustice. They sob through the afternoon, refuse dinner, and go to sleep on tear-soaked pillows. Novice mothers do not sleep at all, only lie awake with the shared burden for a nightlong companion. Experienced ones know better. They realize that if you come down in the morning to renew your solacing, you will meet—what? Refreshed, whole-hearted offspring who can't under*stand* what you're talking about. Beware of making children's griefs your own. They are no more lasting than soap bubbles.

[40] I find myself hoaxed to this day by the recuperative powers of the young, even when they top me by an inch and know all about modern art. More than once I have been called long distance from a college in New England to hear news of impending disaster.

[41] "It's exam time and I'm down with this horrible cold," croaks the sufferer, coughing dramatically. "Can you rush me that prescription of Dr. Murphy's? I don't trust our infirmary."

[42] Envisioning flu, pneumonia, wasting fever, and a lily maid dead before her time, I harry the doctor into scribbling his famous remedy and send it by wire. Then after worrying myself into dyspepsia, I call two days later to find out the worst. An unfogged voice answers me blithely.

[43] "What cold?" it inquires.

[44] Ephemeral tragedies, crises that evaporate overnight are almost certain to coincide with adolescence. Gird yourselves for them. Adolescence is a disease more virulent than measles and difficult to outgrow as an allergy. At its onset parents are bewildered like the victim. They can only stand by with patience, flexibility, and plenty of food in the larder. It's amazing how consoling is a batch of cookies in an emergency. If it doesn't comfort the child, at

least it helps the baker. I stopped in at a neighbor's house the other day and found her busily putting the frosting on a coconut cake.

[45] "It's for Steven," she told me. "His pet skunk just died, and I didn't know what else to do for him."

[46] Food helps more than understanding. Adolescence doesn't really want to be understood. It prefers to live privately in some stone tower of its own building, lonely and unassailable. To understand is to violate. This is the age—at least for girls—of hidden diaries, locked drawers, unshared secrets. It's a trying time for all concerned. The only solace is that they do outgrow it. But the flaw there is that eventually they outgrow being children too, becoming expatriates of their own tribe.

[47] For, impossible as it seems when one first contemplates diapers and croup, then tantrums, homework, scouting, dancing class, and finally the terrible dilemmas of the teens, childhood does come inexorably to an end. Children turn into people. They speak rationally if aloofly, lecture you on manners, condescend to teach you about eclectic criticism, and incline to get married. And there you are, left with all that learning you have so painfully accumulated in twenty-odd years and with no more progeny on whom to lavish it.

[48] Small wonder we love our grandchildren. The old sage recognized the effect but not the cause. Enemies of our enemies indeed! They are our immortality. It is they who will inherit our wisdom, our experience, our ingenuity.

[49] Except, of course, that the grandchildren's parents will listen benevolently (are they not courteous adults?) and not profit by a word we tell them. They must learn for themselves how to speak in another language and with an alien race.

COMMENT

"The two nations, child and grown-up, don't behave alike or think alike or even see with the same eyes," Phyllis McGinley says toward the start of the essay. Her statement suggests a relative estimate of the two worlds—much like that of Mead and Metraux in their contrast of American and European friendships. McGinley's contrast of child and grown-up world is, however, mainly for the purpose of illustration. We are asked throughout the essay whether we recognize the behavior of children in our own grown-up behavior. Assuming that our answer is no, McGinley does not develop the differences. At several points in the essay, the contrast is implied: "You need a sense of proportion when dealing with children, as you also need a sense of humor. Yet you must never expect the very young to have a sense of humor of their own." The statement tells us that grown-ups do have a sense of proportion and can laugh at themselves. The strength of McGinley's essay is in its lively examples drawn from her own experience; no idea in the essay is without illustration. She also maintains a clear and consistent focus on those qualities that distinguish children from grown-ups—her central topic.

QUESTIONS FOR STUDY AND DISCUSSION

1. According to McGinley, in what ways are children different from grown-ups? Through what transitions and topic sentences does she remind the reader of these differences?

2. What kind of transitions does she use? How many of them refer to the ideas of the immediately preceding paragraph?

3. In what order are the qualities of children presented?

4. What point is McGinley making about the differences between children and grown-ups? Is this point stated or implied?

5. Look up the word *reactionary*. In what sense are boys "natural reactionaries" (paragraph 9)? How does the context explain the statement? If boys are reactionaries, what are girls? Do you agree with this distinction?

6. How many of the qualities of children discussed in the essay illustrate their "proper business of discovery"?

VOCABULARY STUDY

Use each of the following pairs of words in sentences that reveal their difference. If you can, use the pair in a sentence that contrasts them:
   a. *premature, early*
   b. *withered, worn out*
   c. *babbled, raved*
   d. *formidable, threatening*
   e. *inanities, absurdities*
   f. *saunter, dawdle*
   g. *exasperating, annoying*
   h. *blithely, happily*

SUGGESTIONS FOR WRITING

1. Develop one of the following statements from your own experience. Explain why you agree or disagree with it:
   a. "Boys, being natural reactionaries, cling longer than girls to their first loves."
   b. "Children in comfortable positions are uncomfortable."
   c. "Children, in their hearts, like laws."
   d. "Children are forced to live very rapidly in order to live at all."
   e. "Children are seldom resentful."
   f. "The ability to forget a sorrow is childhood's most enchanting feature."
   g. "Adolescence doesn't really want to be understood."

2. The author distinguishes between boys and girls, childhood and adolescence, children and grown-ups. Provide illustrations of your own for one of these distinctions. If you wish, distinguish between them in your own way.

3. Compare the rules set for you as a child or adolescent with those you would set for your own children. Be sure to explain the reasons for the differences.

example

In explaining ideas, we fit our examples to the knowledge and experience of our readers or listeners. In explaining to a child that points of light in the night sky are really very large distant objects, we first have to explain why large objects can appear small. An example suited to the child's experience might be a ball that seems to get smaller as it flies through the air. In explaining to college physics students why the space of the universe is said to be "curved," the professor draws on mathematical formulas and scientific observations, but for the person who knows little or nothing about science, the professor would look for analogies in everyday experience.

The word *example* carries the meaning of typical; that is, the example represents the many occurrences or forms of the idea. Examples are essential in exposition, particularly to the explanation of complex ideas. For instance, it would be difficult to explain the following idea without an example:

> The attitude that produces the pseudo-technical tone is made up of a desire to dignify the subject and the writer, coupled with the belief that important matters require a special vocabulary.
> —Jacques Barzun, *Simple and Direct*

Barzun provides this example of pseudo-technical tone:

> I am sorry not to be able to accept the experience of more intensive interaction with your group and its constituency.

No amount of definition and descriptive detail can replace an effective example such as this. At the same time, many examples do require explanation or analysis, particularly when the idea is a complex one.

PURGING STAG WORDS

Russell Baker

Russell Baker was born in 1925 in Loudon County, Virginia, and studied at Johns Hopkins University. Later he joined the staff of the *Baltimore Sun,* and from 1954 to 1962 he was with the *New York Times'* Washington office. Since 1962 he has been a columnist for the *Times.* Baker is a keen and witty observer of American life, and has written much about popular language. His books include *All Things Considered* (1965), *Our Next President* (1968), and *Poor Russell's Almanac* (1972). In 1979 Baker was awarded a Pulitzer Prize for his journalism.

[1] Everybody at some time has probably felt blood pressure rise and pulse when loaded words have been used to diminish him. The laborer who is called "a hardhat," the poor white who is called "a redneck," the black man who is called "boy," the intellectual who is called "an egghead," the liberal who is called "a bleeding heart," the policeman who is called "a pig"—all these and many others are painfully aware how brutally the English language can be used to humiliate them.

[2] In such instances, words become weapons. Their victims see English as an enemy to be disarmed and, so, when they acquire political muscle one of their first goals commonly is to purge the language.

[3] This is what feminists are now struggling to do in their assault on the heavily masculine freight that has been built into English from the time of Angles, the Saxons, and the Normans. When sensible adults are called "the weaker sex," or "the girls," they are apt to feel at least mildly ridiculed and possibly assaulted.

[4] Hearing men refer to "the little woman," "the better half," "the ball and chain" or "a sweet young thing" may make them suspect they are being crushed in a velvet vise. Not surprisingly, then, the feminist movement is heavily engaged in a language purge.

[5] It is not easy once they get beyond putting the taboo on "weaker sex," "ball and chain," "sweet young thing" and similar

ancient clichés that were ready for retirement anyhow, for masculine primacy is deeply entrenched in English.

[6]Some of the difficulties are illustrated in McGraw-Hill's "Guidelines for Equal Treatment of the Sexes in McGraw-Hill Book Company Publications," an admirable analysis of how firmly modern English confines women to the masculine mentality. The author, Timothy Yohn, describes the mental trap very persuasively but is less successful in suggesting how to break out.

[7]The most awkward problem arises with all those words that are compounds of "man." Mr. Yohn tackles "Congressman" and suggest "member of Congress" as a better alternative. His "businessman" becomes "business executive" or "business manager." His "fireman" is a "fire fighter," his "mailman" a "mail carrier," his "salesman" a "sales representative," "salesperson" or "sales clerk," his "insurance man" an "insurance agent," his "statesman" a "leader" or "public servant," his "chairman" a "presiding officer," "the chair," "head," "leader," "coordinator" or "moderator," his "cameraman" a "camera operator" and his "foreman" a "supervisor."

[8]In almost every case the alternative for the "sexist" word to be purged is either a longer word or a combination of words. Instead of "sexism," we have verbosity. It is a dilemma that feminists will have no trouble resolving, but whether it is a good idea to encourage more windiness in an age when most of us already talk like politicians on television is arguable.

[9]One of feminism's goals, presumably, is to establish woman's right, too, to speak in words of one syllable. It will be a pity if everybody has forgotten how by the time equality is finally attained.

[10]The trouble with most of Mr. Yohn's "nonsexist" alternatives—although "fire fighter" isn't bad—is that they abolish "man" only to bring on a Latin-root substitute, and Latin-root words tend to be not only pompous but also vague and long-winded.

[11]Feminists with a classic turn of mind might object that the "or" endings on "operator," "supervisor," "moderator" and "coordinator" smack heavily of the masculine "or" ending common on Latin nouns and are, thus, merely "sexist" words concealed in a toga.

[12]Ideally, someone should invent brand new words that are devoid of gender implication in their job descriptions without weighting the language down like lead settling into swamp water.

A scouring of the dictionaries might even turn up some good old words that would serve.

[13] Mr. Yohn suggests one when, in cautioning against "language that assumes all readers are male," he rules out "you and your wife" and suggests, instead, "you and your spouse." The trouble with "spouse" is that nobody but a lawyer can say it with a straight face. It belongs to W. C. Fields and dry wits in sawdust saloons, and in the plural who could resist saying, "you and your spice"?

[14] Why not "you and your mate," Mr. Yohn? "Mate" has the strength of one unequivocal syllable. It also has sex in it, without gender, and that's what we are looking for, isn't it?

COMMENT

Baker illustrates the attitudes implied in certain words and expressions and the difficulty of finding substitutes for some of these. Through these examples he makes points about language itself—for example, the effect of Latin-root words on English sentences. Without examples, Baker would be stating generalities—essentially, vague opinions unsupported by evidence. Generalizations by contrast are well supported, and can be tested through the examples and evidence amassed. Baker's examples are strong ones, and his ability to amass so many of them shows the seriousness of the problem he discusses.

QUESTIONS FOR STUDY AND DISCUSSION

1. What examples does Baker give of words that are used as weapons? What examples can you give of words used in this way?

2. Are the words cited used only to ridicule women? Or are other attitudes implied in them?

3. What is "verbose" about some of the words suggested as alternatives for sexist words?

4. What general philosophy of language is implied in Baker's comments, as well as stated directly? In other words, what does Baker believe that words should and should not do?

5. Do you agree that substitutes should be found for words that exhibit "masculine primacy"? Do you find yourself belittled or injured by words used about your sex or racial or cultural background?

6. How prevalent do you find sexist language in newspapers and on television? Have you noticed changes in the use of words that apply to men and women equally?

VOCABULARY STUDY

Analyze a newspaper or magazine article or editorial for words that Baker would consider weighted toward the masculine or "loaded" in some other way. Make a list of these words, and be prepared to explain your choice.

SUGGESTIONS FOR WRITING

1. Discuss your agreement or disagreement with Baker on the issues raised in the article. Base your discussion on your experience with these on similar words and expressions.

2. Discuss how the words used to describe teenagers and their behavior and attitudes help to create an image of them—one that you consider inaccurate and unfair.

3. Examine the language referring to men and women in one of your textbooks to determine whether it favors one of the sexes or "slants" the treatment of ideas in any way. Or do the same with letters to the editor of a newspaper or magazine.

SPRING BULLETIN

Woody Allen

Woody Allen has lived in New York City most of his life, and attended New York University and City College of New York. He began his career as a comedy writer for Sid Caesar and Art Carney, among others. More recently, he has been writing, directing, and acting in his own films, including *Bananas, Take the Money and Run, Love and Death, Annie Hall, Interiors,* and *Manhattan.* His humorous essays have appeared in *The New Yorker* and other magazines, and have been collected into two books, *Getting Even* (1971), and *Without Feathers* (1975).

The number of college bulletins and adult-education come-ons that keep turning up in my mailbox convinces me that I must be on a special mailing list for dropouts. Not that I'm complaining; there is something about a list of extension courses that piques my interest with a fascination hitherto reserved for a catalogue of Hong Kong honeymoon accessories, sent to me once by mistake. Each time I read through the latest bulletin of extension courses, I make immediate plans to drop everything and return to school. (I was ejected from college many years ago, the victim of unproved accusations not unlike those once attached to Yellow Kid Weil.) So far, however, I am still an uneducated, unextended adult, and I have fallen into the habit of browsing through an imaginary, handsomely printed course bulletin that is more or less typical of them all:

Summer Session

Economic Theory: A systematic application and critical evaluation of the basic analytic concepts of economic theory, with an emphasis on money and why it's good. Fixed coefficient production functions, cost and supply curves, and nonconvexity comprise the first semester, with the second semester concentrating on spending, making change, and keeping a neat wallet. The Federal Reserve System is analyzed, and advanced students are coached in the proper method of filling out a deposit slip. Other topics include: Inflation and Depression—how to dress for each. Loans, interest, welching.

History of European Civilization: Ever since the discovery of a fossilized eohippus in the men's washroom at Siddon's Cafeteria in East Rutherford, New Jersey, it has been suspected that at one time Europe and America were connected by a strip of land that later sank or became East Rutherford, New Jersey, or both. This throws a new perspective on the formation of European society and enables historians to conjecture about why it sprang up in an area that would have made a much better Asia. Also studied in the course is the decision to hold the Renaissance in Italy.

Introduction to Psychology: The theory of human behavior. Why some men are called "lovely individuals" and why there are others you just want to pinch. Is there a split between mind and body, and, if so, which is better to have? Aggression and rebellion are discussed. (Students particularly interested in these aspects of psychology are advised to take one of these Winter Term courses: Introduction to Hostility; Intermediate Hostility; Advanced Hatred; Theoretical Foundations of Loathing.) Special consideration is given to a study of consciousness as opposed to unconsciousness, with many helpful hints on how to remain conscious.

Psychopathology: Aimed at understanding obsessions and phobias, including the fear of being suddenly captured and stuffed with crabmeat, reluctance to return to volleyball serve, and the inability to say the word "mackinaw" in the presence of women. The compulsion to seek out the company of beavers is analyzed.

Philosophy I: Everyone from Plato to Camus is read, and the following topics are covered:

Ethics: The categorical imperative, and six ways to make it work for you.

Aesthetics: Is art the mirror of life, or what?

Metaphysics: What happens to the soul after death? How does it manage?

Epistemology: Is knowledge knowable? If not, how do we know this?

The Absurd: Why existence is often considered silly, particularly for men who wear brown-and-white shoes. Manyness and oneness are studied as they relate to otherness. (Students achieving oneness will move ahead to twoness.)

Philosophy XXIX-B: Introduction to God. Confrontation with the Creator of the universe through informal lectures and field trips.

The New Mathematics: Standard mathematics has recently been rendered obsolete by the discovery that for years we have been writing the numeral five backward. This has led to a reëvaluation of counting as a method of getting from one to ten. Students are taught advanced concepts of Boolean Algebra, and formerly unsolvable equations are dealt with by threats of reprisals.

Fundamental Astronomy: A detailed study of the universe and its care and cleaning. The sun, which is made of gas, can explode at any moment, sending our entire planetary system hurtling to destruction; students are advised what the average citizen can do in such a case. They are also taught to identify various constellations, such as the Big Dipper, Cygnus the Swan, Sagittarius the Archer, and the twelve stars that form Lumides the Pants Salesman.

Modern Biology: How the body functions, and where it can usually be found. Blood is analyzed, and it is learned why it is the best possible thing to have coursing through one's veins. A frog is dissected by students and its digestive tract is compared with man's, with the frog giving a good account of itself except on curries.

Rapid Reading: This course will increase reading speed a little each day until the end of the term, by which time the student will be required to read *The Brothers Karamazov* in fifteen minutes. The method is to scan the page and eliminate everything except pronouns from one's field of vision. Soon the pronouns are eliminated. Gradually the student is encouraged to nap. A frog is dissected. Spring comes. People marry and die. Pinkerton does not return.

Musicology III: The Recorder. The student is taught how to play "Yankee Doodle" on this end-blown wooden flute, and progresses rapidly to the Brandenburg Concertos. Then slowly back to "Yankee Doodle."

Music Appreciation: In order to "hear" a great piece of music correctly, one must: (1) know the birthplace of the composer, (2) be able to tell a rondo from a scherzo, and back it up with action. Attitude is important. Smiling is bad form unless the composer has intended the music to be funny, as in *Till Eulenspiegel,* which abounds in musical jokes (although the trombone has the best lines). The ear, too, must be trained, for it is our most easily deceived organ and can be made to think it is a nose by bad placement of stereo speakers. Other topics include: The four-bar rest and its potential as a political weapon. The Gregorian Chant: Which monks kept the beat.

Writing for the Stage: All drama is conflict. Character development is also very important. Also what they say. Students learn that long, dull speeches are not so effective, while short, "funny" ones seem to go over well. Simplified audience psychology is explored: Why is a play about a lovable old character named Gramps often not as interesting in the theatre as staring at the back of someone's head and trying to make him turn around? Interesting aspects of stage history are also examined. For example, before the invention of italics, stage directions were often mistaken for dialogue, and great actors frequently found themselves saying, "John rises, crosses left." This naturally led to embarrassment and, on some occasions, dreadful notices. The phenomenon is analyzed in detail, and students are guided in avoiding mistakes. Required text: A. F. Shulte's *Shakespeare: Was He Four Women?*

Introduction to Social Work: A course designed to instruct the social worker who is interested in going out "in the field." Topics covered include: how to organize street gangs into basketball teams, and vice versa; playgrounds as a means of preventing juvenile crime, and how to get potentially homicidal cases to try the sliding pond; discrimination; the broken home; what to do if you are hit with a bicycle chain.

Yeats and Hygiene, A Comparative Study: The poetry of William Butler Yeats is analyzed against a background of proper dental care. (Course open to a limited number of students.)

COMMENT

College students will recognize Allen's satirical targets immediately, because of the accuracy and wit of the examples. Allen assumes that we have all come across pretentious diction and jargon such as he imitates. His humor derives from his observant eye and quick ear for pretentious language of all kinds—in the classroom and outside.

QUESTIONS FOR STUDY AND DISCUSSION

1. How does the introductory paragraph prepare us for the essay—for its humor and satirical intent?

2. What is Allen making fun of in college bulletins? Is he making fun of academic practices and attitudes, in addition to the language of the college bulletin?

3. What voice do you hear as you read the essay? What is the tone of that voice? Does the tone change, or does it remain the same throughout the essay?

4. Allen exposes the pretentions of college bulletins through parody—through imitating the language and exaggerating its qualities. What other uses of language in documents, contracts, and the like might be satirized through parody?

VOCABULARY STUDY

1. One of Allen's satirical targets is pretentious diction ("All drama is conflict") and jargon ("Fixed coefficient production functions"). What examples do you find in the essay of other pretentious diction and jargon? Can you find examples of such language in your textbooks?

2. Find a paragraph in your college bulletin that contains pretentious diction, and rewrite it in plain English.

SUGGESTIONS FOR WRITING

1. Rewrite one or two paragraphs from your college bulletin from a satirical point of view.

2. Write a satirical essay on a series of advertisements that you find unintentionally comical. Convey to your reader, through the examples you choose, why you find them comical.

3. Read one or two humorous essays by one of the following writers: Robert Benchley, Erma Bombeck, Jean Kerr, S. J. Perelman, Frank Sullivan, or Mark Twain. Then write an essay on the kind of humor you find—its sources, humorous devices that the writer employs, the qualities that make it special.

process

When we give a set of directions for changing a tire, we are describing a *process*. The process may be a mechanical one, like the one just mentioned; or a natural one, like the circulation of the blood; or a historical one, like the industrialization of the United States. The stages or steps of the process are usually described according to strict chronology. In mechanical processes, there is sometimes a choice of procedures or tools, and the writer may choose to describe more than one of these—for example, the several kinds of car jack and their operation. Many processes are complex—that is, they contain several related processes, each of which must be carefully distinguished. The process by which a country changes from an agricultural to an industrial economy involves a number of related events occurring at the same time. In the course of our explanation, we may have to define and illustrate terms, make comparisons, and comment on various implications and uses of the process.

BARBED WIRE

John Fischer

John Fischer (1910–78) was born in Texhoma, Oklahoma, and graduated from the University of Oklahoma; he was later a Rhodes Scholar at Oxford University, England. For many years he was editor in chief of *Harper's Magazine,* for which he wrote a regular column called "The Easy Chair." The essay reprinted here draws on experiences of his youth, which he used in his book on the settlement of Texas and Oklahoma, *From the High Plains* (1978).

[1] If you grew up in a city, it is possible that you have never had occasion to look closely at a barbed wire fence. In that case, it might be fun to try to invent it, in imagination, for yourself. It sounds easy. You only have to set two posts in the ground and string between them wires, fitted with barbs at about six-inch intervals. The problem is to fix the barbs so firmly that a heavy animal brushing against the fence will not break them off, or slide them along the wire. If they slide, you will soon have all the barbs shoved up against one post or the other, with a naked wire in between. Another problem is to figure out a way to make your wire cheaply and fast—that is, with machinery requiring a minimum of hand labor.

[2] You might think of soldering on the barbs, but that quickly turns out to be a poor idea. The soldered join is inherently weak, and since each one has to be made by hand, the process would be prohibitively expensive. Another possibility is to take a ribbon of steel about one inch wide, cut zigzags along one side to form sharp points, and then twist the ribbon as you string it. This, too, has been tried and found impractical. The ribbon can be rolled, and cut by machinery, but it is too heavy to handle easily, uses too much expensive steel per foot, and is too weak to resist the impact of a charging bull. Another abortive scheme involved spiked spools strung on a wire.

[3] According to the Bivins Museum in Tascosa, Texas, 401 patents for barbed wire have been recorded, and more than 1,600 variants have been catalogued. Out of all these attempts, only two proved successful. Both were patented at nearly the same time by two neighbors in De Kalb County, Illinois; Joseph F. Glidden and Jacob Haish. Whether they got their ideas independently, and who got his first, are questions that have provoked much expensive litigation. Their concepts were quite similar. Each involved clasping barbs around a wire at appropriate intervals—and then twisting that wire together with another one, so that the barbs are tightly gripped between the two. The only essential difference, to the eye of

anyone but a patent lawyer, was in slightly variant methods of clasping the barb.

[4]Whether or not Glidden was the original inventor, he certainly was the more successful businessman. He made his first wire in 1873, forming the barbs with a converted coffee grinder and twisting the twin wires in his barn with a hand-cranked grindstone. He sold his first wire, and took out his patent, in 1874. That same year he formed a partnership with a neighbor, I. L. Ellwood, and built a factory in De Kalb. Before the end of the next year, their factory was turning out five tons of wire a day, using improved, steam-operated machinery. In 1876 Glidden sold a half interest in his invention to the Washburn and Moen Manufacturing Company of Worcester, Massachusetts, which had been supplying him with plain wire; in payment he got $60,000, plus a royalty of 25 cents for every hundredweight of barbed wire sold.*

[5]How profitable this deal proved to be can be glimpsed from the following figures. In his first year of manufacture, Glidden sold 10,-000 pounds of wire. Two years later, Washburn and Moen sold 2.8 million pounds. Within the next five years, sales mounted to more than 80 million pounds a year—yielding Glidden an income of more than $200,000 annually, the equivalent of at least $1 million today, and that was before the era of income taxes. The manufacturers' profits amounted to many times that.

[6]Much of his wire was being shipped to Texas. Glidden and his money followed it, leaving a permanent impress on the settlement of the High Plains and especially on its main city, Amarillo. There I came across his traces nearly sixty years later.

[7]But in the meantime I had a chance to become well acquainted with his product. When I was eleven years old, my grandfather John Fischer taught me how to string wire during a summer I spent on his homestead near Apache, Oklahoma. To my eyes he seemed a very old man, but he was still wiry, lean, hard-muscled, and accustomed to working from sunup till long after dark.

[8]Like inventing barbed wire, stringing it is a more complex business than you might think. First you find your posts. My grandfather insisted that they be either cedar, locust, or bois d'arc, also known as Osage orange. These woods will last in the ground for many years, while cottonwood or pine will rot quickly unless creo-

---

*Washburn and Moen eventually merged with the American Steel and Wire Company, a subsidiary of U.S. Steel. American Steel and Wire's museum in Worcester is the prime source of information about barbed wire.

soted—and we had no creosote in those days. Some he cut himself along a little creek that ran across one corner of his 160-acre farm; others he bought or bartered from neighbors. Each post had to be exactly six feet long.

⁹When the posts were all collected, with a mule team and wagon, he stacked them near the edge of the pasture he planned to fence, and then marked his line. This he did with a borrowed surveyor's transit, a handful of stakes, and a few rolls of binder twine. At thirty-foot intervals he scratched a mark on the hard prairie soil to indicate where he wanted each post to go. One of my jobs was to make a hole in the ground with a crowbar at each mark, and fill it with water from a five-gallon, galvanized-iron milk can, thus softening the earth for my grandfather, who followed me with his posthole digger.

¹⁰The first post set, to a depth of precisely two feet, was of course at a corner of the tract he was going to enclose. It had to be braced in both directions of the future fence lines. For braces he used two other posts planted diagonally in the earth with their feet anchored against heavy stones; their top ends he sawed at the proper angle and fastened to the corner post with tenpenny nails. Then we set about the weary labor of digging holes and setting intermediate posts until we came to the place he had marked for his next corner. We had to do only three sides of the forty-acre pasture, because the fourth side abutted a field enclosed years earlier; but at that, the post-setting took us the best part of two weeks.

¹¹Then we drove the wagon into Apache to get a load of wire. It came on big wooden spools, so heavy that the hardware dealer had to help us load them. Grandfather let me drive back, a proud and nervous assignment for me, although the mules—named Pete and Repeat—were gentle enough.

¹²At the rear end of the wagon bed he rigged a pole, crosswise, to serve as a spindle on which a spool of wire could be mounted and easily unwound. We drove the wagon close to a corner post, twisted the end of the wire around it one foot above the ground, and stapled it fast. Next we drove along the line of posts for about 200 yards, unreeling wire on the ground behind us. There Grandpa stopped, unhitched the team, blocked three wheels of the wagon with rocks, and jacked up the fourth wheel, the rear one next to the fence line. He cut the wire and twisted the loose end around the axle of the jacked-up wheel, fastening it to a spoke for additional security. By turning the wheel, we wound the wire around the axle until it was

taut. (There were patent wire-stretchers, but Grandpa did not own one. The wheel-stretching method worked just as well, and saved money.) After he had lashed the wheel to maintain the tension, we went back down the line and stapled the wire to each post. Then we repeated the process, time after time, until we had the pasture enclosed with a standard fence of four strands, spaced a foot apart. We finished up by making a wire gate at the corner nearest the house.

[13] Three tips for fence-stringers:

—Wear the heaviest leather gauntlets you can find. Even so, you are bound to get your hands and arms torn, so carry some iodine and bandages with you.

—Staple the wire on the side of the posts facing into the pasture. When a heavy animal runs into the fence, he will press the wire against the posts, not the staples. If the wire were on the other side, the staples might pop out.

—Hang the expense, and use two staples for each fastening of the wire. One of them might someday rust or work loose.

[14] I haven't seen that fence in decades, but my brother told me a few years ago that it was still standing and tight. Probably it is the most nearly permanent thing I have ever worked on. Certainly its useful life has been far longer than that of any article or book I have written.

COMMENT

In the course of his essay, Fischer answers three essential questions about barbed wire—what, why, and how. He is writing for two kinds of reader—the person who wants to learn about barbed wire, and, as the final comments show, for the person who wants to string it. Thus he is careful to provide enough background as well as detail about handling barbed wire; background and detail are joined in exposition, allowing the reader to visualize the process. Fischer does more than provide instructions for the beginner: he creates the world in which barbed wire is used, and relates it to his personal experience with that world.

QUESTIONS FOR STUDY AND DISCUSSION

1. What details about barbed wire help you to visualize both the wire and the process of stringing it?

2. Which of the steps in stringing it are the most difficult, and how do

you know? On which does Fischer give the least information? Does he assume that the reader has any knowledge about these steps?

3. What does the detail about Glidden contribute to your understanding of barbed wire?

4. How does Fischer answer the "why" of barbed wire in the course of providing other information? Does he answer the three questions in a particular order?

VOCABULARY STUDY

Give the specific dictionary meaning important to the sentence and paragraph in which each word appears: *barb* (paragraph 1); *solder* (paragraph 2); *clasping* (paragraph 3); *transit, galvanized* (paragraph 9); *abutted* (paragraph 10); *rigged* (paragraph 12); *gauntlet* (paragraph 13).

SUGGESTIONS FOR WRITING

1. Describe how to change a bicycle or automobile tire or how to thread and operate a sewing machine or how to knit or crochet—or a similar process. Assume that your reader knows nothing about the tools or machinery required. Before writing consider what details must be provided and what terms defined at each stage of the process.

2. Certain jobs can be performed in more than one way—for example, training a dog not to jump on people. Discuss the various ways of doing a similar job. Keep these ways distinct for your reader.

3. Trace a historical process like making the decision to attend college. Comment on the implications of some of the stages of this process as you describe it.

HOW TO EAT AN ICE-CREAM CONE

L. Rust Hills

Rust Hills was born in 1924 in Brooklyn, New York, and attended the United States Merchant Marine Academy and Wesleyan University. He was fiction editor of *Esquire* and *The Saturday Evening Post,* has taught writing, and is now a free lance writer. His books include *How to Do Things Right* (1972), *How to Retire at 41* (1973), and *How to Be Good* (1976).

[1] Before you even get the cone, you have to do a lot of planning about it. We'll assume that you lost the argument in the car and that the family has decided to break the automobile journey and stop at an ice-cream stand for cones. Get things straight with them right from the start. Tell them that after they have their cones there will be an imaginary circle six feet away from the car and that no one—man, woman, or especially child—will be allowed to cross the line and reënter the car until his ice-cream cone has been entirely consumed and he has cleaned himself up. Emphasize: Automobiles and ice-cream cones don't mix. Explain: Melted ice cream, children, is a fluid that is eternally sticky. One drop of it on a car-door handle spreads to the seat covers, to trousers, to hands, and thence to the steering wheel, the gearshift, the rearview mirror, all the knobs of the dashborad—spreads *everywhere* and lasts *forever,* spreads from a nice old car like this, which might have to be abandoned because of stickiness, right into a nasty new car, in secret ways that even scientists don't understand. If necessary, even make a joke: "The family that eats ice-cream cones together sticks together." Then let their mother explain the joke and tell them you don't mean half of what you say, and no, we won't be getting a new car.

[2] Blessed are the children who always eat the same flavor of ice cream or always know beforehand what kind they will want. Such good children should be quarantined from those who want to "wait and see what flavors there are." It's a sad thing to observe a beautiful young child who has always been perfectly happy with a plain vanilla ice-cream cone being subverted by a young schoolmate who has been invited along for the weekend—a pleasant and polite visitor, perhaps, but spoiled by permissive parents and scarred by an overactive imagination. This schoolmate has a flair for contingency planning: "Well, I'll have banana if they have banana, but if they don't have banana then I'll have peach, if it's fresh peach, and if they don't have banana or fresh peach I'll see what else they have that's like that, like maybe fresh strawberry or something, and if they don't have that or anything like that that's good I'll just have

chocolate marshmallow chip or chocolate ripple or something like that." Then—turning to one's own once simple and innocent child, now already corrupt and thinking fast—the schoolmate invites a similar rigmarole. "What kind are *you* going to have?"

[3] I'm a great believer in contingency planning, but none of this is realistic. Few adults, and even fewer children, are able to make up their minds beforehand what kind of ice-cream cone they'll want. It would be nice if they could all be lined up in front of the man who is making up the cones and just snap smartly when their turn came, "Strawberry, please," "Vanilla, please," "Chocolate, please." But of course it never happens like that. There is always a great discussion, a great jostling and craning of necks and leaning over the counter to see down into the tubs of ice cream, and much interpersonal consultation—"What kind are *you* having?"—back and forth, as if that should make any difference. Until finally the first child's turn comes and he asks the man, "What kinds do you have?"

[4] Now, this is the stupidest question in the world, because there is always a sign posted saying what kinds of ice cream they have. As I tell the children, that's what they put the sign up there for—so you won't have to ask what kinds of ice cream they have. The man gets sick of telling everybody all the different kinds of ice cream they have, so they put a sign up there that *says*. You're supposed to read it, not ask the man.

[5] "All right, but the sign doesn't say strawberry."

[6] "Well, that means they don't have strawberry."

[7] "But there *is* strawberry, right there."

[8] "That must be raspberry or something." (Look again at the sign. Raspberry isn't there, either.)

[9] When the child's turn actually comes, he says, "Do you have strawberry?"

[10] "Sure."

[11] "What other kinds do you have?"

[12] The trouble is, of course, that they put up that sign saying what flavors they have, with little cardboard inserts to put in or take out flavors, way back when they first opened the store. But they never change the sign—or not often enough. They always have flavors that aren't on the list, and often they don't have flavors that *are* on the list. Children know this—whether innately or from earliest experience it would be hard to say. The ice-cream man knows it, too. Even grownups learn it eventually. There will always be

chaos and confusion and mind-changing and general uproar when ice-cream cones are being ordered, and there has not been, is not, and will never be any way to avoid it.

[13] Human beings are incorrigibly restless and dissatisfied, always in search of new experiences and sensations, seldom content with the familiar. It is this, I think, that accounts for people wanting to have a taste of your cone, and wanting you to have a taste of theirs. "*Do* have a taste of this fresh peach—it's delicious," my wife used to say to me, very much (I suppose) the way Eve wanted Adam to taste her delicious apple. An insinuating look of calculating curiosity would film my wife's eyes—the same look those beautiful, scary women in those depraved Italian films give a man they're interested in. "How's *yours?*" she would say. For this reason, I always order chocolate chip now. Down through the years, all those close enough to me to feel entitled to ask for a taste of my cone— namely, my wife and children—have learned what chocolate chip tastes like, so they have no legitimate reason to ask me for a taste. As for tasting other people's cones, never do it. The reasoning here is that if it tastes good, you'll wish you'd had it; if it tastes bad, you'll have had a taste of something that tastes bad; if it doesn't taste either good or bad, then you won't have missed anything. Of course no person in his right mind ever *would* want to taste anyone else's cone, but it is useful to have good, logical reasons for hating the thought of it.

[14] Another important thing. Never let the man hand you the ice-cream cones for the whole group. There is no sight more pathetic than some bumbling disorganized papa holding four ice-cream cones in two hands, with his money still in his pocket, when the man says, "Eighty cents." What does he do then? He can't hand the cones back to the man to hold while he fishes in his pocket for the money, for the man has just given them to *him.* He can start passing them out to the kids, but at least one of them will have gone back to the car to see how the dog is doing, or have been sent round in back by his mother to wash his hands or something. And even if papa does get them distributed, he's still going to be left with his own cone in one hand while he tries to get his money with the other. Meanwhile, of course, the man is very impatient, and the next group is asking him, "What flavors do you have?"

[15] No, never let the man hand you the cones of others. Make him hand them out to each kid in turn. That way, too, you won't get

those disgusting blobs of butter pecan and black raspberry on your own chocolate chip. And insist that he tell you how much it all costs and settle with him *before* he hands you your own cone. Make sure everyone has got paper napkins and everything *before* he hands you your own cone. Get *everything* straight before he hands you your own cone. Then, as he hands you your own cone, reach out and take it from him. Strange, magical, dangerous moment! It shares something of the mysterious, sick thrill that soldiers are said to feel on the eve of a great battle.

[16] Now, consider for a moment just exactly what it is that you are about to be handed. It is a huge, irregular mass of ice cream, faintly domed at the top from the metal scoop, which has first produced it and then insecurely balanced it on the uneven top edge of a hollow inverted cone made out of the most brittle and fragile of materials. Clumps of ice cream hang over the side, very loosely attached to the main body. There is always much more ice cream than the cone could hold, even if the ice cream were tamped down into the cone, which of course it isn't. And the essence of ice cream is that it melts. It doesn't just stay there teetering in this irregular, top-heavy mass; it also melts. And it melts *fast*. And it doesn't just melt—it melts into a sticky fluid that *cannot* be wiped off. The only thing one person could hand to another that might possibly be more dangerous is a live hand grenade from which the pin had been pulled five seconds earlier. And of course if anybody offered you that, you could say, "Oh. Uh, well—no thanks."

[17] Ice-cream men handle cones routinely, and are inured. They are like professionals who are used to handling sticks of TNT; their movements are quick and skillful. An ice-cream man will pass a cone to you casually, almost carelessly. Never accept a cone on this basis! Too many brittle sugar cones (the only good kind) are crushed or chipped or their ice-cream tops knocked askew, by this casual sort of transfer from hand to hand. If the ice-cream man is attempting this kind of brusque transfer, keep your hands at your side, no matter what effort it may cost you to overcome the instinct by which everyone's hand goes out, almost automatically, whenever he is proffered something delicious and expected. Keep your hands at your side, and the ice-cream man will look up at you, startled, questioning. Lock his eyes with your own, and *then*, slowly, calmly, and above all deliberately, take the cone from him.

[18] Grasp the cone with the right hand firmly but gently between

thumb and at least one but not more than three fingers, two-thirds of the way up the cone. Then dart swiftly away to an open area, away from the jostling crowd at the stand. Now take up the classic ice-cream-cone-eating stance: feet from one to two feet apart, body bent forward from the waist at a twenty-five-degree angle, right elbow well up, right forearm horizontal, at a level with your collarbone and about twelve inches from it. But don't start eating yet! Check first to see what emergency repairs may be necessary. Sometimes a sugar cone will be so crushed or broken or cracked that all one can do is gulp at the thing like a savage, getting what he can of it and letting the rest drop to the ground, and then evacuating the area of catastrophe as quickly as possible. Checking the cone for possible trouble can be done in a second or two, if one knows where to look and does it systematically. A trouble spot some people overlook is the bottom tip of the cone. This may have been broken off. Or the flap of the cone material at the bottom, usually wrapped over itself in that funny spiral construction, may be folded in a way that is imperfect and leaves an opening. No need to say that through this opening—in a matter of perhaps thirty or, at most, ninety seconds—will begin to pour hundreds of thousands of sticky molecules of melted ice cream. You know in this case that you must instantly get the paper napkin in your left hand under and around the bottom of the cone to stem the forthcoming flow, or else be doomed to eat the cone far too rapidly. It is a grim moment. No one wants to eat a cone under that kind of pressure, but neither does anyone want to end up with the bottom of the cone stuck to a messy napkin. There's one other alternative—one that takes both skill and courage: Forgoing any cradling action, grasp the cone more firmly between thumb and forefinger and extend the other fingers so that they are out of the way of the dripping from the bottom, then increase the waist-bend angle from twenty-five degrees to thirty-five degrees, and then eat the cone, *allowing* it to drip out of the bottom onto the ground in front of you! Experienced and thoughtful cone-eaters enjoy facing up to this kind of sudden challenge.

[19] So far, we have been concentrating on cone problems, but of course there is the ice cream to worry about, too. In this area, immediate action is sometimes needed on three fronts at once. Frequently the ice cream will be mounted on the cone in a way that is perilously lopsided. This requires immediate corrective action to move it back into balance—a slight pressure downward with the teeth and lips to

seat the ice cream more firmly in and on the cone, but not so hard, of course, as to break the cone. On other occasions, gobs of ice cream will be hanging loosely from the main body, about to fall to the ground (bad) or onto one's hand (far, far worse). This requires instant action, too; one must snap at the gobs like a frog in a swarm of flies. Sometimes, trickles of ice cream will already (already!) be running down the cone toward one's fingers, and one must quickly raise the cone, tilting one's face skyward, and lick with an upward motion that pushes the trickles away from the fingers and (as much as possible) into one's mouth. Every ice-cream cone is like every other ice-cream cone in that it potentially can present all of these problems, but each ice-cream cone is paradoxically unique in that it will present the problems in a different order of emergency and degree of severity. It is, thank God, a rare ice-cream cone that will present all three kinds of problems in exactly the same degree of emergency. With each cone, it is necessary to make an instanta-

neous judgment as to where the greatest danger is, and to *act!* A moment's delay, and the whole thing will be a mess before you've even tasted it *(Fig. 1)*. If it isn't possible to decide between any two of the three basic emergency problems (i.e., lopsided mount, dangling gobs, running trickles), allow yourself to make an arbitrary adjudication; assign a "heads" value to one and a "tails" value to the other, then flip a coin to decide which is to be tended to

Fig. 1

first. Don't, for heaven's sake, *actually* flip a coin—you'd have to dig in your pocket for it, or else have it ready in your hand before you were handed the cone. There isn't remotely enough time for anything like that. Just decide *in your mind* which came up, heads or tails, and then try to remember as fast as you can which of the problems you had assigned to the winning side of the coin. Probably, though, there isn't time for any of this. Just do something, however arbitrary. Act! *Eat!*

[20] In trying to make wise and correct decisions about the ice-cream cone in your hand, you should always keep the objectives in mind. The main objective, of course, is to get the cone under control. Secondarily, one will want to eat the cone calmly and with pleasure. Real pleasure lies not simply in eating the cone but in eating it *right.* Let us assume that you have darted to your open space and made your necessary emergency repairs. The cone is still dangerous—still, so to speak, "live." But you can now proceed with it in an

orderly fashion. First, revolve the cone through the full three hundred and sixty degrees, snapping at the loose gobs of ice cream; turn the cone by moving the thumb away from you and the forefinger toward you, so the cone moves counterclockwise. Then, with the cone still "wound," which will require the wrist to be bent at the full right angle toward you, apply pressure with the mouth and tongue to accomplish overall realignment, straightening and settling the whole mess. Then, unwinding the cone back through the full three hundred and sixty degrees, remove any trickles of ice cream. From here on, some supplementary repairs may be necessary, but the cone is now defused.

[21] At this point, you can risk a glance around you. How badly the others are doing with their cones! Now you can settle down to eating yours. This is done by eating the ice cream off the top. At each bite, you must press down cautiously, so that the ice cream settles farther and farther into the cone. Be very careful not to break the cone. Of course, you never take so much ice cream into your mouth at once that it hurts your teeth; for the same reason, you never let unmelted ice cream into the back of your mouth. If all these procedures are followed correctly, you should shortly arrive at the ideal—the way an ice-cream cone is always pictured but never actually is when it is handed to you *(Fig. 2)*. The ice cream should now form a small dome whose circumference exactly coincides with the large circumference of the cone itself—a small skullcap that fits exactly on top of a larger, inverted dunce cap. You have made order out of chaos; you are an artist. You have taken an unnatural, abhorrent, irregular, chaotic form, and from

Fig. 2

it you have sculpted an ordered, ideal shape that might be envied by Praxiteles or even Euclid.

[22] Now at last you can begin to take little nibbles of the cone itself, being very careful not to crack it. Revolve the cone so that its rim remains smooth and level as you eat both ice cream and cone in the same ratio. Because of the geometrical nature of things, a constantly reduced inverted cone still remains a perfect inverted cone no matter how small it grows, just as a constantly reduced dome held within a cone retains *its* shape. Because you are constantly reshaping the dome of ice cream with your tongue and nibbling at the cone, it follows in logic—and in actual practice, if you are skillful and careful—that the cone will continue to look exactly the

same, except for its size, as you eat it down, so that at the very end you will hold between your thumb and forefinger a tiny, idealized replica of an ice-cream cone, a thing perhaps one inch high. Then, while the others are licking their sticky fingers, preparatory to wiping them on their clothes, or going back to the ice-cream stand for more paper napkins to try to clean themselves up—*then* you can hold the miniature cone up for everyone to see, and pop it gently into your mouth.

COMMENT

Hills is writing about the joys of eating ice-cream cones, and he is writing humorously. The problems he describes are real ones, but these are part of the fun of eating ice-cream cones, and he knows that his readers will share this view. Though he gives instructions for each stage in the process, he also knows that his readers are probably familiar with all of the details. The purpose of the essay, then, is to give the pleasure of recognition. The many kinds of analysis—from comparison and contrast to process—can be used for many different purposes, as this delightful essay shows.

QUESTIONS FOR STUDY AND DISCUSSION

1. What in the description of the process depends on the reader's recognition of the problem? How does Hills remind the reader of these problems?

2. What explains the order of the steps in the process? Is Hills moving from the easier to the more difficult steps, or has he chosen another principle of order?

3. What is the overall tone of the essay? How do the drawings contribute to it?

4. Are the various statements about human nature to be taken seriously, though they are presented humorously?

5. The most effective humor develops out of genuine problems and observations—not out of invented ones. Is this true of the humor of this essay?

6. What impression do you get of the writer—his personality, his outlook on life, his sense of humor?

VOCABULARY STUDY

Formal words will often seem humorous in an informal setting: "This schoolmate has a flair for *contingency* planning. . . ." Identify formal words of this sort in the essay, and explain the humor they provide.

SUGGESTIONS FOR WRITING

1. Write a humorous description of a process similar to eating an ice-cream cone—perhaps wrapping a large gift, or eating an unfamiliar food for the first time. Let your details reveal something unusual and important about human beings.

2. Write a set of instructions for a job that involves a number of related processes, for example, changing a flat tire. Keep each of the processes distinct, and be careful to define important terms for the person who has not performed the process before.

TAKE THE PLUNGE . . .

Gloria Emerson

Gloria Emerson worked as a foreign correspondent for the *New York Times* from 1965 to 1972, reporting on Northern Ireland, on the Nigerian Civil War, and, from 1970 to 1972, on Vietnam. She received the 1971 George Polk Award for excellence in her reporting from Vietnam, and the 1978 National Book Award for her book about the Vietnam war, *Winners and Losers*.

[1] It was usually men who asked me why I did it. Some were amused, others puzzled. I didn't mind the jokes in the newspaper office where I worked about whether I left the building by window, roof or in the elevator. The truth is that I was an unlikely person to jump out of an airplane, being neither graceful, daring nor self-possessed. I had a bad back, uncertain ankles and could not drive with

competence because of deficient depth perception and a fear of all
buses coming toward me. A friend joked that if I broke my bones I
would have to be shot because I would never mend.

[2]I never knew why I did it. It was in May, a bright and dull
May, the last May that made me want to feel reckless. But there
was nothing to do then at the beginning of a decade that changed
almost everything. I could not wait that May for the Sixties to
unroll. I worked in women's news; my stories came out like little
cookies. I wanted to be brave about something, not just about love,
or a root canal, or writing that the shoes at Arnold Constable looked
strangely sad.

[3]Once I read of men who had to run so far it burned their chests
to breathe. But I could not run very far. Jumping from a plane,
which required no talent or endurance, seemed perfect. I wanted to
feel the big, puzzling lump on my back that they promised was a
parachute, to take serious strides in the absurd black boots that I
believed all generals wore.

[4]I wanted all of it: the rising of a tiny plane with the door off,
the earth rushing away, the plunge, the slap of the wind, my hands
on the back straps, the huge curve of white silk above me, the drift
through the space we call sky.

[5]It looked pale green that morning I fell into it, not the baby
blue I expected. I must have been crying; my cheeks were wet. Only
the thumps of a wild heart made noise; I did not know how to keep
it quiet.

[6]That May, that May my mind was a clear as clay. I did not
have the imagination to perceive the risks, to understand that if the
wind grew nasty I might be electrocuted on high-tension wires,
smashed on a roof, drowned in water, hanged in a tree. I was sure
nothing would happen, because my intentious were so good, just as
young soldiers start out certain of their safety because they know
nothing.

[7]Friends drove me to Orange, Massachusetts, seventy miles
west of Boston, for the opening of the first U.S. sports parachuting
center, where I was to perform. It was the creation, the passion, of a
Princetonian and ex-Marine named Jacques Istel, who organized
the first U.S. jumping team in 1956. Parachuting was "as safe as
swimming," he kept saying, calling it the "world's most stimulating
and soul-satisfying sport." His center was for competitions and the
teaching of skydiving. Instead of hurtling toward the earth, sky

divers maintain a swan-dive position, using the air as a cushion to support them while they maneuver with leg and arm movements until the rip cord must be pulled.

[8] None of that stuff was expected from any of us in the little beginners class. We were only to jump, after brief but intense instruction, with Istel's newly designed parachute, to show that any dope could do it. It was a parachute with a thirty-two-foot canopy; a large cutout hole funneled escaping air. You steered with two wooden knobs instead of having to pull hard on the back straps, or risers. The new parachute increased lateral speed, slowed down the rate of descent, reduced oscillation. We were told we could even land standing up but that we should bend our knees and lean to one side. The beginners jumped at eight A.M., the expert sky divers performed their dazzling tricks later when a crowd came.

[9] Two of us boarded a Cessna 180 that lovely morning, the wind no more than a tickle. I was not myself, no longer thin and no longer fast. The jump suit, the equipment, the helmet, the boots, had made me into someone thick and clumsy, moving as strangely as if they had put me underwater and said I must walk. It was hard to bend, to sit, to stand up. I did not like the man with me; he was eager and composed. I wanted to smoke, to go to the bathroom, but there were many straps around me that I did not understand. At twenty-three hundred feet, the hateful, happy man went out, making a dumb thumbs-up sign.

[10] When my turn came, I suddenly felt a stab of pain for all the forgotten soldiers who balked and were kicked out, perhaps shot, for their panic and for delaying the troops. I was hooked to a static line, an automatic opening device, which made it impossible to lie down or tie myself to something. The drillmaster could not hear all that I shouted at him. But he knew the signs of mutiny and removed my arms from his neck. He took me to the doorway, sat me down, and yelled "Go!" or "Now!" or "Out!" There was nothing to do but be punched by the wind, which knocked the spit from my mouth, reach for the wing strut, hold on hard, kick back the feet so weighted and helpless in those boots, and let go. The parachute opened with a plop, as Istel had sworn to me that it would. When my eyelids opened as well, I saw the white gloves on my hands were old ones from Saks Fifth Avenue, gloves I wore with summer dresses. There was dribble on my chin; my eyes and nose were leaking. I wiped everything with the gloves.

[11]There was no noise; the racket of the plane and wind had gone away. The cold and sweet stillness seemed an astonishing, undreamed-of gift. Then I saw what I had never seen before, will never see again; endless sky and earth in colors and textures no one had ever described. Only then did the parachute become a most lovable and docile toy: this wooden knob to go left, this wooden knob to go right. The pleasure of being there, the drifting and the calm, rose to a fever; I wanted to stay pinned in the air and stop the ground from coming closer. The target was a huge arrow in a sandpit. I was cross to see it, afraid of nothing now, for even the wind was kind and the trees looked soft. I landed on my feet in the pit with a bump, then sat down for a bit. Later that day I was taken over to meet General James Gavin, who had led the 82nd Airborne in the D-day landing at Normandy. Perhaps it was to prove to him that the least promising pupil, the gawkiest, could jump. It did not matter that I stumbled and fell before him in those boots, which walked with a will of their own. Later, Mr. Istel's mother wrote me a charming note of congratulations. Everyone at the center was pleased; in fact, I am sure they were surprised. Perhaps this is what I had in mind all the time.

COMMENT

The process of skydiving involves more than the mechanics of opening the parachute in the air—the operation that probably grips the attention of people who know nothing about the sport. The physical and mental preparation for the parachute jump is of greater significance to Emerson, for these are the steps she concentrates on. She does, however, provide enough details about the jump—details essential to her purpose in writing. These are not presented separately from the physical and mental preparation: they are part of the total narrative, and are properly subordinated and focused.

QUESTIONS FOR STUDY AND DISCUSSION

1. What is Emerson's purpose in writing? Does she state her purpose directly, or do you discover it from her approach to the subject and her focus? What were her motives in making the jump?

2. What details does she provide about the operation of the parachute,

the descent, and the landing? How are these details fitted to the discussion of her feelings at various stages in her experience? What are these stages?

3. How does she maintain the focus on her feelings throughout the essay? Do these feelings change?

4. What kind of definition does she use in the course of the essay? What is the purpose of this definition?

5. Would you have reacted to the parachute jump as Emerson did? What comparable experience aroused similar expectations and feelings in you.

VOCABULARY STUDY

1. Emerson uses a number of technical terms, among them *rip cord, static line* and *wing strut.* See whether your dictionary—or an unabridged dictionary—contains these. If you do not find them listed, state how the essay clarifies their meaning. Notice that we do not always require a complete definition of a term to understand its purpose or role in the process. Is that true of these terms?

2. Explain the italicized words and phrases:
   a. The truth is that I was an unlikely person to jump out of an airplane, being neither graceful, daring nor *self-possessed.*
   b. That May, that May my mind was as *clear as clay.*
   c. Instead of *hurtling* toward the earth, sky divers maintain a *swan-dive position,* using the air *as a cushion* to support them while they *maneuver with leg and arm movements* until the rip cord must be pulled.

SUGGESTIONS FOR WRITING

1. Describe a process that uses equipment such as a parachute, and that contains a series of steps. Write for a particular audience, and define only those terms that they would need to know. Fit these details to an account of your feelings at various stages of the process.

2. Describe an experience comparable to the one Emerson describes. Explain your motives in undertaking the experience, and trace the stages of the experience as Emerson does, giving an account of your feelings at each stage.

cause and effect

Reasoning about *cause and effect* is often a simple matter of connecting two events. When I get wet during a thunderstorm, I know that rain is the cause. But making other connections is usually not this simple. If I catch a cold the same day, I may blame it on the rain. However, I might have caught cold even if I had stayed indoors; and if I had been in the rain, the rain alone may not have been the single cause. A number of conditions together probably produced the cold: a run-down state arising from overwork or lack of sleep, poor eating habits, getting wet—these may have triggered a virus in the body.

The sum of these conditions is generally what we mean by *cause*. We ordinarily speak loosely of one of these conditions as the cause. Except where an immediate action (exposure to the storm) produces a direct consequence (getting wet), my reasoning about cause and effect is probable rather than certain. Having identified conditions that produced colds in the past, I cannot be sure that they *must* produce one in the present. The identical conditions may be present, without producing a cold.

In all discussions of cause and effect, formal and informal, are hidden or unstated assumptions or beliefs about people, society, the ways things happen in nature; human beings are naturally aggressive; adolescents are naturally rebellious; the Irish have hot tempers; the English are cold and reserved; opposites attract. Many who hold these beliefs unquestioningly seldom think about them, nor do they feel it necessary to test them through observation. In cause-and-effect reasoning such assumptions are hidden in the explanation and may be decisive.

WHY SMALLER REFRIGERATORS CAN PRESERVE THE HUMAN RACE

Appletree Rodden

Appletree Rodden did research in biochemistry at Stanford University and has been a member of the Staatstheater Ballet Company, in West Germany.

[1] Once, long ago, people had special little boxes called refrigerators in which milk, meat, and eggs could be kept cool. The grandchildren of these simple devices are large enough to store whole cows, and they reach temperatures comparable to those at the South Pole. Their operating costs increase each year, and they are so complicated that few home handymen attempt to repair them on their own.

[2] Why has this change in size and complexity occurred in America? It has not taken place in many areas of the technologically advanced world (the average West German refrigerator is about a yard high and less than a yard wide, yet refrigeration technology is Germany is quite advanced). Do we really need (or even want) all that space and cold?

[3] The benefits of a large refrigerator are apparent: a saving of time (one grocery-shopping trip a week instead of several), a saving of money (the ability to buy expensive, perishable items in larger, cheaper quantities), a feeling of security (if the car breaks down or if famine strikes, the refrigerator is well stocked). The costs are there, too, but they are not so obvious.

[4] Cost number one is psychological. Ever since the refrigerator began to grow, food has increasingly become something we buy to store rather than to eat. Few families go to market daily for their daily bread. The manna in the wilderness could be gathered for only one day at a time. The ancient distaste for making food a storage item is echoed by many modern psychiatrists who suggest that such psychosomatic disorders as obesity are often due to the patient's inability to come to terms with the basic transitoriness of life. Research into a relationship between excessive corpulence and the size of one's refrigerator has not been extensive, but we might suspect one to be there.

[5] Another cost is aesthetic. In most of Europe, where grocery marketing is still a part of the daily rhythm, one can buy tomatoes, lettuce, and the like picked on the day of purchase. Many European families have modest refrigerators for storing small items (eggs, milk, butter) for a couple of days, but the concept of buying large quantities of food to store in the refrigerator is not widely accepted. Since fresh produce is easily available in Europe, most people buy it daily.

[6] Which brings to mind another price the large refrigerator has cost us: the friendly neighborhood market. In America, time is money. A large refrigerator means fewer time-consuming trips to the grocery store. One member of a deep-freeze-owning family can do the grocery shopping once or twice a month rather than daily. Since shopping trips are infrequent, most people have been willing to forego the amenities of the little store around the corner in favor of the lower prices found in the supermarket.

[7] If refrigerators weren't so large—that is, if grocery marketing were a daily affair—the "entertainment surcharge" of buying farm-fresh food in a smaller, more intimate setting might carry some weight. But as it is, there is not really that much difference between eggs bought from Farmer Brown's wife and eggs bought from the supermarket which in turn bought them from Eggs Incorporated, a firm operated out of Los Angeles that produces 200,000 eggs a day from chickens that are kept in gigantic warehouses lighted artificially on an eighteen-hour light-and-dark cycle and produce one-and-a-half times as many eggs—a special breed of chickens who die young and insane. Not much difference if you don't mind eating eggs from crazy chickens.

[8] Chalk up Farmer and Mrs. Brown as cost number four of the

big refrigerator. The small farmer can't make it in a society dominated by supermarkets and big refrigerators; make way for super-farmers, super yields, and pesticides (cost number five).

[9] Cost number six of the big refrigerator has been the diminution of regional food differences. Of course the homogenization of American fare cannot be blamed solely on the availability of frozen food. Nonetheless, were it not for the trend toward turning regional specialties into frozen dinners, it might still be possible to experience novelty closer to home.

[10] So much for the disadvantages of the big refrigerator. What about the advantages of the small one? First of all, it would help us to "think small," which is what we must learn anyway if the scary predictions of the Club of Rome *(The Limits of Growth)* are true. The advent of smaller refrigerators would set the stage for reversing the "big-thinking" trends brought on with the big refrigerator, and would eventually change our lives.

[11] Ivan Illich makes the point in *Tools for Conviviality* that any tool we use (the automobile, standardized public education, public-health care, the refrigerator) influences the individual, his society, and the relationship between the two. A person's automobile is a part of his identity. The average Volkswagen owner has a variety of characteristics (income, age, occupation) significantly different from those of the average Cadillac owner. American society, with more parking lots than parks, and with gridded streets rather than winding lanes, would be vastly different without the private automobile. Similar conclusions can be drawn about any of the tools we use. They change us. They change our society. Therefore, it behooves us to think well before we decide which tool to use to accomplish a given task. De we want tools that usurp power unto themselves, the ones called "non-convivial" by Illich?

[12] The telephone, a "convivial tool," has remained under control; it has not impinged itself on society or on the individual. Each year it has become more efficient, and it has not prevented other forms of communication (letter writing, visits). The world might be poorer without the telephone, but it would not be grossly different. Telephones do not pollute, are not status symbols, and interact only slightly (if at all) with one's self-image.

[13] So what about the refrigerator? Or back to the more basic problem to which the refrigerator was a partial answer: what about our supply of food? When did we decide to convert the emotion-laden

threat of starvation from a shared community problem (of societal structure: farm-market-home) to a personal one (of storage)? How did we decide to accept a thawed block taken from a supermarket's freezer as a substitute for the voluptuous shapes, smells, and textures of fresh fruits and vegetables obtained from complex individual sources?

[14] The decision for larger refrigerators has been consistent with a change in food-supply routes from highly diversified "trails" (from small farms to neighborhood markets) to uniform, standardized highways (from large farms to centrally located supermarkets). Desirable meals are quick and easy rather than rich and leisurely. Culinary artistry has given way to efficiency, the efficiency of the big refrigerator.

[15] People have a natural propensity for running good things into the ground. Mass production has been a boon to mankind, but its reliance on homogeneity precludes its being a paradigm for all areas of human life. Our forebears and contemporaries have made it possible to mass-produce almost anything. An equally challenging task now lies with us: to choose which things of this world should be mass-produced, and how the standards of mass production should influence other standards we hold dear.

[16] Should houses be mass-produced? Should education? Should food? Which brings us back to refrigerators. How does one decide how large a refrigerator to buy, considering one's life, one's society, and the world, and not simply the question of food storage?

[17] As similar questions are asked about more and more of the things we mass-produce, mass production will become less of a problem and more of a blessing. As cost begins to be measured not only in dollars spent and minutes saved, but in total richness acquired, perhaps smaller refrigerators will again make good sense. A small step backward along some of the roads of "technological progress" might be a large step forward for mankind, and one our age is uniquely qualified to make.

COMMENT

If Rodden were trying to persuade West German readers to buy large refrigerators, the benefits they provide would be emphasized. Writing to persuade Americans to give up large refrigerators, he focuses on one cause of their preference for them, the attitude that "time is money." If this attitude is one necessary condition of the American preference—that is, a condition that must be present for this preference to exist—attacking the attitude may help to diminish the incentive. Rodden attacks this attitude by showing the disadvantages of thinking about life in this way; these include the sacrifice of fresh food and the fun of buying it, the gradual disappearance of the small farmer, the use of dangerous pesticides—in general, the limits of choice imposed by technology. There may be other necessary conditions, but Rodden need not identify all of them and does not claim to have done so. The "natural propensity for running good things into the ground" is a necessary condition that would be difficult to eliminate. Writers seldom try to identify all the causes of a situation or attitude—not only because it would be difficult to do so, but because they need not do so to make their point.

QUESTIONS FOR STUDY AND DISCUSSION

1. In what order does Rodden present the costs of large refrigerators?

2. What other causes does Rodden state or imply for the American preference? What is the thesis of the essay, and where is it first stated?

3. Does Rodden explain why Europeans prefer small refrigerators? Is Rodden implying that Americans are more easily captivated by "technological progress"?

4. What in Rodden's comments on storing food and the problem of obesity shows that he is stating some of the reasons for practices and attitudes, not all of them?

5. Does Rodden assert or imply that the greater efficiency a tool has, the greater control it exerts over people?

6. Do you agree that the telephone is a "convivial tool" and do you agree with Rodden's theory of tools?

7. How formal are the transitions of the essay? What is the overall tone? Do you find shifts in tone?

VOCABULARY STUDY

Find synonyms for the following words: *psychosomatic, transitoriness, corpulence, aesthetic, amenities, homogenization, convivial, usurp, culinary, propensity.*

SUGGESTIONS FOR WRITING

1. Analyze your preference for a certain make or size of automobile, or your opinion about the role of the telephone or a comparable tool. Discuss as many causes of your preference or opinion as you can, and present them in the order of their importance.

2. Discuss your eating habits, or those of your family, with attention to the role of the refrigerator in shaping these habits.

3. Discuss a possible change in American eating or consumption habits or recreation that in your opinion would improve the quality of American life. Explain your reasons as Rodden does.

VIOLENCE: TV'S CROWD-CATCHER

Robert Lewis Shayon

Robert Lewis Shayon was born and educated in New York City. He has worked as a producer for CBS and NBC, written for television, and written a column on television and other media for *Saturday Review*. He teaches at the Annenberg School of Communications at the University of Pennsylvania. His books include *Open to Criticism* (1969) and *The Crowd-Catchers: Introducing Television* (1973).

[1] The President's Commission on the Causes and Prevention of Violence continues to hold hearings and to conduct studies on the subject of violence in TV programs. The commission's activities have energized the press to make surveys of its own. The editors of *McCall's* recently urged its readers to write letters to television executives to protest against the outpouring of TV violence. *The Christian Science Monitor* has reported the results of a six-week survey that show that video violence "still rides high on the air-waves, in spite of assurances by network chiefs that they are doing all they

can to minimize the incidence of shootings, stabbings, killings, and beatings."

[2] Social scientists discuss for the commission members the subtleties of defining violence, calculating its effects in terms of aggression, catharsis, and impact on social norms. Some witnesses have urged regulation and control even though research has as yet established no clear, causal relationship between violence in the media and in real life. Nobody, however, seems willing to talk about the true options that are available to the public, as it tries to decide what ought to be done about the problem of violence on TV. The implicit assumptions are that networks could cut down violence if they really wanted to do it; that corporations and advertising agencies have the power to reform the networks if they wished.

[3] Thus, Dr. Leo Bogart, general manager of the Bureau of Advertising of the American Newspaper Publishers Association, told the Commission on Violence that "it must appeal to top managers of corporations . . . in order to induce change in TV programing, and other advertiser-supported media. There is still among them an overwhelming acceptance of the need to do what is right." Perhaps so, but the question is not one of regulation by the industry, government, or any other constituted authority of "them" (people in TV). The real question is whether we—all of us—wish to regulate the American way of life, which is inextricably interwoven with violence on TV.

[4] To understand what the game is all about, one has to get rid of the notion that television is in the program business; nothing could be further from the truth. Television is in the crowd-catching business. The networks and stations are instant crowd-catchers who deliver their catch to the advertisers who inoculate them with consumer messages. Proof of this is at hand in any broadcasting or advertising trade journal, where broadcasters, addressing their real clients, boast of what great crowd-catchers they are at how cheap a cost.

[5] The catching of instant crowds is necessary for the sale of instant tea, coffee, headache relief, spot remover, and other assorted goods and services—not for profit maximization, as John Kenneth Galbraith has argued, but for the instant managing of demand. Planned growth, in his theory, is the driving rod of our industrial state; growth depends on assured flow of capital for long-term projections. Corporations cannot depend on the whims of the old "free

market"—where the consumer was sovereign—for steady, reliable demand. Therefore, demand has to be "managed." Advertising is the manager, and broadcasting is the crowd-catcher.

[6] Now, the essence of the art of catching crowds is conflict—the most contagious of all human experiences, the universal language. Of conflict there are many varieties, ranging from parliamentary debates and elections to strikes, games, and fights. Television could, and occasionally does, present conflicts of ideas, but you can't run a crowd-catching business at this level. Instant crowds require simple phenomena, quickly grasped. Furthermore, ideas are controversial, dangerous; people have convictions, they take sides, are easily offended. Crowd-catchers want only happy consumers.

[7] The type of conflict that will deliver instant crowds most efficiently is physical violence. Consider what would happen if a crowd had three viewing choices on a street: watching a clown, a nude woman, or a no-holds-barred fight—which do you think would attract the biggest crowd? Physical violence grows in mesmeric power, while sex and humor diminish relatively. Violence, internal and external, is the young generation's hang-up, not sex. This is the way our world is; TV tells us so—TV is the true curriculum of our society. We fear violence and enjoy it with guilt, because it calls to our own deeply latent potential for violence in response to a violent world. With such a sure-fire, instant crowd-catcher providing the essential energy which runs our industries, our networks, our advertising agencies—in short, our style of life—to call for the voluntary or involuntary regulation of violence on TV is to call for instant self-destruction of the system. By "system," I mean TV based on advertiser support. Television can run on a different system, of course; it does so in other countries. Public funds can support TV directly; license-fees on sets, along with marginal income from controlled advertising, can provide another basis. But to choose another system is to opt for another style of life, one where corporate and consumer acquisitions are not the dominant values.

[8] If the American citizen is to be addressed maturely on the subject of violence in TV, he ought, at least, to be accorded the dignity of being told what his real choices are. Anything less—any talk of regulating and minimizing physical violence on TV, while retaining the present advertiser-supported crowd-catching system—is to contribute to instant self-delusion.

COMMENT

Shayon is concerned with several cause-and-effect relationships in his discussion of television violence. The cause, he tries to show, is "the American way of life"—which he identifies with the "advertiser-supported crowd-catching system." The relationship is not, however, a direct one, nor does Shayon suggest it is. Advertisers support physical violence on television not because they want to promote violence but because it can best "deliver instant crowds." American business executives make certain assumptions about people—and so does Shayon. We know that his argument is merely probable, not certain, for he appeals to experience for support; it is from experience that he has drawn his own assumptions. The strength of his reasoning depends on the strength of his one example—the probable behavior of the street crowd. He does not try to probe deeply into the "hang-up" with violence. He can merely assert that this hang-up exists and ask his reader to consider his "real choices." The discussion is informal; Shayon does not try to deal with the problem as the social scientists mentioned in paragraph 2 probably would.

QUESTIONS FOR STUDY AND DISCUSSION

1. How does Shayon identify the "implicit assumptions" in the public discussion of television violence?

2. What does Shayon assume about the viewing habits and attitudes of his reader toward television violence? Is he addressing himself to readers who share the views of *McCall's* and *The Christian Science Monitor?*

3. In what ways is "the American way of life . . . inextricably interwoven with violence on TV"? Is Shayon saying that Americans are basically prone to violence, and always have been?

4. Is Shayon opposing planned growth in his comments on the "system," or is his analysis a limited one? Is he suggesting that it is possible to change the system, or that it is possible only to change one's thinking about television violence? What exactly is Shayon recommending?

5. How would you answer the question he asks about the street crowd? If you disagree with his comments on Americans today, need you disagree with his analysis of television violence? Do you think he has identified its cause?

VOCABULARY STUDY

Write a paraphrase of paragraphs 2 and 7. Be sure to explain the following in your own words: *catharsis, social norms,* and *true curriculum.*

SUGGESTIONS FOR WRITING

1. Draw on your experience with and attitudes toward physical violence on television and in everyday life to answer Shayon's question and comment on his views.

2. Shayon wrote his essay in 1969. Discuss how much you believe the situation he describes has changed since then.

3. Discuss what you believe are the false causes of a current problem like the energy crisis. Then analyze what you believe are the probable causes.

argument

Argument, unlike explanation, seeks to prove. Proof becomes necessary when disagreement arises over an issue or principle. Here is an argument that proves its conclusion from well-established *facts:*

> Since large cars use more gas than small ones, and since supplies of crude oil are growing scarce, a car tax should be levied, based on the weight and fuel economy of the car. Such a tax will probably discourage purchase of large cars and reduce the demand on a valuable natural resource.

And here is an argument that proves its conclusion from a different kind of evidence, long-held *assumptions* or *beliefs* that the writer considers unquestionably true:

> Since a high standard of living depends on continuing economic growth, and since continuing economic growth depends on the manufacture of large cars, a car tax will be harmful to the economy and the living standard of Americans.

These arguments are different not only in the kind of evidence presented, but also in the probability or certainty claimed for the conclusion. The first argument is an *inductive* one, the second *deductive:* the first claims to be probable only, the second claims to be certain.

Inductive arguments reason from observations or particulars of experience to general conclusions:

> The Salk vaccine has reduced polio in the United States.
> Smallpox vaccination has virtually eradicated the disease.
> Vaccination for German measles has reduced the incidence of birth defects resulting from the disease.
> *Vaccination is an effective method of fighting contagious diseases.*

The conclusions of inductive arguments are only as strong as the evidence warrants. The evidence above does not, for example, warrant the conclusion that vaccination is the *most* effective method available.

The cause-and-effect reasoning described in the previous section is one form of inductive argument: identifying the "conditions" that produce an event is the same as drawing a conclusion from particulars of experience. Another inductive form is the argument from analogy, a special kind of comparison. I might argue that a certain senator should be elected President because he resembles President Truman in several important ways. My analogy consists of a point-by-point comparison: personality, traits of character, policies, and actions. For an effective argument, the points of similarity adduced should be pertinent to the issue: qualifications for the Presidency. It would be immaterial, for example, if the senator were shorter than Truman. Similarly, important differences would weaken the analogy: it would be a material difference if the senator had served only one month and had no previous government experience. With these cautions in mind, I conclude that since the senator resembles Truman in the ways noted, he probably would make a good a President.

Notice the qualification *probably*. That qualification applies to all inductive arguments. While inductive arguments can be highly probable, they can never be certain, for we cannot be sure that we have discovered all the facts—that an exception may not exist to the generalization we have drawn. Some contagious diseases may be resistant even to vaccination, and when and if that fact is discovered, our conclusion would have to be severely qualified.

Deductive arguments, by contrast, derive conclusions from statements assumed to be self-evident or well enough established to provide certain and decisive evidence for the conclusion:

> We hold these truths to be self-evident; that all men are created equal; that they are endowed by their creator with certain unalienable rights; that among these are life, liberty, and the pursuit of happiness . . .

The following are held as unquestioned truths by many people today, and serve as decisive evidence in deductive arguments such as the one quoted above:

> A high standard of living depends on continuing economic growth.
> A strong automobile industry, engaged in the manufacture of large cars, is essential to that growth.

In formal logic, statements (or premises) and conclusion are arranged in what is called a syllogism, and they must be worded strictly:

> Devices that use large amounts of gas waste a natural resource.
> Eight-cylinder engines are devices that use large amounts of gas.
> Eight-cylinder engines waste a natural resource.

Usually, however, such a deductive argument is worded less formally and more concisely:

> Eight-cylinder engines, like all devices that use large amounts of gas, waste a natural resource.

To repeat, a deductive argument depends on the evident truth of its statements to establish its conclusion; and more than this, deductive evidence is considered to be certain enough to establish the conclusion without qualification. When writing a deductive argument, we may choose to explain or illustrate our statements, perhaps as a way of reminding our readers of what they already know to be true. But that explanation or illustration is not presented as *proof* of our statements, as in inductive arguments.

We must understand that not everyone will agree with our premises: we may have to defend them in the course of a deductive argument. However we do so, the argument is deductive as long as the premises themselves provide the decisive evidence for the conclusion. In some arguments, statements may be implied rather than made explicitly, as was mentioned in the previous discussion. Appletree Rodden *implies* that people need not be victims of technology: they need not own large refrigerators just because they exist. These assumptions are basic to his argument, and yet they are unstated in the essay. When we disagree with an argument, yet cannot say why we do, we may be in disagreement with such implied assumptions. Identifying hidden assumptions—for example, prejudices that may color an argument in subtle ways—is of course a more difficult job.

Deductive arguments must be developed and written with care. For if the premises are not well-established truths, but rather "glittering generalities"—statements that cannot be defended and do not cover all instances they presume to—the argument will be unsound. In inductive arguments, remember that the major problem is not to claim more in the conclusion than the evidence presented warrants.

TWO ESSAYS ON WORK

Eric Hoffer

Eric Hoffer was born in 1902 in New York City. He had learned to read by the age of five, but his education was interrupted at seven when he became blind. Recovering his sight at fifteen, Hoffer read widely and intensively. In later years he worked as a migratory laborer and as a longshoreman on the San Francisco docks, experiences that are the source of his ideas on work and on American society. His many books include *The True Believer* (1951) and *Reflections on the Human Condition* (1974).

Dull Work

¹There seems to be a general assumption that brilliant people cannot stand routine; that they need a varied, exciting life in order to do their best. It is also assumed that dull people are particularly suited for dull work. We are told that the reason the present-day young protest so loudly against the dullness of factory jobs is that they are better educated and brighter than the young of the past.

[2] Actually, there is no evidence that people who achieve much crave for, let alone live, eventful lives. The opposite is nearer the truth. One thinks of Amos the sheepherder, Socrates the stonemason, Omar the tentmaker. Jesus probably had his first revelations while doing humdrum carpentry work. Einstein worked out his theory of relativity while serving as a clerk in a Swiss patent office. Machiavelli wrote *The Prince* and the *Discourses* while immersed in the dull life of a small country town where the only excitement he knew was playing cards with muleteers at the inn. Immanuel Kant's daily life was an unalterable routine. The housewives of Königsberg set their clocks when they saw him pass on his way to the university. He took the same walk each morning, rain or shine. The greatest distance Kant ever traveled was sixty miles from Königsberg.

[3] The outstanding characteristic of man's creativeness is the ability to transmute trivial impulses into momentous consequences. The greatness of man is in what he can do with petty grievances and joys, and with common physiological pressures and hungers. "When I have a little vexation," wrote Keats, "it grows in five minutes into a theme for Sophocles." To a creative individual all experience is seminal—all events are equidistant from new ideas and insights— and his inordinate humanness shows itself in the ability to make the trivial and common reach an enormous way.

[4] An eventful life exhausts rather than stimulates. Milton, who in 1640 was a poet of great promise, spent twenty sterile years in the eventful atmosphere of the Puritan revolution. He fulfilled his great promise when the revolution was dead, and he in solitary disgrace. Cellini's exciting life kept him from becoming the great artist he could have been. It is legitimate to doubt whether Machiavelli would have written his great books had he been allowed to continue in the diplomatic service of Florence and had he gone on interesting missions. It is usually the mediocre poets, writers, etc., who go in search of stimulating events to release their creative flow.

[5] It may be true that work on the assembly line dulls the faculties and empties the mind, the cure only being fewer hours of work at higher pay. But during fifty years as a workingman, I have found dull routine compatible with an active mind. I can still savor the joy I used to derive from the fact that while doing dull, repetitive work on the waterfront, I could talk with my partners and compose sentences in the back of my mind, all at the same time. Life seemed

glorious. Chances are that had my work been of absorbing interest I could not have done any thinking and composing on the company's time or even on my own time after returning from work.

[6] People who find dull jobs unendurable are often dull people who do not know what to do with themselves when at leisure. Children and mature people thrive on dull routine, while the adolescent, who has lost the child's capacity for concentration and is without the inner resources of the mature, needs excitement and novelty to stave off boredom.

A Meaningful Life

[1] One of the lessons of the 1960s has been that abundance, freedom, equality and justice are not the most vital ingredients of a satisfactory individual existence. We begin to realize that from now on a society will be able to stay on an even keel only when it makes it possible for a majority of its people to live meaningful lives.

[2] Now, there is no doubt that in a modern society there is not enough meaningful work to make it possible for most people to derive the meaning in their lives from the work they do to earn a living. For it is a peculiarity of a modern society that the existence of millions depends on being paid for doing what seems like nothing when done. The demand that the work we do for a living should be worth doing, though not "a human impertinence," as Santayana thinks, is unrealizable.

[3] There is a widely held assumption that the way to inject meaning into an individual existence is by participation in communal affairs. Good citizenship, it is true, involves a concern for the welfare of one's community, one's country and probably of humanity in general. But to make such a concern the main content of an individual life is, in normal times, unnatural and unhealthy. With the majority of people, participation in communal affairs cannot be more than a condiment.

[4] In a healthy society the craving for acting with others becomes an aid to the realization and cultivation of the individual. One joins others in a relatively small circle to learn a skill, master a subject or exercise a talent. It is the acquisition of skills in particular, irrespective of their utility, that is potent in making life meaningful. Since man has no inborn skills, the survival of the species has depended on the ability to acquire and perfect skills. Hence the

mastery of skills is a uniquely human activity and yields deep satisfaction.

⁵ I am also convinced that the mastery of skills can be therapeutic. Skill-healing should be particularly effective in the reconstruction and human renewal of the chronically poor, the unemployable and people who cannot cope with life. The acquisition of a skill generates confidence and, since people enjoy doing what they are good at, it may have an energizing effect.

⁶ Were I the mayor of San Francisco, I would have a square or a street lined with small shops where subsidized experts would practice and display every imaginable skill. I would comb the globe for little-known or half-forgotten skills in order to revive them. And I would have children apprenticed to the experts. It is most fitting that in an automated world the human hand, a most unique organ, should come back into its own and again perform wonders. It may well be the hand that will save us.

COMMENT

"Dull Work" is a deductive argument. Hoffer states his basic ideas as unqualified truths: "The outstanding characteristic of man's creativeness is the ability to transmute trivial impulses into momentous consequences. The greatness of man is in what he can do with petty grievances and joys, and with common physiological pressures and hungers." From these truths Hoffer makes the deduction that dull work can be eventful (not that it always is). His examples illustrate these ideas: they are not intended to prove them, though Hoffer does not deny that many creative people have lived eventful lives. His concern is rather with those whose lives have not been eventful. The same kind of argument is developed in "A Meaningful Life." Here Hoffer presents the essential argument briefly: "Since man has no inborn skills, the survival of the species has depended on the ability to acquire and perfect skills. Hence the mastery of skills is a uniquely human activity and yields deep satisfaction." From this essential argument he draws other conclusions that relate to the exercise of skills in a healthy society.

QUESTIONS FOR STUDY AND DISCUSSION

1. Is "dull" work necessarily uninteresting work, or does Hoffer mean something else by this word?

2. What other conclusions can be drawn from Hoffer's premise that creative acts develop out of "trivial impulses"?

3. What is Hoffer's conception of a healthy society? What other ideas about work and community life do you think he would favor?

4. Do you agree with Hoffer about the need to master skills? What is the basis of your opinion—personal experience, observation, long-held beliefs, or a combination of these?

VOCABULARY STUDY

1. Examine the dictionary definitions of the following words to discover denotative and connotative differences in meaning. Then write a sentence for each, using the word in a way that suggests its distinctive meaning: *work, labor, drudgery, grind.*

2. Use your dictionary to investigate the etymology of the following words. Then write a sentence for each, stating what its etymology contributes to your understanding of one or more of its current meanings:
   a. routine
   b. transmute
   c. inordinate
   d. vexation
   e. impertinence
   f. therapeutic

SUGGESTIONS FOR WRITING

1. Discuss your own views on the role of work in a meaningful life. Discuss also the extent to which you agree with Hoffer, and the basis of your views—personal experience, the influences of home and school, your friends, and the like.

2. Discuss one of the following statements from personal experience, to show the extent of your agreement with it:
   a. "An eventful life exhausts rather than stimulates."
   b. " . . . the adolescent, who has lost the child's capacity for concentration and is without the inner resources of the mature, needs excitement and novelty to stave off boredom."
   c. "For it is a peculiarity of a modern society that the existence of millions depends on being paid for doing what seems like nothing when done."

d. "One joins others in a relatively small circle to learn a skill, master a subject or exercise a talent."

e. "The acquisition of a skill generates confidence and, since people enjoy doing what they are good at, it may have an energizing effect."

3. Hoffer states that in an "automated world" the human hand "may well be the hand that will save us." Explain this statement in light of other statements in the two essays, and provide your own examples of Hoffer's point.

STRIKE OUT LITTLE LEAGUE

Robin Roberts

Robin Roberts was born in Springfield, Illinois, in 1926. After his graduation from high school in 1944, he joined the Air Force Student Training Reserve Unit at Michigan State University, where he played basketball and baseball while he earned his Bachelor of Science degree. In 1946 he was named Michigan's Outstanding Basketball Player. Two years later he joined the Philadelphia Phillies and played with that baseball team until 1962. In 1976, he was made a member of the National Baseball Hall of Fame.

[1] In 1939, Little League baseball was organized by Bert and George Bebble and Carl Stotz of Williamsport, Pa. What they had in mind in organizing this kid's baseball program, I'll never know. But I'm sure they never visualized the monster it would grow into.

[2] At least 25,000 teams, in about 5,000 leagues, compete for a chance to go to the Little League World Series in Williamsport each summer. These leagues are in more than fifteen countries, although recently the Little League organization has voted to restrict the competition to teams in the United States. If you judge the success of a program by the number of participants, it would appear that Little League has been a tremendous success. More than 600,000

boys from 8 to 12 are involved. But I say Little League is wrong—and I'll try to explain why.

[3] If I told you and your family that I want you to help me with a project from the middle of May until the end of July, one that would totally disrupt your dinner schedule and pay nothing, you would probably tell me to get lost. That's what Little League does. Mothers or fathers or both spend four or five nights a week taking children to Little League, watching the game, coming home around 8 or 8:30 and sitting down to a late dinner.

[4] These games are played at this hour because the adults are running the programs and this is the only time they have available. These same adults are in most cases unqualified as instructors and do not have the emotional stability to work with children of this age. The dedication and sincerity of these instructors cannot be questioned, but the purpose of this dedication should be. Youngsters eligible for Little League are of the age when their concentration lasts, at most, for five seconds—and without sustained concentration organized athletic programs are a farce.

[5] Most instructors will never understand this. As a result there is a lot of pressure on these young people to do something that is unnatural for their age—so there will always be hollering and tremendous disappointment for most of these players. For acting their age, they are made to feel incompetent. This is a basic fault of Little League.

[6] If you watch a Little League game, in most cases the pitchers are the most mature. They throw harder, and if they throw strikes very few batters can hit the ball. Consequently, it makes good baseball sense for most hitters to take the pitch. Don't swing. Hope for a walk. That could be a player's instruction for four years. The fun is in hitting the ball; the coach says don't swing. That may be sound baseball, but it does nothing to help a young player develop his hitting. What would seem like a basic training ground for baseball often turns out to be a program of negative thoughts that only retards a young player.

[7] I believe more good young athletes are turned off by the pressure of organized Little League than are helped. Little Leagues have no value as a training ground for baseball fundamentals. The instruction at that age, under the pressure of an organized league program, creates more doubt and eliminates the naturalness that is most important.

[8]If I'm going to criticize such a popular program as Little League, I'd better have some thoughts on what changes I would like to see.

[9]First of all, I wouldn't start any programs until the school year is over. Any young student has enough of a schedule during the school year to keep busy.

[10]These programs should be played in the afternoon—with a softball. Kids have a natural fear of a baseball; it hurts when it hits you. A softball is bigger, easier to see and easier to hit. You get to run the bases more and there isn't as much danger of injury if one gets hit with the ball. Boys and girls could play together. Different teams would be chosen every day. The instructors would be young adults home from college, or high-school graduates. The instructor could be the pitcher and the umpire at the same time. These programs could be run on public playgrounds or in schoolyards.

[11]I guarantee that their dinner would be at the same time every night. The fathers could come home after work and relax; most of all, the kids would have a good time playing ball in a program in which hitting the ball and running the bases are the big things.

[12]When you start talking about young people playing baseball at 13 to 15, you may have something. Organize them a little, but be careful; they are still young. But from 16 and on, work them really hard. Discipline them, organize the leagues, strive to win championships, travel all over. Give this age all the time and attention you can.

[13]I believe Little League has done just the opposite. We've worked hard with the 8- to 12-year-olds. We overorganize them, put them under pressure they can't handle and make playing baseball seem important. When our young people reach 16 they would appreciate the attention and help from the parents, and that's when our present programs almost stop.

[14]The whole idea of Little League baseball is wrong. There are alternatives available for more sensible programs. With the same dedication that has made the Little League such a major part of many of our lives, I'm sure we'll find the answer.

[15]I still don't know what those three gentlemen in Williamsport had in mind when they organized Little League baseball. I'm sure they didn't want parents arguing with their children about kids' games. I'm sure they didn't want to have family meals disrupted for three months every year. I'm sure they didn't want young athletes

hurting their arms pitching under pressure at such a young age. I'm sure they didn't want young boys who don't have much athletic ability made to feel that something is wrong with them because they can't play baseball. I'm sure they didn't want a group of coaches drafting the players each year for different teams. I'm sure they didn't want unqualified men working with the young players. I'm sure they didn't realize how normal it is for an 8-year-old boy to be scared of a thrown or batted baseball.

[16] For the life of me, I can't figure out what they had in mind.

COMMENT

Roberts does not begin with general truths about boys and girls. He begins with and presents his specific experience and observations and draws limited conclusions from them. How much evidence he presents for these depends on how he views his reader. He clearly expects the reader to know from experience that eight-year-old boys are scared of hard balls, and that most adults who instruct the boys are unqualified; on other points he presents more evidence. In an inductive argument of this sort, depending on particulars of experience, the strength of the argument depends on the amount and variety. It depends, too, on the reputation of the author. Roberts has a claim to authority in writing about Little League baseball; an author with less impressive credentials may need to cite more particulars and verify them.

QUESTIONS FOR STUDY AND DISCUSSION

1. What audience does Roberts have in mind? Is his purpose to inform them of the situation, or to inform and persuade them to take action?

2. How does Roberts establish his authority on the subject? Does he make direct reference to his experience in baseball? Does he ask his audience to accept his views on the basis of his authority alone?

3. Roberts anticipates an objection sometimes called a *dilemma:* either we have Little Leage baseball, or we have no organized baseball for boys and girls. How does he "go between the horns" of this dilemma by suggesting a third possibility?

4. How might Roberts answer those who object that only parents with children playing Little Leage baseball currently have a right to judge the sport?

VOCABULARY STUDY

1. Identify those words in the essay that you consider negative in connotation. Use your dictionary to find neutral words that could be substituted for them.

2. Use your dictionary to find antonyms—words opposite in their meaning—to the following. Use the antonyms in sentences of your own:
   a. restrict
   b. compete
   c. retard
   d. relax

SUGGESTIONS FOR WRITING

1. Discuss your experience with and attitude toward an organized sport like Little League baseball. Use this discussion to state the extent of your agreement or disagreement with Roberts on planned sports for children.

2. Discuss how supporters of Little League baseball might answer the charges Roberts makes. Then discuss how Roberts might answer these people, given his statements in the essay.

3. Write your own essay, using the title "Strike Out _____," to persuade your readers of the disadvantages of an organization or activity. Remember that you will not convince readers without strong evidence based on your experience and observations.

4. Roberts discusses some mistaken ideas that adults have about children and adolescents. Discuss other such mistaken ideas that affect the lives of children in important ways—perhaps in school activities or home life.

. . . MEANWHILE, HUMANS EAT PET FOOD

Edward H. Peeples Jr.

Edward H. Peeples Jr. was born in 1935 in Richmond, Virginia. He attended the Richmond Professional Institute, the University of Pennsylvania, and the University of Kentucky, where he received his Ph.D. in 1972. He is associate professor of preventive medicine at Virginia Commonwealth University. In the sixties he gained knowledge of urban poverty as a social worker in Richmond and South Philadelphia. He has been a leader of the Richmond Human Rights Coalition and Council on Human Relations and is deeply concerned with the nutritional problems and medical care of poor people.

[1] The first time I witnessed people eating pet food was among neighbors and acquaintances during my youth in the South. At that time it was not uncommon or startling to me to see dog-food patties sizzling in a pan on the top of a stove or kerosene space heater in a dilapidated house with no running water, no refrigerator, no heat, no toilet and the unrelenting stench of decaying insects. I simply thought of it as the unfortunate but unavoidable consequence of being poor in the South.

[2] The second time occurred in Cleveland in the summer of 1953. Like many other Southerners, I came to seek my fortune in one of those pot-at-the-end-of-the-rainbow factories along Euclid Avenue. Turned away from one prospective job after another ("We don't hire hillbillies," employers said), I saw my nest egg of $30 dwindle to nothing. As my funds diminished and my hunger grew, I turned to pilfering food and small amounts of cash. With the money, I surreptitiously purchased, fried and ate canned dog and cat food as my principal ration for several weeks.

[3] I was, of course, humiliated to be eating something that, in my experience, only "trash" consumed. A merciless pride in self-sufficiency kept me from seeking out public welfare or asking my friends or family for help. In fact, I carefully guarded the secret from everyone, because I feared being judged a failure.

[4] Except for the humiliation I experienced, eating canned pet food did not at the time seem to be particularly unpleasant. The dog food tasted pretty much like mealy hamburger, while the cat food was similar to canned fish that I was able to improve with mayonnaise, mustard or catsup.

[5] The next time I ate dog food was in 1956 while struggling through a summer session in college without income for food. Again,

I was ashamed to admit it, fearing that people would feel sorry for me or that others who had even less than I would feel compelled to sacrifice for my comfort. I never again had to eat pet food.

[6] Later, while working as a hospital corpsman at the Great Lakes Illinois Naval Training Center in the late 1950's I had the opportunity to ask new recruits about their home life and nutrition practices. While I was not yet a disciplined scientist, I was able to estimate that about 5 to 8 percent of the thousands of young men who came to Great Lakes annually consumed pet foods and other materials not commonly thought to be safe or desirable for humans. Among these substances were baking soda, baking powder, laundry starch, tobacco, snuff, clay, dirt, sand and various wild plants.

[7] My later experience as a public assistance caseworker in Richmond, a street-based community worker in South Philadelphia, and my subsequent travels and studies as a medical sociologist throughout the South, turned up instances of people eating pet food because they saw it as cheaper than other protein products. Through the years, similar cases found in the Ozarks, on Indian reservations and in various cities across the nation have also been brought to my attention.

[8] While there do exist scattered scientific reports and commentary on the hazards and problems associated with eating such things as laundry starch and clay, there is little solid epidemiological evidence that shows a specific percentage of American households consume pet food. My experience and research, however, suggest that human consumption of pet food is widespread in the United States. My estimate, one I believe to be conservative, is that pet foods constitute a significant part of the diet of at least 225,000 American households, affecting some one million persons. Who knows how many more millions supplement their diet with pet-food products? One thing that we can assume is that current economic conditions are increasing the practice and that it most seriously affects the unemployed, poor people, and our older citizens.

[9] There are those who argue that we do not have enough hard data on the human consumption of pet foods. Must we wait for incontrovertible data before we seriously seek to solve the problems of hunger and malnutrition in America? I submit that we have data enough. Isn't it sufficient to know that one American child or a single elderly person in this bountiful land is reduced to eating the forage of animals or exposed to unknown toxic levels of mercury,

lead or salmonella to know that something very extraordinary must be done?

COMMENT

The writer of an inductive argument must decide how much evidence is needed to draw a well-founded conclusion—to make the "inductive leap." There is, of course, no end to the amount of evidence that could be presented for a conclusion such as Peeples reaches in his final sentence; the writer makes the decision at some point in conducting an investigation that enough evidence has been found. The phrase "inductive leap" sometimes means that the writer has drawn a conclusion too soon, on the basis of incomplete evidence. Probably few writers are satisfied that they have found all the evidence needed to make the argument convincing to everyone. Like Peeples, they may feel it necessary to draw conclusions from a smaller amount of evidence because a current situation is growing critical and must be exposed at once. Notice that Peeples admits the limitation his personal experience imposes on his conclusions. He is careful to state this limitation and also the basis of his estimate—a conservative estimate, he notes—that about a million people in the United States eat pet food in significant amounts. If writers have wide and expert experience in their subject, as Peeples has, their experience alone may be sufficient to give weight to their conclusions. As in all inductive arguments, the conclusion Peeples reaches is probable only, not absolutely certain.

QUESTIONS FOR STUDY AND DISCUSSION

1. Why do people eat pet food, according to Peeples?

2. What is his purpose in writing, and where does he state it? What makes the essay inductive?

3. To what audience is he writing, and how do you know? Were he writing to public health officials only, would he approach the subject in a different way, or present different evidence?

4. How does Peeples qualify his conclusion that people who eat pet food are affected by it seriously—that is, how does he indicate the degree of probability that this is so?

5. Has Peeples persuaded you that the situation he describes is serious

and that something must be done about it? If not, what other evidence would persuade you?

VOCABULARY STUDY

1. Complete the following to show the meaning of the italicized words:
   a. His *disciplined* way of living was shown by
   b. A *conservative* action is one that
   c. An *incontrovertible* proof can never
   d. The *bountiful* harvest

2. Identify the denotative and connotative meanings of the following: paragraph 1: *sizzling, dilapidated, stench;* paragraph 2: *pilfering, surreptitious;* paragraph 3: *"trash";* paragraph 7: *cheaper;* paragraph 9: *extraordinary, forage.*

SUGGESTIONS FOR WRITING

1. Write an essay that builds to a thesis through a series of observations and experiences. Qualify your thesis by stating the limitations of your experience and knowledge of the subject.

2. Discuss an experience that resulted when you found yourself short of or without money. Discuss not only what you did but also what you learned about yourself and perhaps about other people.

3. Discuss how your ideas about people different from you in some way changed through experiences in a world different from that you grew up in. Use this experience to persuade a particular audience to change their thinking about these people.

THE TRUTH ABOUT THE BLACK MIDDLE CLASS

Vernon E. Jordan Jr.

Vernon E. Jordan Jr. was born in Atlanta, Georgia, in 1935. He studied at De Pauw University and at the Howard University law school. Later he practiced law, worked for the NAACP and the United Negro College Fund, and served as adviser to the U.S. government on selective service and civil rights. In 1972 he succeeded Whitney M. Young Jr. as executive director of the National Urban League.

[1] Recent reports of the existence of a vast black middle class remind me of daring explorers emerging from the hidden depths of a strange, newly discovered world bearing tales of an exotic new phenomenon. The media seem to have discovered, finally, black families that are intact, black men who are working, black housewives tending backyard gardens and black youngsters who aren't sniffing coke or mugging old ladies.

[2] And out of this "discovery" a new black stereotype is beginning to emerge. Immaculately dressed, cocktail in hand, the new black stereotype comes off as a sleek, sophisticated professional light-years away from the ghetto experience. As I turn the pages of glossy photos of these idealized, fortunate few, I get the feeling that this new black image is all too comforting to Americans weary of the struggle against poverty and racism.

[3] But this stereotype is no more real than was the old image of the angry, fire-breathing militant. And it may be just as damaging to black people, for whom equal opportunity is still a theory and for whom a national effort to bring about a more equitable distribution of the fruits of an affluent society is still a necessity. After all, who can argue the need for welfare reform, for guaranteed jobs, for integrated schools and better housing, when the supposed beneficiaries are looking out at us from the pages of national magazines, smiling at the camera between sips from their Martinis?

[4] The "new" black middle class has been seen recently in prime time on a CBS News documentary; it has adorned the cover of *The New York Times Magazine*, and it has been the subject of a *Time* cover story. But its much ballyhooed emergence is more representative of wishful thinking than of reality. And important as it is for the dedication and hard work of countless black families finally to receive recognition, the image being pushed so hard may be counterproductive in the long run.

[5] The fact is that the black middle class of 1974, like that of earlier years, is a minority within the black community. In 1974, as

in 1964, 1954 and in the decades stretching into the distant past, the social and economic reality of the majority of black people has been poverty and marginal status in the wings of our society.

⁶The black middle class traditionally included a handful of professionals and a far larger number of working people who, had they been white, would be solidly "working class." The inclusion of Pullman porters, post-office clerks and other typical members of the old black middle class was due less to their incomes—which were well below those of whites—than to their relative immunity from the hazards of marginal employment that dogged most blacks. They were "middle class" relative to other black people, not to the society at large.

⁷Despite all the publicity, despite all the photos of yacht-club cocktail parties, that is where the so-called black middle class stands today. The CBS broadcast included a handyman and a postal worker. Had they been white they would be considered working class, but since they were black and defied media-fostered stereotypes, they were given the middle-class label.

⁸Well, is it true that the black community is edging into the middle class? Let's look at income, the handiest guide and certainly the most generally agreed-upon measurement. What income level amounts to middle-class status? Median family income is often used, since that places a family at the exact midpoint in our society. In 1972 the median family income of whites amounted to $11,549, but black median family income was a mere $6,864.

⁹That won't work. Let's use another guide. The Bureau of Labor Statistics says it takes an urban family of four $12,600 to maintain an "intermediate" living standard. Using that measure, the average black family not only is *not* middle class, but it earns far less than the "lower, non-poverty" level of $8,200. Four out of five black families earn less than the "intermediate" standard.

¹⁰What about collar color? Occupational status is often considered a guide to middle-class status, and this is an area in which blacks have made tremendous gains, breaking into occupations unheard of for non-whites only a decade ago. When you look at the official occupation charts, there is a double space to separate higher-status from lower-status jobs such as laborer, operative and service worker. That gap is more than a typographical device. It is an indicator of racial separation as well, for the majority of working whites hold jobs above that line, while the majority of blacks are still con-

fined to the low-pay, low-status jobs below it. At the top of the job pinnacle, in the elite categories of the professions and business, the disparity is most glaring, with one out of four whites in such middle-class jobs in contrast to every tenth black worker.

[11] Yes, there are black doctors, dentists and lawyers, but let no one be fooled into thinking they are typical—these professions include only 2 percent blacks. Yes, there are black families that are stable, who work, often at more than one job, and who own cars and homes. And yes, they are representative of the masses of black people who work the longest hours at the hardest jobs for the least pay in order to put some meat on the table and clothes on their backs. This should be emphasized in every way possible in order to remind this forgetting nation that there is a dimension of black reality that has never been given its due.

[12] But this should not blind us to the realization that even with such superhuman efforts, the vast majority of blacks are still far from middle-class status. Let us not forget that the gains won are tenuous ones, easily shaken from our grasp by an energy crisis, a recession, rampant inflation or nonenforcement of hard-won civil-rights laws.

[13] And never let us fall victim to the illusion that the limited gains so bitterly wrenched from an unwilling nation have materially changed the conditions of life for the overwhelming majority of black people—conditions still typified by discrimination, economic insecurity and general living conditions inferior to those enjoyed by the majority of our white fellow citizens.

COMMENT

Jordan attacks the mistaken confidence of those who write about the black middle class; he then draws conclusions from his own observations. His main point is that "the black middle class of 1974, like that of earlier years, is a minority within the black community." To establish this point, he must show that, in the past at least, the black middle class was *defined* differently from the white middle class; he is, in fact, exposing the fallacy of "hasty generalization"—generalizing from exceptional rather than typical instances. Jordan's evidence of this difference is the inclusion of the handyman and postal worker in the CBS broadcast: "Had they been white they would be considered working class, but since they were black and defied media-fostered stereotypes they were given the middle-class label." He then measures black people by the standards of white middle-class status—median family income, "intermediate" living standard, "collar color." Not only do fewer black families meet these standards, but the few that do are untypical of American blacks. Jordan uses this inductive argument to drive home his point: "There is a dimension of black reality that has never been given its due." The concern with the definition of the black middle class is inductive also because Jordan is concerned with an implied analogy between the white and black middle class that he shows to be false.

QUESTIONS FOR STUDY AND DISCUSSION

1. What is the implied analogy that the media make between the white and black middle class? How does Jordan show the analogy to be false?

2. How does Jordan show that the media have generalized about the black middle class from exceptional instances?

3. Does Jordan attribute a motive to those who generalize hastily or use a false analogy? Or is he blaming the stereotype on widespread ignorance about black people?

4. How does Jordan show that it is important to define the black middle class properly?

VOCABULARY STUDY

The following words and phrases have exact denotative meanings and strong connotative ones. Show how both types of meaning are used in the essay: *immaculately dressed, stereotype, affluent, militant, dogged, elite, tenuous, recession.*

SUGGESTIONS FOR WRITING

1. Explore the effects of a stereotype—possibly of black teenagers, or high school students, or motorcyclists—for those being stereotyped. You might discuss the view they hold of themselves, or their relations to other people, as these are affected by the stereotype.

2. Discuss an "illusion" people hold about a group you belong to, and state the real facts as Jordan does. You might discuss the consequence of this illusion for you personally.

3. Trace the growth of your feelings toward a particular minority. Discuss the various influences that shaped your feelings, including perhaps television and movies.

DIALOG: JOB PROSPECTS AND COLLEGE MAJORS

Dialog is a regular feature in *Change Magazine,* a periodical devoted to current issues in American education in which teachers, administrators, and students respond to a topic announced in the magazine. The question that resulted in the dialog reprinted here is: "Should students be advised against majoring in areas of study where job prospects are weak?" The respondents are David A. Fedo, Massachusetts College of Pharmacy; E. Michael Walsh, Southern Illinois University at Carbondale; Pamela M. Bischoff, Ramapo College of New Jersey; Harriet C. Seligsohn, University of South Florida; and Nancy Tobin, Wellesley College.

DOUBLE MAJORS

David A. Fedo

[1] Some weeks ago, riding in a cab from Boston to Cambridge, my driver turned and asked me what I did for a living. "Teach English," I said. "Is that so?" the young man continued. "I was an English major." But then, instead of chatting idly about Joyce or dropping the subject altogether, this driver caught me short. "You guys," he said, turning back so that his furry face pressed into the glass partition, "ought to be shot." I think he meant it.

[2] The guilty party in this present state of affairs is not really the academic discipline. It is not the fault of English and philosophy

and biology that engineering and accounting and computer science afford students better job opportunities and increased flexibility in career choice. Literature and an understanding of, say, man's evolutionary past are as important as ever. They simply are no longer perceived in today's market as salable. That is the harsh economic fact. And it is not only true in the United States. Employment prospects for liberal arts graduates in Canada, for example, are said to be the worst since the 1930s.

[3] What to do? I think it would be shortsighted for colleges and universities to advise students against majoring in certain subjects that do not appear linked (at least directly) to careers. Where our energies should be directed instead is toward the development of educational programs that combine course sequences in the liberal arts with course sequences in the viable professions. Double majors—one for enrichment, one for earning one's bread—have never been promoted very seriously in our institutions of higher learning, mainly because liberal arts and professional-vocational faculties have long been suspicious or contemptuous of one another. Thus students have been directed to one path or the other, to the disadvantage of both students and faculty.

[4] A hopeful cue could be taken, it seems to me, from new attempts in the health professions (nursing and pharmacy, for example), where jobs are still plentiful, to give the humanities and social sciences a greater share of the curriculum. Why could not the traditional history major in the college of arts and sciences be pointed toward additional courses in the business school, or to engineering, or to physical therapy? This strategy requires a new commitment from both the institution and the student and demands a much harder look at the allocation of time and resources. But in an age of adversity, double majors are one way liberal arts students can more effectively prepare for the world outside.

ACCOUNTABILITY EXAMINED

E. Michael Walsh

[1] The question points most obviously to liberal arts education. Everyone is painfully aware of the minimal demand not only for

philosophers and students of English literature but also for the graduates of many other arts and science programs that do not prepare students for specific occupations. Because this type of education does not consist of preparation for a specific occupation, many conclude that it is useless.

[2] Such programs, however, are not meant to be job preparation: Sociology majors are not being prepared for positions as sociologist trainees, and philosophy majors are not being prepared for positions in the philosophy industry in the way that education majors are being prepared to teach and automotive technology students are being prepared for work in the automotive industry.

[3] The assumption that labor market demand is the measure of the value of higher education is a fallacy. Labor market demand—meaning the match between an educational program and a specific occupational slot—is a suitable criterion only for those programs which have preparation for employment as their goal. Based on this premise, students should not be advised against majoring in arts and science programs unless they are interested in receiving preparation for a specific job while in college. The question, in short, is irrelevant to a liberal arts education.

[4] Although the criterion of employability is not, strictly speaking, applicable to arts and science education at the undergraduate level, it is most applicable to programs such as education, business, engineering, and journalism that are preparing students for jobs. These fields have as their goal job preparation and they should be held accountable to this goal. Not only should students be advised against majoring in programs that do not achieve their outcomes, but state colleges and universities and private colleges funded by public subsidies (such as VA benefits) have no business spending public funds on activities that do not achieve their goals.

[5] This same accountability holds true for all graduate education, not just graduate education in such fields as business and education. While an undergraduate English major should be receiving a liberal education, a graduate student in English is receiving job preparation is teaching or scholarship (or both). Unless positions involving teaching or scholarship in English are in evidence, a graduate program in English is questionable.

[6] The distinction made here puts accountability for employment where it belongs—on those programs which have preparation for employment as a goal.

INCREASING EMPLOYABILITY

Pamela M. Bischoff

[1] We need only superficially examine recent undergraduate enrollment statistics showing the steady increase in the popularity of business administration courses to know that many students believe that choosing the "right" major will lead to obtaining a "good" job upon graduation. Similarly, we need only listen briefly to the deliberations of many faculty groups to know that the students' concerns are not always shared (and indeed are sometimes deprecated) by those who teach them.

[2] The consumerism movement has given impetus to the notion that educational institutions should provide present and prospective students with descriptive data, including placement statistics. Many students, particularly women, those who are physically disabled, and a high percentage of minority group students, believe they cannot afford the luxury of making a poor career decision. In addition, many students fear that the "wrong" major will lead to underemployment, to an inadequate salary, or to a job which does not involve self-growth. Disclosure of information is thus thought to be helpful in decision making.

[3] But faculty members rightly protest that our knowledge concerning which fields have good job prospects is woefully inadequate, that our understanding of how many persons are preparing for various career areas is even less certain, and that, in any event, the purposes of a liberal arts education go far beyond simply preparing students for specific careers. What is taught, these faculty argue, is both critical and problem-solving modes of thought, as well as a close familiarity with at least one field. All are useful, they claim, in preparation for a variety of careers.

[4] What then can we tell students if our own college communities are so divided? We can teach them that neither self-assessment techniques alone (skills, interests, and values inventories) nor job availability predictions by themselves should be the deciding factors in making rational career decisions. More than in the past we of the faculty and professional staff can work cooperatively to provide helpful direction to students. We can tell them that employers of all kinds look for resourceful and imaginative applicants. We can focus

their concerns on increasing their employability without changing majors. There are a variety of means to accomplish this, including helping students to acquire well-developed communications skills, research capabilities, and analytical abilities; fluency in a foreign language; familiarity with computer applications; quantitative competence; and the ability to complete independent research projects. Above all we should strongly encourage college-sponsored work internship programs and field study experiences for credit as well as seeking out and supporting career-related part-time or summer jobs. These provide a good means of entry to specific jobs while they have the salutary side effect of helping students make more reasoned personal career decisions based upon actual work experiences.

SELF-KNOWLEDGE FOR STUDENTS

Harriet C. Seligsohn

[1] Having been an academic adviser and the administrator of an advising unit for almost eight years, I faced this question as part of my daily routine. Generally speaking, I would have to answer "no." In practice, however, I have advised students to analyze their reasons for selecting a particular major; to evaluate their own potential for that field; to talk with people already employed in appropriate fields; to consider willingness to relocate; and to obtain some exposure to related working environments either by doing volunteer or paid work or simply by obtaining permission to observe those employed. Very often, the student who has made an uneducated selection decides the major was a poor choice. The initial selection is typically based on reasons such as, "My parents want me to be a_____," with no consideration of the student's own motivations and abilities. Also, the freshman student comes to the university or college with little knowledge of the world of work and has stereotyped impressions of what is involved in common careers. Or the student has no idea what he or she wants to do and, if pressured to select a major, picks something popular among peers.

[2] Once the student has learned how to investigate major fields, the activities and functions involved with careers in those fields,

and the job market—and it is critical that the student understand the chances of obtaining a position in a selected field at a given educational level—then motivation should be the determining factor. A student who is willing to work hard and excel in order to compete in a tight job market should not be discouraged if all other indicators point in the direction of that major. A student who does not have the drive to compete should be discouraged from entering a highly competitive field.

[3] However, any student who wishes to compete in a crowded field should be further advised to get preparation in a second area either as an alternative or as a complement to the first. It could also be helpful for the individual to develop some specific skills appropriate to lower-level positions as a means of entering the appropriate environment with the prospect of advancement. This could be particularly valuable if there is less competition at levels just below the one at which the student desires employment.

[4] In all cases, students should be encouraged to have a broad general education. I'm not sure if I'm one of a dying breed which believes in the value of general education or if I'm part of a new movement to reinstate the concept as an important part of education. But in regard to the present issue, since it is not possible to predict long-range market trends with any degree of precision, it is my strong belief that the person who "learns to learn" and is well educated in the broad sense will be better situated to take advantage of future opportunities than a person who overspecializes.

[5] Perhaps the most valuable function educators can perform in helping students select a field of study is to assist them to know themselves, to investigate career options, and to match the two. Knowledge of job prospects is only one of many elements that must be considered toward this choice.

DATA LIMITATIONS

Nancy Tobin

[1] Counselors who believe it is possible to guide students in their choice of major on the basis of job prospects overlook two important points. First, choosing a major is not tantamount to choosing a

career. Second, for most career fields occupational projections are not sufficiently comprehensive to predict weak or strong prospects.

[2] The relationship between subject major and occupational choice is tenuous at best. A direct correlation can be determined only by counting the number of persons in a particular major who enter a similarly labeled occupation. Since art history, psychology, and philosophy majors, for example, often spread out over diverse occupations like marketing, banking, and business management, this kind of counting is not always feasible. While it is true that many accounting majors will become accountants and education majors will be teachers, Ann Stouffer Bisconti and Lewis Solmon point out in their follow-up survey of over 12,000 college graduates who entered college in 1961 that more English majors employed as business administrators used their field content than did economics and engineering majors. Although employers often seem to prefer a particular major, this attitude may not be based on knowledge concerning job content, skill requirements and transferability of skills.

[3] Although the Bureau of Labor Statistics provides a great deal of data on projected employment, these data have serious limitations as a basis for career counseling. While estimates concerning demand for various occupations are based on assumptions, subject to change, about present trends continuing, supply estimates are even less reliable. Numerous occupations, such as marketing and personnel work, are entered by persons from different training programs and a significant amount of training can be acquired on the job. In addition, in many fields there are many more workers possessing entry-level skills than there are job openings. Also, data on annual openings exclude those arising from occupational transfers. Projections also lack flexibility; a field with long-run expansion projections may have limited job openings. Finally, advising students to study for a field with a projected deficit may produce a surplus, as occurred in the teaching field in the 1960s.

[4] Prospects of relatively few openings, or of strong competition in a field, should not prevent one from pursuing a particular career if one's interests and aptitudes justify one's goal. Counseling literature repeatedly warns students not to be trapped by the question, "Where do I fit into the existing job market?" Eli Ginsburg, among others, points out that educational preparation for a specific career is generally impractical, since few people stay with their first job. The more serious problem facing college graduates is not whether

they are going to find jobs related to their major, but whether there will be enough jobs that will fully utilize their level of education.

COMMENT

Arguments usually develop as a response to an event or proposal that will affect people's lives. Those who engage in dialog begin with a discussion of the "givens"—the extent of their agreement on assumptions and the proper questions to raise and deal with. The dialog reprinted here is somewhat different, for the respondents to the question do not engage in discussion with one another. They all approach the topic in their own way, reflecting their personal experiences and special interests in education.

Fedo, for example, accepts the assumption implied in the question that students in college must at least consider their major in light of the present job market. He thus begins with the assumption that both cultural "enrichment" and employable skills should be goals for the student and the college in planning curriculum and allocating resources. The issue for Fedo is whether both are possible and attainable through changes in curriculum. By contrast, Walsh does not deal with the desirability of "enrichment" and occupational skill. The issue for him is the "accountability" of programs designed to make the student employable. Rejecting the premise that all educational programs have a duty to make students employable, he asserts that liberal arts education has a different purpose—and he turns immediately to the pertinent question. Walsh thus deals with the question by analyzing its underlying assumptions and rejecting at least one of them.

Bischoff goes further in analyzing the situation. Analyzing the two main viewpoints or positions, she goes between the horns of the dilemma to show that the complex employment situation today suggests no easy solution such as a double major; students who choose a double major may be without a job if they lack abilities that lie beyond specific academic fields. The issue for Bischoff is whether the question as stated misleads by oversimplifying the decision to be faced and closing off other solutions. Going between the horns means suggesting one or more alternative solutions to those presented.

These differences in the points taken to be at issue arise probably from differences in the experience of the respondents, as well as in their basic educational philosophy. The matter of cultural enrichment is not discussed, perhaps because it is of no concern, or more likely because it is irrelevant to the problem being discussed.

QUESTIONS FOR STUDY AND DISCUSSION

1. Are Fedo and Walsh in disagreement over the desirability of cultural enrichment and the nature of liberal arts education? Would Walsh agree that liberal arts education can have secondary aims?

2. Does Bischoff show agreement with Walsh on liberal arts education? That is, does she believe that its aims have nothing to do with making students employable?

3. How does Seligsohn's experience as an academic adviser shape or influence her approach to the question? What does she assume about the purpose of education generally? Does she, for example, consider employment prospects to be irrelevant to some academic fields like liberal arts?

4. What is at issue in the dialog for Tobin, and where does she state it? How does she define it as the issue? To what extent does she agree with Seligsohn's assumptions?

5. Do you find assumptions shared by all five writers? Do you find different conclusions arising from any shared assumptions?

6. Which of the writers comes closest to your concerns about your education and future employment, and best states the questions you have been asking yourself? With which of the writers are you in most agreement or disagreement, and why?

VOCABULARY STUDY

Explain the italicized words as used in the following sentences:
   a. "The guilty party in this present state of affairs is not really the academic *discipline*." (Fedo)
   b. "Where our energies should be directed instead is toward the development of education programs that combine course *sequences* in the liberal arts with course sequences in the *viable* professions." (Fedo)
   c. "This *strategy* requires a new *commitment* from both the institution and the student and demands a much harder look at the *allocation* of time and resources." (Fedo)

d. "The *assumption* that labor market demand is the measure of the value of higher education is a *fallacy*." (Walsh)

e. "This same *accountability* holds true for all graduate education. . . ." (Walsh)

f. "There are a variety of means to accomplish this, including helping students to acquire well-developed *communications skills, research capabilities,* and *analytical abilities; fluency* in a foreign language; familiarity with computer applications; *quantitative competence;* and the ability to complete independent research projects." (Bischoff)

g. "In practice, however, I have advised students to analyze their reasons for selecting a particular major; to *evaluate* their own *potential* for that field; to talk with people already employed in *appropriate* fields; to consider willingness to relocate; and to obtain some exposure to *related* working *environments* either by doing volunteer or paid work or simply by obtaining permission to observe those employed." (Seligsohn)

h. "First, choosing a major is not *tantamount* to choosing a career." (Tobin)

i. "*Projections* also lack *flexibility;* a field with long-run expansion projections may have limited job openings." (Tobin)

SUGGESTIONS FOR WRITING

1. Write a statement of your own in answer to the question of the dialog. In the course of your statement, indicate which of the five writers you agree and disagree with the most.

2. Develop an argument of your own on a current issue at your college—perhaps the financing of athletic programs for women or the reduction of electives and reintroduction of certain requirements. State both sides of the argument before arguing your agreement with one of them and disagreement with the other.

3. Write an analysis of your present educational goals—defending the choices you have made to a person skeptical of your choices and ideas.

4. Write a letter of application for a position that you consider yourself qualified to fill. Explain how your previous education and work experience qualify you for it.

persuasion

Most arguments are directed to a particular audience and organized in light of that audience's knowledge and beliefs; in other words, most arguments are meant to be *persuasive*. For example, if the argument is deductive, the conclusion may be stated first as a way of focusing attention on the point of most concern. Or the essay may begin with the least controversial statement, proceed to the more controversial, and end with the most controversial. Basic to an argument in favor of gun control may be the premise that the rights of society have precedence over the rights of the individual. Though this premise would be stated first in the formal argument, the writer may save it for last in addressing an audience opposed to gun control since it is the idea they may find least acceptable. In addressing an audience that favors gun control, the writer may choose to begin with it. In short, the premises and conclusion of a deductive argument may be presented in the order most persuasive to a particular audience.

The persuasiveness of the inductive argument depends, as we have seen, on the strength of the facts presented. Precise definition of terms and a clear thesis statement in a position of prominence—at the end of the opening paragraph, for example—will heighten the force of the argument. Though the inductive argument usually builds through details to the conclusion, the writer may anticipate it through a partial statement early in the essay.

In contrast to the logical order of deductive or inductive ideas, then, there is a rhetorical order of ideas—an order determined by the audience being addressed. Having thought out their ideas logically, writers may arrange them in the most effective order, given a particular audience. Over many years a basic form of argument has emerged, deriving from the legal orations of the ancient Greeks. Here is a brief outline of it:

Introduction or exhortation—an urging or plea to the audience to listen to the evidence and judge it fairly

Narrative—a statement of the facts of the case or appropriate background

Division of proofs—a summary of the main arguments or evidence to be presented

Thesis—the central proposition

Confirmation—arguments presented in support of the thesis

Refutation—arguments and evidence against opponents, or answers to opposing arguments

Recapitulation—a summary of the main arguments and evidence

Final appeal to the audience for their fair consideration of the argument

An argument may include all of these, or it may omit some. The order of parts shown may of course be altered to fit a particular audience; the refutation, for example, may precede the confirmation or be combined with it.

LIMITING HANDGUNS

Robert di Grazia

Robert J. di Grazia was born in 1928 in San Francisco, and studied at the University of San Francisco, Michigan State University, and Sonoma State College in California. He has served in various law enforcement posts, including sheriff of Marin County, California; chief of police in St. Louis, Missouri; and, later, superintendent of police there; police commissioner of Boston, Massachusetts; and police chief of Montgomery County, Maryland.

[1] We buried Donald Brown in May. He was murdered by three men who wanted to rob the supermarket manager he was protecting. Patrolman Brown was 61 years old, six months from retirement. He and his wife intended to retire to Florida at the end of the year. Now there will be no retirement in the sun, and she is alone.

[2] Donald Brown was the second police officer to die since I became commissioner here on Nov. 15, 1972.

[3] The first was John Schroeder, a detective shot in a pawnshop robbery last November. John Schroeder was the brother of Walter Schroeder, who was killed in a bank robbery in 1970. Their names are together on the honor roll in the lobby of Police Headquarters.

[4] John Murphy didn't die. He was shot in the head last February as he chased a robbery suspect into the Washington Street subway station. He lived, but he will be brain-damaged for the rest of his life, unable to walk or talk.

[5] At least two of these police officers were shot by a handgun, the kind one can buy nearly everywhere for a few dollars. Those who don't want to buy one can steal one, and half a million are stolen each year. There are forty million handguns circulating in this country; two and half million are sold each year.

[6] Anybody can get a gun. Ownership of handguns has become so widespread that the gun is no longer merely the instrument of crime; it is now a cause of violent crime. Of the eleven Boston police officers killed since 1962, seven were killed with handguns; of the seventeen wounded by guns since 1962, sixteen were shot with handguns.

[7] Police officers, of course, are not the only people who die. Ten thousand other Americans are dead at the price of our promiscuous right to bear arms. Gun advocates are fond of saying that guns don't kill, people do. But guns do kill.

[8] Half of the people who commit suicide do so with handguns. Fifty-four percent of the murders committed in 1972 were committed with handguns. Killing with handguns simply is a good deal easier than killing with other weapons.

[9] Rifles and shotguns are difficult to conceal. People can run away from knife-wielding assailants. People do die each year by drownings, bludgeonings and strangulation. But assaults with handguns are five times more likely to kill.

[10] No one can convince me, after returning from Patrolman Brown's funeral, after standing in the rain with hundreds of others from this department and others, that we should allow people to own handguns.

[11] I know that many people feel deeply and honestly about their right to own and enjoy guns. I realize that gun ownership and self-protection are deeply held American values. I am asking that people give them up.

[12] I am committed to doing what I can to take guns away from the people. In my view, private ownership of handguns must be banished from this country. I am not asking for registration or licensing or outlawing cheap guns. I am saying that no private citizen, whatever his claim, should possess a handgun. Only police officers should.

COMMENT

Robert di Grazia recognizes that gun ownership and self-protection are "givens" for people who oppose confiscation: "I realize that gun ownership and self-protection are deeply held American values." He might have focused on these givens, showing them to be unsound, but he chooses not to do so; for he wishes to make the point-at-issue the question of whether gun ownership can be tolerated in face of the hazards named and illustrated in the essay. Some of di Grazia's opponents would make these values the issue, specifically the claim of individual rights versus the claim of society and its appointed representatives, police officers. In ordinary arguments, the main dispute is often over what is at issue. In the courtroom, rulings on the admissibility of evidence are in effect determinations of the point-at-issue in the case; in his instructions to the jury following the presentation of evidence, the judge defines it in stating the basis on which the defendant is to be judged innocent or guilty. Though di Grazia stakes out his argument by focusing on the hazards of gun ownership, he is fair to his opponents and his readers in saying he has done so, and mentioning the reasons for gun ownership. He does not attack the character or motives of his opponents, nor does he appeal to prejudice or to "force," that is, through the argument that guns will be confiscated with or without the consent of their owners. His essay is a model of fair reasoning.

QUESTIONS FOR STUDY AND DISCUSSION

1. Di Grazia builds his case against gun ownership through particulars of experience. What are these particulars?

2. Is he arguing against gun ownership on the ground that people intend to wound or kill with guns? What is his answer to the slogan in favor of gun ownership, "Guns don't kill, people do"?

3. Why does he oppose registration, licensing, and outlawing cheap guns, and why does he limit his recommendation to handguns?

4. What parts of the essay constitute the narrative, the confirmation, and the refutation? Where is the thesis first stated? Where is it restated?

VOCABULARY STUDY

Look up the following words and determine their exact meaning in the essay: *instrument, promiscuous, advocates, assailants, banished.*

SUGGESTIONS FOR WRITING

1. State your agreement or disagreement with di Grazia—specifically, whether you agree or disagree with his assumptions, the point-at-issue in the essay, his recommendations. Defend your own assumptions and attitudes in the course of your discussion.

2. Organize a persuasive essay in defense of or in opposition to a current controversy. Include in your essay an introduction, a narrative or statement of the backgrounds, a division of arguments, a statement of your proposition or thesis, your confirming argument, a refutation of your opponents, possibly a summary of your main points, and finally a conclusion. These need not be presented in this order. Write to a specific audience and keep in mind the knowledge and beliefs of that audience.

A LETTER ON STRIP MINING

Harvey and Nancy Kincaid

Harvey and Nancy Kincaid live with their seven children in Fayetteville, West Virginia, near Buffalo Creek. On February 26,

1972, a dam consisting of slag from the mines and owned by a local coal company burst. The ensuing flood killed 125 people and injured many thousands, most of the victims working and disabled coal miners and members of their families. In 1971 Mrs. Kincaid spoke about strip mining to the Congress Against Strip Mining, in Washington, D.C. Her letter was read before the West Virginia State Legislature and it helped to pass the Anti-Strip-Mining Bill. Mrs. Kincaid told an interviewer:

It used to be that the kids could keep fish, catfish, and minnows in the creeks. Now you can see the rocks in the creek where the acid has run off the mountains, off the limestone rocks. The rocks in the creek are reddish-looking, like they're rusted. There's nothing living in the creek now.

Gentlemen:

¹ I don't believe there could be anyone that would like to see the strip mines stopped any more than my husband and myself. It just seems impossible that something like this could happen to us twice in the past three and one half years of time. We have been married for thirteen years and worked real hard at having a nice home that was ours and paid for, with a nice size lot of one acre. Over the thirteen years, we remodeled this house a little at a time and paid for it as we worked and did the work mostly ourselves. The house was located about a quarter of a mile off the road up Glenco Hollow at Kincaid, Fayette County, West Virginia, where it used to be a nice, clean neighborhood.

² Then the strippers came four years ago with their big machinery and TNT. I know that these men need jobs and need to make a living like everyone else, but I believe there could be a better way of getting the coal out of these mountains. Have you ever been on a mountaintop and looked down and seen about five different strips on one mountain in one hollow?

³ My husband owns a Scout Jeep and he can get to the top of the strip mines with the Scout. I would like to invite you to come and visit us sometime and go for a ride with us. It would make you sick to see the way the mountains are destroyed.

⁴ First they send in the loggers to strip all the good timber out and then they come with their bulldozers. If their engineers make a

From *Hillbilly Women*, copyright © 1973 by Kathy Kahn. Reprinted by permission of Doubleday & Co., Inc.

mistake in locating the coal they just keep cutting away until they locate the seam of coal. When the rains come and there isn't anything to stop the drainage, the mountains slide, and the spoil banks fall down to the next spoil bank and so on until the whole mountain slides. There is a small creek in the hollow and when the spring rains come, its banks won't hold the water.

[5] So where does it go?—into people's yards, into their wells, under and into their houses. You have rocks, coal, and a little bit of everything in your yards. When the strippers came they started behind our house in the fall sometime before November. There was a hollow behind our house and we asked them not to bank the spoil the way they did, because we knew what would happen when the spring rains came. My father-in-law lived beside us and the property all ran together in a nice green lawn—four acres.

[6] But the rains came in the spring and the spoil bank broke and the water and debris came into our property every time it rained. It would only take a few minutes of rain and this is what we had for three years.

[7] Then the damage comes to your house because of so much dampness. The doors won't close, the foundation sinks and cracks the walls in the house, your tile comes up off your floors, your walls mold, even your clothes in your closets. Then your children stay sick with bronchial trouble, then our daughter takes pneumonia—X-rays are taken, primary T.B. shows up on the X-ray. This is in July of two years ago. About for a year this child laid sick at home. In the meantime we have already filed suit with a lawyer in Oak Hill when the water started coming in on us, but nothing happens. For three years we fight them for our property—$10,000. The lawyer settles out of court for $4,500. By the time his fee comes out and everything else we have to pay, we have under $3,000 to start over with.

[8] So what do we have to do? Doctor's orders, move out for child's sake and health. We sell for a little of nothing—not for cash, but for rent payments, take the $3,000 and buy a lot on the main highway four miles up the road toward Oak Hill.

[9] The $3,000 goes for the lot, digging of a well and a down payment on a new house. Here we are in debt for thirty years on a new home built and complete by the first of September. We moved the first part of September and was in this house *one month* and what happens? The same strip company comes up the road and puts a blast off and damages the new house—$1,400 worth. When they put one blast off that will crack the walls in your house, the foundation

cracked the carport floor straight across in two places, pull a cement stoop away from the house and pull the grout out of the ceramic tile in the bathroom. This is what they can get by with.

[10] How do they live in their $100,000 homes and have a clear mind, I'll never know. To think of the poor people who have worked hard all their lives and can't start over like we did. They have to stay in these hollows and be scared to death every time it rains. I know by experience the many nights I have stayed up and listened to the water pouring off the mountains and the rocks tumbling off the hills.

[11] I remember one time when the strippers put a blast off up the hollow a couple years ago and broke into one of the old mines that had been sealed off for 30 years. They put their blast off and left for the evening. Around seven o'clock that evening it started. We happened to look up the hollow; and thick mud—as thick as pudding—was coming down the main road in the hollow and made itself to the creek and stopped the creek up until the creek couldn't even flow.

[12] The water was turned up into the fields where my husband keeps horses and cattle. I called the boss and told him what was happening and the danger we were in and what did he say? "There isn't anything I can do tonight. I'll be down tomorrow." I called the agriculture and they told us, whatever we did, not to go to bed that night because of the water backed up in those mines for miles.

[13] This is just some of the things that happen around a strip mine neighborhood. But they can get by with it, unless they are stopped. Even if they are stopped it will take years for the trees and grass—what little bit they put on them—to grow enough to keep the water back and stop the slides.

Mr. and Mrs. Harvey Kincaid

COMMENT

A French writer, Amiel, wrote in his journal: "Truth is the secret of eloquence and of virtue, the basis of moral authority." The Kincaids' great letter is an example of eloquence achieved through simple words that state facts plainly and exactly. Instead of reviewing the rights and wrongs of strip mining, Mr. and Mrs. Kincaid describe what happened to them and the land—in enough detail for the reader to imagine the life of people in the hollow. At the end of the letter they state the issue simply and without elaboration: "But they can get by with it, unless they are stopped."

QUESTIONS FOR STUDY AND DISCUSSION

1. The KIncaids state how their life was changed by strip mining. How do they show that their experiences were typical of people in the area?

2. Is the damage caused by strip mining the result of neglect or careless-ness, or is it inherent in the process itself—given the details of the letter? Are the Kincaids mainly concerned with this question?

3. What is the central issue for them? Are they arguing against strip min-ing on moral grounds? Or are they concerned only with the practical consequences? What assumptions about the rights of individuals underlie their argument?

4. Are the KIncaids addressing a general or a special audience? How do you know?

5. What is the tone of the letter, and what in the letter creates it? What do the various questions asked in the letter contribute?

VOCABULARY STUDY

Consult a dictionary of American English or Americanisms on the exact meaning of the following words and phrases and explain their use in the letter: *hollow, strips, spoil banks, grout, pudding.*

SUGGESTIONS FOR WRITING

1. Write a letter protesting an activity that has changed your life in some way. Let the details of the change carry the weight of your protest.

2. Look through magazines and newspapers for a defense of strip mining. You will find authors and titles in the *Reader's Guide to Periodical Literature.* Analyze the assumptions and reasoning of the writer. (For a general review of the debate, pro and con, see *Business Week,* November 4, 1972.)

A STORY WITH A HAPPY ENDING

Lucie Prinz

Lucie Prinz lived for many years in New York City, where she worked as a journalist and publicist, and did public relations for health and welfare agencies. She previously wrote book reviews for the *St. Louis Post-Dispatch* and operated a book store. She lives now in Ipswich, Massachusetts. Her short essay shows how important ideas can develop out of personal experience and observation, sharply focused and reported.

[1] Last year the sidewalk at our corner was resurfaced. As soon as it was dry, the youngest of the children who hang out at the corner sat on the sidewalk squares. They looked like country kids enjoying the new grass in the fields, but to some of my neighbors these children and their friends, ranging in age from 8 to 18, were dangerous.

[2] When the children first began to appear they caused little comment. It was a gradual process. In ones and twos and then in larger numbers they began to congregate around the phone booth, on the cars and in the doorways and steps. They played frisbee and tossed a ball occasionally. There was a good deal of flirting. Once in a while a friendly scuffle would break out. But primarily they were performing the traditional rite of city kids—hanging out, doing nothing in a group.

[3] Our corner was ideal. While it didn't have the candy store my generation considered a necessity, it had wide sidewalks and the telephone. It also had bright lights and a guard who discouraged muggers. But as summer came the number of kids on the corner increased and my neighbors grew alarmed. An elderly lady walking her dog was struck by a frisbee. The kids were noisy; they were often there late at night making noise. They crowded the sidewalks and sometimes used obscenities. They were, in fact, annoying at times.

[4] Beneath the legitimate complaints was a fear all out of proportion to reality. These kids hadn't made a single threatening gesture. They weren't defacing the new sidewalks with graffiti. Regardless, the adults talked about "an outside element" invading the neighborhood. Some of the kids were black, some Hispanic and a few Oriental. Some lived on the block, others didn't. We had become a community afraid of its children.

[5] A notice in our elevator announced a meeting to discuss "the kids on the corner." A representative of the 24th Precinct came. The cops, having been called on several particularly noisy nights, knew many of the kids by name. Now they told the block association that

the kids had a right to be on the corner. It was not a police matter. The adults would have to deal with them in a more traditional manner. They would have to approach the kids and talk to them, directly, without fear.

[6] The police administered a dose of old-fashioned common sense and the tension in the neighborhood slowly began to disappear. The kids were, after all, just kids.

[7] They still hang out at the corner. They have a new obsession now—the skateboard. Using large cans they set up a skateboard slalom on our sloping sidewalk. I suppose it made it hard for some people to walk down the street but I loved seeing the kids swooping, like so many birds, around the intricacies of the slalom. The cans are gone now. Did someone complain? Or did the kids just tire of it?

[8] Undoubtedly there are dangerous kids in our city. But their existence almost poisoned my neighborhood and its children. We have learned that a community that is afraid of its kids has no future; a community that needs to use the police to communicate with its children is in deep trouble.

[9] On a lamppost at our corner two dozen pairs of tennis shoes, tied by their laces, swing in the wind. To me they are a symbol of the exuberance of youth, not of urban terrorism. Like the noisy kids at my corner, they signal that my block is populated. Far from being dangerous, the kids enhance our block, keeping it alive at night with young, active people and making it safe for the adults who, only a year ago, were so afraid.

COMMENT

Prinz is addressing a particular audience: people who have become afraid of children. Wishing to convince these people that problems are often imagined or exaggerated, and that simple solutions are available, she chooses to report her own experience in a New York City neighborhood. She does not deal with the issue abstractly, as might be done in a textbook discussion of grownups, children, and urban community relations. The episode teaches a number of important lessons through a simple but vivid presentation of what happened. As a result, the ideas of paragraph 8—the thesis paragraph of the essay—seem neither abstract nor remote. Prinz clinches her argument with a final memorable lesson: streets are safer when they are alive with children.

QUESTIONS FOR STUDY AND DISCUSSION

1. Prinz does not develop what is called in logic an *ad hominem* argument (literally, an argument "to the man"); that is, she does not attack the character and motives of her neighbors, though she is concerned with the reasons for their fear. How precisely does she explore these reasons without ascribing motives?

2. What are the stated and implied solutions to the problem described?

3. Has Prinz persuaded you that the episode is typical of the *general* problem of relations between grownups and children? What examples would you cite if you were dealing with the same problem?

VOCABULARY STUDY

Explain how the words in brackets change the meaning of the sentences:
   a. "Once in a while a friendly scuffle [*argument*] would break out."
   b. "The kids were noisy [*rowdy*]; they were often there late at night making noise."
   c. "They were, in fact, annoying [*threatening*] at times."
   d. "They have a new obsession [*interest*] now—the skateboard."
   e. "To me they are a symbol of the exuberance [*flamboyance*] of youth, not of urban terrorism."

SUGGESTIONS FOR WRITING

1. Write an essay on the "generation gap," focusing on one or more episodes that define a problem. Build your essay to a discussion of possible solutions. In the course of the essay, discuss the implications of the various episodes, as Prinz does. Use this discussion to persuade a particular audience to accept the solutions you propose.

2. Discuss a problem that arose in your high school because of a misunderstanding between the students and the administration. State what could have been done to remedy the problem—and what was actually done. Draw a conclusion from your discussion about high-school life as you experienced it.

3. Defend or attack one of the following propositions. Answer objections to your views on the issue:
   a. High-school students should control the contents of the student newspaper and yearbook.

b. Parents should approve the television programs teenagers watch.
c. The names of teenagers arrested by the police should not be published in the newspaper.

HOMEMAKING

William Raspberry

William Raspberry comes from Okolona, in northeastern Mississippi, where his parents taught school. He attended Indiana Central College in Indianapolis, and after army service began reporting for the *Washington Post*. He became a columnist for that newspaper in 1966, and is syndicated widely in the United States. He has written on a wide range of subjects including Washington politics, urban problems, and black education in America. His recent columns urging an examination of attitudes toward black education have been much discussed.

[1] Since my wife was out of town last weekend—leaving me to look after our children and the house—I suppose I could make the case that I now have a better appreciation of what homemaking is about.

[2] Well, if I do, it isn't because of what I had to do in her absence but because of what I didn't have to do. I had to cook and make sure that the little ones were warmly clothed, that they spent some time playing outside, that they got baths, picked up after themselves, and so on. In short, I took over a series of chores, many of which I would have performed even if my wife had been home.

[3] But I didn't have to plan anything, schedule anything, or fit anything into an overall design. I didn't have to see to my children's overall nutrition; I only had to see that they weren't too bored and didn't tear the house down. What I did was episodic, a combination of housework and babysitting. What my wife does is part of an ongoing enterprise: homemaking. Hers is an executive role, though neither she nor I had ever thought to describe it as such.

[4] I strongly suspect that the failure to make the distinction between homemaking and chores is one of the chief reasons why homemaking has fallen into such disrepute of late. As Jinx Melia, founder and director of the Martha Movement,* observed in a recent interview, "ethnic" homemakers, as a rule, have managed to retain a higher sense of respect for their calling, partly, she suspects, because their husbands may be somewhat more likely to work at blue-collar jobs that hold no attraction for their wives.

[5] A larger part, though, may be that "traditional" husbands—whatever jobs they work at—are likelier to be ignorant (perhaps deliberately so) of homemaking skills. Homemaking may involve as much a sense of mystique for these husbands as outside work holds for their wives. Men of all classes are increasingly likely these days to help out with the chores, or even take over for a spell, as I did last weekend. And if we aren't careful, we come to believe that we can do easily everything our wives do—if we can only survive the boredom of it. The result is that we lose respect for what they do. Think of homemaking as a series of more or less unpleasant chores and the disrespect is virtually automatic.

[6] Well, most jobs are a series of more or less unpleasant chores. But it doesn't follow that that's all they are. Looking up cases and precedents, trying to draw information out of a client who doesn't quite understand what you need to know, keeping records, writing "boiler-plate" contracts—all these things are routine, and a bright high school graduate could quickly learn to do them all. The chores are a drag; but lawyering is a fascinating career. Reducing a career to a series of chores creates this additional problem of perspective: Any time not spent on one or another of the chores is viewed as time wasted.

[7] As Melia also pointed out, the men who work at professions spend an enormous amount of time doing the mirror image of what their non-career wives may be chided or even openly criticized for doing. They talk on the phone a lot (perhaps about business, but they often aren't doing business). They hold staff meetings or unit meetings that are hardly different from coffee klatches. A business lunch with a client you've already sold (or for whom you have no specific proposal at the moment) is not vastly different from a gathering of homemakers in somebody's kitchenette.

* This movement, founded to give a voice to housewives and homemakers in the United States, now has 75 chapters in fifty states. Ed.

[8]The main difference is that a man gets to call all these things "work." One reason for the difference is that the details of home-making are far more visible (to the spouse) than the details of work done outside. As a result, husbands often not only devalue their wives' work but also feel perfectly free to question the wisdom of what they do as part of that work. Wives generally know too little about their husbands' work to question any aspect of it. They are more likely to magnify its importance.

[9]None of this should be taken as a proposal that women be kept out of the labor market. There are women whose talents are so far removed from home and hearth that it would be criminal to encourage them to become homemakers. There are women who need to earn income, for reasons ranging from fiscal to psychic. Women who choose careers outside the home, or who have no choice but to pursue careers, ought to be free to do so without any discrimination of any sort.

[10]But there are also women who seek outside work primarily because they know their homemaking role is undervalued, by their husbands and by themselves. There is nothing intrinsic about producing income, on the one hand, or nuturing children and managing a household, on the other, that would lead to a natural conclusion that income-production is of greater value. The opposite conclusion would appear likelier, as in the distinction between worker and queen bees, for instance. But worker bees don't claim sole ownership and discretion over what they produce; they work for the hive. It would go a long way toward changing the onerous working conditions of homemakers if we could learn to think of family income as belonging to the family, not primarily to the person who happens to bring it home.

[11]Maybe there is a logical reason why the marriage partner who doesn't produce income should be the fiscal dependent of the one who does. Off hand, I can't think what it might be.

COMMENT

Raspberry is addressing chiefly those homemakers who need to be persuaded that their work is complex and important. They need not, he is saying, seek work outside the home in the mistaken belief that they are not performing important work. His central argument uses *analogy* in showing that there are important similarities between taking care of a home and performing an "executive" job. In developing this analogy, Raspberry defines the nature of work in each sphere. He also rejects a false analogy—that between producing income and the work done by worker bees. He reminds us that "worker bees don't claim sole ownership and discretion over what they produce; they work for the hive." Raspberry has developed a complex argument in simple, lucid language, with the help of striking illustrations.

QUESTIONS FOR STUDY AND DISCUSSION

1. How early in the essay does Raspberry state his thesis? Where in the essay does he restate it?

2. In distinguishing between routine chores and the "ongoing enterprise" of home and office, Raspberry has employed division. What is his principle of division of work?

3. What specific conclusions is he drawing about women and work? What general conclusions is he drawing about attitudes toward work in America?

4. What other illustrations might he have used to make his distinctions? Can you think of other work situations to which his distinctions apply?

VOCABULARY STUDY

1. Use your dictionary to determine the exact difference between the words in each pair. Then determine how the first word given is used in the paragraph indicated:
   a. paragraph 3: *episodic, occasional; enterprise, vocation*
   b. paragraph 4: *disrepute, unpopularity*
   c. paragraph 5: *mystique, belief*
   d. paragraph 6: *precedents, procedures; perspective, view*
   e. paragraph 7: *chided, criticized*
   f. paragraph 10: *discretion, concern; onerous, exhausting*

2. What are the possible meanings of *ethnic,* according to your dictionary? In what sense does Raspberry use this word in the essay?

SUGGESTIONS FOR WRITING

1. Describe and analyze the various kinds of work you perform every day, and define your attitude toward them. In the course of your essay, draw support or definitions from one or two of the writers in this book

who discuss work—Heckscher, Hoffer, Raspberry—or use your discussion to disagree with one of their ideas.

2. Discuss whether Heckscher and Raspberry define chores in the same way and share the same view of them.

3. Describe work that many people mistakenly consider routine and uninteresting. Persuade these people that they are mistaken in their view of it. You might use an analogy for this purpose, as Raspberry does.

coordination and subordination

Making our sentences express our exact meaning requires long practice and attention to sentence coordination and subordination. When we *coordinate,* we use words like *and, but, or,* and *yet* to connect words, phrases and clauses of the same weight and importance in the sentence, or clauses that can stand by themselves. The first three clauses in the following sentence are coordinate ones:

> The cold night had come, *and* Ukwane in the frosty grass was shivering, *yet* he sat for an hour keeping his patience, putting his hands into the cold blood of the springbok to trace veins to their source, prefacing all his answers with positive, qualifying remarks.—Elizabeth Marshall Thomas, *The Harmless People*

When we *subordinate,* we attach phrases and clauses that usually do not stand by themselves to independent clauses that complete their meaning. In the Thomas sentence above, the concluding phrases beginning with the words *putting* and *prefacing* are subordinate to the independent clause that precedes them. As in this sentence, subordinate sentence elements sometimes contain specific details that expand or explain the independent clause.

In writing and revising sentences, whether simple or very complex, we need to keep in mind the possibilities that English sentences offer the speaker and writer for focus and emphasis.

A simple rule to keep in mind is that English sentences tend to reserve the end of the sentence for the most important idea. This end focus is seen in the stress we give final words, as in this spoken sentence:

> My wife's parents live in NEWark.

Even if we have to stress another word in the sentence, we still give a degree of stress to the final word:

> My WIFE's parents live in NEWark. (my wife's parents, not my own)

This rule has important consequences for the way we build and vary sentences. It means, simply, that we can "load" the end of the sentence, as we cannot the beginning. We speak or write the following sentence, for example, without thinking twice about its structure:

> (1) I know that they won't come because they're out of town.

We would not say or write:

> (2) That they won't come because they're out of town I know.

But we can and do on occasion open the sentence with a shorter complement:

> (3) That he is coming I have no doubt.

Notice that the complement *that they won't come* in (1) is itself modified by a subordinate clause and therefore cannot appear at the beginning of the sentence, whereas the unmodified complement in (3)—*That he is coming*—can so appear. This is one limitation we face in beginning a sentence, as every speaker and writer knows without being told. By contrast, we can add complex modifiers to the end of the sentence without difficulty, owing to the capacity of the English sentence to carry weight at the end. In the following sentence, the main clause has been italicized. Notice the relatively short and simple opening modifying phrase and the relatively long concluding subordinate clause:

> Despite the Gestapo terror led by Himmler and Heydrich after the Anschluss *Germans flocked by the hundreds of thousands to Austria,* where they could pay with their marks for sumptuous meals not available in Germany for years and for bargain-priced vaca-

tions amid Austria's matchless mountains and lakes.—William
L. Shirer, *The Rise and Fall of the Third Reich*

Compound sentences, in which independent clauses are
coordinated, can run on indefinitely:

> John loves Mary, and Mary loves Bill, but Bill loves Sally, and
> Sally loves Harry . . .

A simple sentence can be modified endlessly through subordinate
phrases and clauses:

> The dog that is lying on the rug in the living room will be taken
> for a walk around the block after we have finished supper and
> then . . .

There is no logical reason why these sentences must end; many
English sentences continue for considerable length. The old
definition of a sentence as a complete thought is of no use in
deciding when to end sentences of this kind, for the completeness of
the thought lies in the mind of the speaker or writer, who alone
knows when everything necessary has been said. Sentence length
is thus often determined by how much can be included without
losing the reader's attention. In general, a sentence should be
ended when no idea is left hanging; the sentence should not seem
to run on or drift monotonously. Proper sentence coordination and
subordination help to prevent this from happening.

JURY DUTY

William K. Zinsser

William Zinsser teaches at Yale University. He was born in
1922 in New York City, and has written much about life there
in numerous articles and books. He attended Princeton University, and later was a feature writer, film critic, and drama editor

for the *New York Herald Tribune* and a columnist for *Look* and *Life*. His books include *Pop Goes America* (1966) and *On Writing Well* (1976).

[1] Jury duty again. I'm sitting in the "central jurors' room" of a courthouse in lower Manhattan, as I do every two years, waiting to be called for a jury, which I almost never am. It's an experience that all of us have known, in one form or another, as long as we can remember: organized solitude.

[2] The chair that I sit in is a little island of apartness. I sit there alone, day after day, and I go out to lunch alone, a stranger in my own city. Strictly, of course, I'm not by myself. Several hundred other men and women sit on every side, as closely as in a movie theater, also waiting to be called for a jury, which they almost never are. Sometimes we break briefly into each other's lives, when we get up to stretch, offering fragments of talk to fill the emptiness. But in the end each of us is alone, withdrawn into our newspapers and our crossword puzzles and our sacred urban privacy.

[3] The room intimidates us. It is a dreary place, done in thirties Bureaucratic, too dull to sustain more than a few minutes of mental effort. On the subconscious level, however, it exerts a strong and uncanny hold. It is the universal waiting room. It is the induction center and the clinic; it is the assembly hall and the office where forms are filled out. Thoughts come unbidden there, sneaking back from all the other moments—in the army, at camp, on the first day of school—when we were part of a crowd and therefore lonely.

[4] The mere taking of roll call by a jury clerk will summon back the countless times when we have waited for our name to be yelled out—loud and just a little wrong. Like every person whose job is to read names aloud, the jury clerk can't read names aloud. Their shapes mystify him. They are odd and implausible names, as diverse as the countries that they came from, but surely the clerk has met them all before. *Hasn't* he? Isn't that what democracy—and the jury system—is all about? Evidently not.

[5] We are shy enough, as we wait for our name, without the extra burden of wondering what form it will take. By now we know most of the variants that have been imposed on it by other clerks in

other rooms like this, and we are ready to answer to any of them, or to some still different version. Actually we don't want to hear our name called at all in this vast public chamber. It is so private, so vulnerable. And yet we don't want to *not* hear it, for only then are we reassured of our identity, really certain that we are known, wanted, and in the right place. Dawn over Camp Upton, 1943: Weinberg, Wyzanski, Yanopoulos, Zapata, Zeccola, Zinsser . . .

⁶ I don't begin my jury day in such a retrospective state. I start with high purpose and only gradually slide into mental disarray. I am punctual, even early, and so is everybody else. We are a conscientious lot—partly because we are so surrounded by the trappings of justice, but mainly because that is what we are there to be. I've never seen such conscientious-looking people. Observing them, I'm glad that American law rests on being judged by our peers. In fact, I'd almost rather be judged by my peers than judged by a judge.

⁷ Most of us start the day by reading. Jury duty is America's gift to her citizens of a chance to catch up on "good" books, and I always bring *War and Peace*. I remember to bring it every morning and I keep it handy on my lap. The only thing I don't do is read it. There's something about the room . . . the air is heavy with imminent roll calls, too heavy for tackling a novel that will require strict attention. Besides, it's important to read the newspaper first: sharpen up the old noggin on issues of the day. I'm just settling into my paper when the clerk comes in, around ten-twenty-five, and calls the roll ("Zissner?" "Here!"). Suddenly it is 1944 and I am at an army base near Algiers, hammering tin to make a hot shower for Colonel McCloskey. That sort of thing can shoot the whole morning.

⁸ If it doesn't, the newspaper will. Only a waiting juror knows how infinite the crannies of journalism can be. I read "Arrival of Buyers," though I don't know what they want to buy and have nothing to sell. I read "Soybean Futures," though I wouldn't know a soybean even in the present. I read classified ads for jobs that I didn't know were jobs, like "keypunch operators." What keys do they punch? I mentally buy 4bdrm 1½bth splt lvl homes w/fpl overlooking Long Island Sound and dream of taking ½bath there. I read dog news and horoscopes ("bucking others could prove dangerous today") and medical columns on diseases I've never heard of, but whose symptoms I instantly feel.

⁹ It's an exhausting trip, and I emerge with eyes blurry and

mind blank. I look around at my fellow jurors. Some of them are trying to work—to keep pace, pitifully, with the jobs that they left in order to come here and do nothing. They spread queer documents on their knees, full of graphs and figures, and they scribble on yellow pads. But the papers don't seem quite real to them, or quite right, removed from the tidy world of filing cabinets and secretaries, and after a while the workers put the work away again.

[10] Around twelve-forty-five the clerk comes in to make an announcement. We stir to attention: we are needed! "Go to lunch," he says. "Be back at two." We straggle out. By now the faces of all my fellow jurors are familiar (we've been here eight days), and I keep seeing them as we poke around the narrow streets of Chinatown looking for a restaurant that isn't the one where we ate yesterday. I smile tentatively, as New Yorkers do, and they smile tentatively back, and we go our separate ways. By one-fifty-five we are seated in the jurors' room again, drowsy with Chinese food and American boredom—too drowsy, certainly, to start *War and Peace.* Luckily, we all bought the afternoon paper while we were out. Talk about remote crannies of journalism!

[11] Perhaps we are too hesitant to talk to each other, to invite ourselves into lives that would refresh us by being different from our own. We are scrupulous about privacy—it is one of the better gifts that the city can bestow, and we don't want to spoil it for somebody else. Yet within almost every New Yorker who thinks he wants to be left alone is a person desperate for human contact. Thus we may be as guilty as the jury system of not putting our time to good use.

[12] What we want to do most, of course, is serve on a jury. We believe in the system. Besides, was there ever so outstanding a group of jurors as we, so intelligent and fairminded? The clerks have told us all the reasons why jurors are called in such wasteful numbers: court schedules are unpredictable; trials end unexpectedly; cases are settled at the very moment when a jury is called; prisoners plead guilty to a lesser charge rather than wait years for a trial that might prove them innocent. All this we know, and in theory it makes sense.

[13] In practice, however, somebody's arithmetic is wrong, and one of America's richest assets is being dribbled away. There must be a better way to get through the long and tragic list of cases awaiting a solution—and, incidentally, to get through *War and Peace.*

COMMENT

Zinsser's first paragraph illustrates important kinds of sentence emphasis. The brief opening phrase—"Jury duty again"—which serves as a topic sentence, contrasts with the two longer sentences that follow. The first of these adds a series of qualifying clauses to the opening main clause:

> I'm sitting in the "central jurors' room" of a courthouse in lower Manhattan, as I do every two years, waiting to be called for a jury, which I almost never am.

The final sentence of the paragraph does the same, but with an important difference: the concluding phrase—"'organized solitude'"—complements the opening clause: "It's an experience that all of us have known." This concluding phrase gains special emphasis at the end of the sentence. In many of his sentences Zinsser takes advantage of this kind of terminal emphasis. But he uses this effect sparingly. His sentences have the ring of spoken sentences, depending on coordination and occasionally italics to convey vocal inflection:

> They are odd and implausible names, as diverse as the countries that they came from, but surely the clerk has met them all before. *Hasn't* he? Isn't that what democracy—and the jury system—is all about?

QUESTIONS FOR STUDY AND DISCUSSION

1. Which sentences in paragraph 5 are coordinate only? How many sentences consist of one introductory main clause, and one or more subordinate clauses? Do any of the sentences join subordinate to coordinate clauses?

2. Paragraph 6 contains a series of short emphatic opening sentences. Does Zinsser maintain this kind of emphasis in the rest of the paragraph?

3. How different is paragraph 7 from paragraph 6 in sentence construction? What use does Zinsser make of ellipsis? How much emphasis (through pitch and volume) should the parenthetical statements be given?

4. How much subordination do you find in paragraph 8? How many sentences are built through modification?

5. How does Zinsser establish a point of view and a dominant tone? Or do you find changes in tone throughout the essay?

6. Why would Zinsser "almost rather be judged by [his] peers than judged by a judge"?

VOCABULARY STUDY

Write a sentence using each of the following pairs of words, and explain the difference between them:
   a. fragments, parts
   b. intimidates, threatens
   c. bureaucratic, governmental
   d. uncanny, strange
   e. implausible, unconvincing
   f. vulnerable, weak
   g. scrupulous, careful
   h. bestow, give

SUGGESTIONS FOR WRITING

1. Describe a waiting room and your feelings in it. Make your details specific, and use your description to make a comment about your general situation. Develop several of your sentences with modification, as Zinsser does. Where you can, combine coordinate clauses with subordinate phrases and clauses.

2. Analyze two of the final paragraphs, showing how coordination and subordination are used to give emphasis to particular ideas.

THE FIGHT WITH GUY HAWKINS

Jesse Stuart

Born in 1907, the American writer and teacher Jesse Stuart was raised and educated in rural Tennessee, and he later attended Vanderbilt University in Nashville. His book *The Thread That Runs So True,* from which the essay reprinted here is taken, describes his experiences as a young teacher in a rural Southern community. Stuart was seventeen at the time of the experience he describes here; the school had one room, in which he taught all eight grades. Later in his life, he served as principal and superintendent in rural and city high schools and school systems. "I left teaching, the profession I loved, because I thought I couldn't make enough to live. I raised sheep, lectured, wrote novels and made money, but my heart was always in the schoolroom. And it still is."

¹The following Monday I had stayed at the schoolhouse to do some work on my school records, and Don Conway had gone home with his sister and brothers. This was the first afternoon I had stayed at school after all my pupils had gone. The room was very silent and I was busy working when I heard soft footsteps walking around the building. I looked through the window on my left and I saw Guy Hawkins' head. His uncombed, tousled hair was ruffled by the Lonesome Valley wind.

²I wondered why he was coming back. I wondered if he had forgotten something.

³Then I realized this was the first time he had been able to catch me by myself. And I remembered a few other incidents in Greenwood County's rural schools where a pupil had come back to the school when the teacher was there alone, and had beaten heck out of him. I could recall three or four such incidents. But I didn't have time to think about them. Not now. Guy came in the door with his cap in his hand. I didn't want him to see me looking up at him, but I did see him coming down the broad middle aisle, taking long steps and swinging his big arms. He looked madder than any man or animal I had ever seen. He walked up to my desk and stood silently before me.

⁴"Did you forget something, Guy?" I asked.

⁵"Naw, I've never forgot nothin'," he reminded me.

⁶"Then what do you want?" I asked.

⁷"Whip you," he said.

⁸"Why do you want to fight me?" I asked him. I dropped my pencil and stood up facing him.

⁹"I don't like you," he said. "I don't like teachers. I said never another person with your name would teach this school. Not as long as I'm here."

From *The Thread That Runs So True* by Jesse Stuart. Reprinted by permission of Charles Scribner's Sons. Copyright © 1949 by Jesse Stuart.

[10] "It's too bad you don't like me or my name," I said, my temper rising.

[11] "I won't be satisfied until I've whipped you," he said.

[12] "Can you go to another school?" I asked him. "The Valley School is not too far from where you live."

[13] "Naw, naw," he shouted, "if anybody leaves, you'll leave. I was in Lonesome Valley first. And I ain't a-goin' to no other school because of you!"

[14] "Then there's nothing left for us to do but fight," I said. "I've come to teach this school and I'm going to teach it!"

[15] "Maybe you will," he snarled. "I have you penned in this schoolhouse. I have you where I want you. You can't get away! You can't run! I aim to whip you right where you stand! It's the same place where I whipped your sister!"

[16] "I looked at his face. It was red as a sliced beet. Fire danced in his pale-blue, elongated eyes. I knew Guy Hawkins meant every word he said. I knew I had to face him and to fight. There was no other way around. I had to think quickly. How would I fight him?

[17] "Will you let me take my necktie off?" I said, remembering I'd been choked by a fellow pulling my necktie once in a fight.

[18] "Yep, take off that purty tie," he said. "You might get it dirty by the time I'm through with you."

[19] "I slowly took off my tie.

[20] "Roll up the sleeves of your white shirt too," he said. "But they'll be dirty by the time I sweep this floor up with you."

[21] "Sweep the floor up with me," I said.

[22] He shot out his long arm but I ducked. I felt the wind from his thrust against my ear.

[23] I mustn't let him clinch me, I thought.

[24] Then he came back with another right and I ducked his second lick. I came around with my first lick—a right—and planted it on his jaw, not a good lick but just enough to jar him and make him madder. When he rushed at me, I sidestepped. He missed. By the time he had turned around, I caught him a haymaker on the chin that reeled him. Then I followed up with another lick as hard as I had ever hit a man. Yet I didn't bring him down. He came back for more. But he didn't reach me this time. He was right. I did get my shirt dirty. I dove through the air with a flying tackle. I hit him beneath the knees. I'd tackled like this in football. I'd tackled hard. And I never tackled anybody harder than Guy. His feet went from

under him, and I scooted past on the pine floor. I'd tackled him so quickly when he had expected me to come back at him with my fists, that he went down so fast he couldn't catch with his hands. His face hit flat against the floor and his nose was flattened. The blood spurted as he started to get up.

[25] I let him get to his feet. I wondered if I should. For I knew it was either him or me. One of us had to whip. When he did get to his feet after that terrible fall, I waded into him. I hit fast and I hit hard. He swung wild. His fingernail took a streak of hide from my neck and left a red mark that smarted and the blood oozed through. I pounded his chin. I caught him on the beardy jaw. I reeled him back and followed up. I gave him a left to the short ribs while my right in a split second caught his mouth. Blood spurted again. Yet he was not through. But I knew I had him.

[26] "Had enough?" I panted.

[27] He didn't answer. I didn't ask him a second time. I hit him hard enough to knock two men down. I reeled him back against a seat. I followed up. I caught him with a haymaker under the chin and laid him across the desk. Then he rolled to the floor. He lay there with blood running from his nose and mouth. His eyes were rolled back. I was nearly out of breath. My hand ached. My heart pounded. If this is teaching school! I thought. If this goes with it! Then I remembered vaguely I had asked for it. I'd asked for this school. I would take no other.

[28] Guy Hawkins lay there sprawled on the unswept floor. His blood was mingled with the yellow dirt carried into the schoolroom by seventy bare feet. I went back and got the water bucket. With a clean handkerchief, I washed blood from his mouth and nose. I couldn't wash it from his shirt. I put cool water to his forehead.

[29] I worked over a pupil—trying to bring him back to his senses—who only a few hours before I had stood beside and tried to teach how to pronounce words when he read. "Don't stumble over them like a horse stumbles over frozen ground," I told him, putting it in a language he would understand. I had promoted him. I'd sent Guy and Ova after water when other pupils had wanted to go. On their way to get water, I knew they chewed tobacco and thought they were putting something over on me. I had known I couldn't allow them to use tobacco at school. I had known the time would eventually come. But I wanted to put it off as long as I could. Now I had whipped him and I wondered as I looked at him stretched on the

floor how I'd done it. He was really knocked out for the count. I knew the place where we had fought would always be marked. It was difficult to remove bloodstain from pine wood. It would always be there, this reminder, as long as I taught school at Lonesome Valley.

30 When Guy Hawkins came to his senses, he looked up at me. I was applying the wet cool handkerchief to his head. When he started to get up, I helped him to his feet.

31 "Mr. Stuart, I really got it poured on me," he admitted. "You're some fighter."

32 This was the first time he had ever called me "Mr. Stuart." I had heard, but had pretended not to hear, him call me "Old Jess" every time my back was turned. He had never before, when he had spoken directly to me, called me anything.

33 "I'm not much of a fighter until I have to fight, Guy," I said. "You asked for it. There was no way around. I had to fight you."

34 "I know it," he said. I've had in mind to whip you ever since I heard you's a-goin' to teach this school. But you win. You winned fair too," he honestly admitted. "I didn't think you could hit like that."

35 Guy was still weak. His nose and mouth kept bleeding. He didn't have a handkerchief and I gave him a clean one.

36 "Think you can make it home all right, Guy?"

37 "I think so," he said.

38 He walked slower from the schoolhouse than he had walked in. I was too upset to do any more work on my recordbook. I stood by the window and watched him walk across the schoolyard, then across the foot log and down the Lonesome Creek Road until he went around the bend and was out of sight. Something told me to watch for Ova Salyers. He might return to attack me. I waited several minutes and Ova didn't come. Guy had come to do the job alone.

39 I felt better now that the fight was over, and I got the broom and swept the floor. I had quickly learned that the rural teacher was janitor as well, and that his janitor work was one of the important things in his school. I believed, after my brief experience, that the schoolhouse should be made a place of beauty, prettier and cleaner than any of the homes the pupils came from so they would love the house and the surroundings, and would think of it as a place of beauty and would want to keep it that way.

40 The floor was easy to sweep. But it was difficult to clean blood from the floor. I carried a coal bucket of sand and poured it on the

blood and then shoveled up the sand and carried it out. I had the blood from the floor. Then I scrubbed the place but the stain was there. I could not get it from the oily, soft pine wood. I knew this was one day in my teaching career I would never forget.

COMMENT

Stuart sometimes presents his thoughts and impressions in short, pointed sentences that convey tension and excitement:

> I looked at his face. It was red as a sliced beet. Fire danced in his pale-blue, elongated eyes. I knew Guy Hawkins meant every word he said. I knew I had to face him and to fight. There was no other way around. I had to think quickly. How would I fight him?

This excitement is diminished when the short sentences are connected:

> I looked at his face, which was red as a sliced beet—fire dancing in his pale-blue, elongated eyes. I knew Guy Hawkins meant every word he said, and that I had to face him and to fight, there being no way around. I had to think quickly about how I would fight him.

Stuart's original passage *shows* him thinking quickly. Short sentences create a similar effect in the following passage:

> When he rushed at me, I sidestepped. He missed. By the time he had turned around, I caught him a haymaker on the chin that reeled him. Then I followed up with another lick as hard as I had ever hit a man. Yet I didn't bring him down. He came back for more.

Here each moment of the action is expressed in a single sentence; the relation of events is clear, the short sentences at the same time conveying the swiftness of the fight. They would be less effective if all the sentences contained two or three words. By contrast, such coordinate sentences as the following express a series of related actions. The two events represented are occurring simultaneously:

> His feet went from under him, and I scooted past on the pine floor.

The following sentences show a different relationship through subordination. The action here is not simultaneous:

> When he rushed at me, I sidestepped.
> By the time he had turned around, I caught him a haymaker on the chin that reeled him.

In general, the length and construction of Stuart's sentences are appropriate to the feelings of the speaker and the action described.

QUESTIONS FOR STUDY AND DISCUSSION

1. Rewrite paragraph 28, using coordination and subordination where possible. How does your revision change the tone and impact of Stuart's sentences?

2. The first sentence of the following group is Stuart's; the second and third are revisions of it. What changes in these revisions—emphasis or meaning? Which of the revisions sounds strange to the ear?

> It would always be there, this reminder, as long as I taught school at Lonesome Valley.
> This reminder would always be there, as long as I taught school at Lonesome Valley.
> As long as I taught school at Lonesome Valley, it would always be there—this reminder.

3. What feelings of Hawkins' and of his own does Stuart express in the course of the narrative? Are these feelings stated or implied?

4. What is Stuart telling us about the situation of a young teacher in a rural school forty or fifty years ago? What may he be suggesting about education more generally?

5. Did Stuart maintain your interest in the episode throughout? If so, how did he do so? Did he arouse your interest in him as a person? Were you surprised by how he responded to the challenge?

SENTENCE STUDY

1. Combine the following sentences through coordination or subordination, depending on which is appropriate. Rearrange the order of ideas if necessary:
   a. "I wondered why he was coming back. I wondered if he had forgotten something."
   b. "I dove through the air with a flying tackle. I hit him beneath the knees."
   c. "I'd tackled like this in football. I'd tackled hard. And I never tackled anybody harder than Guy."
   d. "I let him get to his feet. I wondered if I should. For I knew it was either him or me."

2. The following simple sentences are adapted from the originals in George Orwell's *The Road to Wigan Pier*. Combine each group into a single sentence, subordinating where possible, and using semicolons or colons only when necessary:

   a. Miners are changed from one shift to another. Their families have to make adjustments to these changes. These adjustments are tiresome in the extreme.

   b. If he is on the night shift he gets home in time for breakfast. He gets home in the middle of the afternoon on the morning shift. On the afternoon shift he gets home in the middle of the night. In each case, of course, he wants his principal meal of the day as soon as he returns.

   c. The rate of accidents among miners is high. It is high compared with that in other trades. Accidents are so high that they are taken for granted almost as they would be in a minor war.

   d. The most obviously understandable cause of accidents is explosions of gas. This cause is always more or less present in the atmosphere of the pit.

   e. The gas may be touched off by a spark during blasting operations. It may be touched off by a pick striking a spark from a stone. It may be touched off by a defective lamp. And it may be touched off by "gob fires." These are spontaneously generated fires which smolder in the coal dust and are very hard to put out.

SUGGESTIONS FOR WRITING

1. Fistfights are uncommon today between teachers and students, but both groups still experience the same strong emotions that sometimes bring them into conflict. Describe one such conflict that you experienced. Trace its causes and stages and describe the outcome.

2. Discuss the kinds of relationships between teachers and students today. How do they differ from the relationship between Stuart and Guy Hawkins? Discuss what you think are the reasons for this difference.

3. Compare a number of people you lived or worked with during a period of your life, perhaps two of your teachers. Give enough details so that your readers can see and know them as you did, and discuss the differences in your relationship to each. Draw one or more conclusions from your details and comparison.

parallelism

Words, phrases, and clauses that are similar in structure and perform the same function in a sentence are said to be *parallel:*

> *Skiing, ice skating,* and *tobogganing* are winter sports. (parallel subjects) We learned *to ski, to skate,* and *to toboggan.* (parallel phrases) We learned *that corn is a grain, that the tomato is a fruit,* and *that the potato is a plant tuber.* (parallel clauses)

In the same way, sentences in a paragraph may be parallel in structure:

> *You can watch* the judging of home-baked bread *or listen* to the latest rock group. *You can watch* free every day the teenage talent search *or pay* money to hear the same nationally known acts you can watch free on television.—Paul Engle, The Iowa State Fair

Parallelism makes the reader aware of the similarity in ideas. If the ideas are not similar, the parallel structure may seem awkward. Writers in the past often aimed for strict parallelism in sentences and paragraphs, to the point of using almost the same number of words in phrases and clauses. Modern writers, by contrast, favor a looser parallelism, and may vary the length of elements, to avoid a formal effect:

> He watched Martin slip the lens into his pocket, he sighed, he struggled for something else to say, and silently he lumbered into his bedroom.—Sinclair Lewis, *Arrowsmith*

THE IOWA STATE FAIR

Paul Engle

Paul Engle has lived in Iowa most of his life, and has written much about Iowa life. Born in 1908, in Cedar Rapids, he was educated at Coe College and Iowa State University; he later attended Columbia, and was a Rhodes Scholar at Oxford University in England. He is the author of numerous books of poetry, essays, and fiction, and is the director of the creative writing program at the University of Iowa. His books include *An Old-Fashioned Christmas* (1964) and *Portrait of Iowa* (1974).

[1] If all you saw of life was the Iowa State Fair on a brilliant August day, when you hear those incredible crops ripening out of the black dirt between the Missouri and Mississippi rivers, you would believe that this is surely the best of all possible worlds.

[2] You would have no sense of the destruction of life, only of its rich creativeness: no political disasters, no assassinations, no ideological competition, no wars, no corruption, no atom waiting in its dark secrecy to destroy us all with its exploding energy.

[3] There is a lot of energy at the Fair in Des Moines, but it is all peaceful. The double giant Ferris wheel circles, its swaying seats more frightening than a jet plane flying through a monsoon. Eighty thousand men, women, and children walk all day and much of the night across the fairgrounds. Ponies pick up their feet in a slashing trot as if the ground burned them. Hard-rock music backgrounds the soft lowing of a Jersey cow in the cattle barn over her newborn calf, the color of a wild deer. Screaming speeches are made all around the world urging violence; here there are plenty of voices, but they are calling for you to throw baseballs at Kewpie dolls, to pitch nickels at a dish which won't hold them, to buy cotton candy, corn dogs, a paring knife that performs every useful act save mixing a martini.

[4] Above all, you would believe there was no hunger in the world, for what the Iowa State Fair celebrates is not only peace but food. This is one of the few places in the world where you see every

From *Holiday* (March, 1975). Reprinted by permission of *Travel/Holiday*.

condition of food. It walks by you on the hoof, the Hereford, Angus, Charolais, Shorthorn steer, the meat under its hide produced by a beautifully balanced diet more complicated than a baby's formula. These thousand-pound beef animals look at you with their oval, liquid eyes, not knowing that in human terms they are round steak, rib roast, tenderloin, chuck, and hamburger.

[5] The Fair has always specialized in show-ring competition for swine and cattle, but in recent years this has been extended to the slaughtered and dressed carcass. Often the animal which won on the hoof will not actually be as good a meat specimen as one graded lower on its "figure." Probably the most important single event at the Fair is also the quietest and most hidden: the judging of the carcass by experts in long white coats in a refrigerated room. The months of elaborate feeding, of care to prevent injuries, all have their meaning when the loin eye is measured and the balance between fat and lean is revealed.

[6] At the 1974 Fair, Roy B. Keppy's crossbred hog placed second in the live competition, but first in the pork carcass show. It yielded a chop which measured 6.36 square inches, one of the largest in the history of the Fair. A little more than an inch of fat covered the rib (loin-eye) area.

[7] If you saw close up the boys and girls of 4-H, you would also believe that this world was lived in by the best of all possible people. These are not the drugged youth of the newspapers. They are intelligent and sturdy and have carried into the present the old-fashioned and sturdy ideas: the four-*H* concept means thinking HEAD, feeling HEART, skilled HAND, and strong HEALTH. They walk with the ease of the physically active and the confidence of people who have done serious and useful projects. They understand animals, machines, fibers.

[8] Nor are they the "hicks" of rural legend. Newspapers, radio, television have brought the world into their home; before their eyes they see what is happening not only in the nearest city but in a country five thousand miles away. Nor are they dull. Often a 4-H boy and girl will work together washing down their steers, shampooing the tails and polishing the hooves, and then go off to spend the evening dancing or at a rock concert.

[9] One of the great sights in 4-H at the Fair is the weeping face of a bright, attractive farm girl whose steer has just won a championship. She has raised the animal herself. She has kept a daily

record of how much she fed it each day, of how many pounds of feed it took to make pounds of grain (a corn-fed beef steer's daily growth is frightening and fattening). She has washed and brushed and combed it, taught it to lead with a halter, to stand still on order.

[10] The final moment of truth comes when she leads it into the show-ring and the judge examines it with a hard and expert eye. If a Blue Ribbon is awarded, tears of joy on the cheeks of the 4-H girl, after her months of loving care and the tension of competing. Then the auction, for which she receives much more per pound than the average because she has the champion, with tears of sadness because the creature who had become a pet at home is led off to be slaughtered. Head, Heart, Hand and Health of that devoted girl went into the profitable health of that sexless steer.

[11] One of the dramatic examples of energy at the Fair is in the tractor, draft team and pony "pulls," in which the machine and the animals rear up as they try to pull a weighted sledge. The tractor is the usual case of a souped-up engine performing a task it would never do on a farm, with a great snorting and straining. The fun is in the horse and pony pulls, where the animals dig into the turf and drive themselves beyond their real strength, as if they understood the nature of competition.

[12] Above all, the Fair gives a workout to the body's five senses they could get nowhere else in the U.S.A. Apart from the fact that most people walk far more than they realize in their four-wheeled daily life, one reason for the healthy tiredness at the end of a morning-afternoon-evening at the Fair is that eye, hand, ear, tongue, and nose are exercised more than in all the rest of the year.

[13] *Eye* sees the great, full udders of Holstein cows swaying between those heavy legs, the rounded bellies of hogs unaware that the symmetry will lead to an early death, the sheep struggling under the shearer's hand as he draws red blood on their pink skin in his haste, the giant pumpkin glowing orange as an autumn moon, the Ladies' Rolling Pin Throw contest (you wouldn't argue with one of them), the blue-red-purple-white stalks of gladioli from home gardens, the harness horses pulling goggled drivers as they trot and pace frail sulkies in front of the grandstand.

[14] *Hand* touches surfaces it never meets at home unless it belongs to a farmer: softness of Guernsey hide or of the five-gaited saddle horse sleek from the currycomb, the golden feel of new oat straw, the fleece of Oxford Down or Shropshire lambs, the green

surface of a John Deere eight-row corn picker, smooth as skin and tough as steel, the sweet stickiness of cotton candy.

[15] *Ear* has almost too much to take in: the hog-calling contest with its shrill shrieks, the husband-calling contest combining seduction with threats, the whinnying of Tennessee walking horses, the lowing of cattle bored with standing in the show-ring, the male chauvinist crowing of roosters at the poultry barn, loudest at daybreak (the champion crowed 104 times in half an hour), the merry-go-round playing its old sentimental tunes, the roar of racing cars, the barkers praising the promised beauty to be revealed at the girlie show, the old fiddler's contest quivering the air with "Buffalo Gal," "Texas Star" and "Tennessee Waltz," the clang of horseshoes against each other and against the stake.

[16] *Tongue* learns the taste of hickory-smoked ham, the richness of butter on popcorn with beer, the tang of rhubarb pie, sour elegance of buttermilk served ice cold, the total smack of hamburger with onion, pickle, mustard and horseradish, many-flavored ice cream, chicken fried in sight of their live cousins in the poultry barn, barbecued pork ribs spitting their fat into the fire as fattened hogs waddle by on their way to be judged.

[17] *Nose* has an exhausting time at the Fair. It smells the many odors rising from the grills of men competing in the Iowa Cookout King contest, grilling turkey, lamb, beef, pork, chicken, ham with backyard recipes which excite the appetite, the delicate scents of flowers in the horticulture competition, the smell of homemade foods, the crisp smell of hay. People drive hundreds of miles in air-conditioned cars which filter out smells in order to walk through heavy and hot late summer air across the manure-reeking atmosphere of the hog, cattle, horse and sheep barns, to sniff again the animal odors of their childhood.

[18] You can watch the judging of home-baked bread or listen to the latest rock group. You can watch free every day the teenage talent search or pay money to hear the same nationally known acts you can watch free on television. The 4-H sewing contest, in which contenders wear the clothes they made, was startled in 1974 to have a boy enter himself and his navy blue knit slacks and jacket with white trim (he grew up on a hog farm, but wants to design clothes). A girl won.

[19] The Iowa State Fair is a great annual ceremony of the sane. Young girls still stand all night behind dairy cows with pitch forks

to keep the freshly washed animals from getting dirty before being shown in the morning. Boys milk cows at 10 P.M., 2 A.M., and 3 A.M. to be sure their udders are "balanced" when judges look at them. This is hardly the view of teenagers we often hear. A six-year-old boy wins the rooster crowing contest. There is Indian Wrestling (arm-hand wrestling) with a white and black sweating in immobile silence; the judge was John Buffalo, a real Indian from the Tama reservation.

[20] Year after year this rich and practical ritual of life is repeated. Animals whose ancestors competed many Fairs ago come back. So do people, returning by plane and automobile to the grounds their grandparents visited by train and buggy. Three-hundred-and-fifty-horsepower internal-combustion engines have replaced the one-horse hitch or the two-horse team, but the essential objects of life are the same: the dented ear of corn, the rounded rib of steer and pig, that nourishment of the human race which is the prime purpose of the plowing and harvesting State of Iowa.

[21] To some, the Fair seems corny. To others, the world still needs to catch up to the human and animal decency which each year dignifies a corner of this corrupt world. A few hundred acres of human skill and animal beauty in Des Moines, Iowa, prove to the space capsule of Earth how to live.

COMMENT

Engle arranges his details in parallel order—a means to concision in an essay that is full of observations and details:

> . . . here there are plenty of voices, but they are calling for you to throw baseballs at Kewpie dolls, to pitch nickels at a dish which won't hold them, to buy cotton candy, corn dogs, a paring knife that performs every useful act save mixing a martini.

This large number of parallel phrases increases the tempo and thus the excitement of Engle's sentences—an effect appropriate to what he is saying about the fair. He achieves the same effect in the five paragraphs that begin *Eye, Hand, Ear, Tongue,* and *Nose:* these develop parallel ideas though the details are different in each. Toward the end of the essay Engle arranges parallel phrases in climactic order to provide a striking conclusion:

> Three-hundred-and-fifty-horsepower internal-combustion engines have replaced the one-horse hitch or the two-horse team, but the essential objects of life are the same: *the dented ear of corn, the rounded rib of steer and pig, that nourishment of the human race which is the prime purpose of the plowing and harvesting State of Iowa.*

Notice that the much longer concluding phrase contributes most to the sense of climax.

QUESTIONS FOR STUDY AND DISCUSSION

1. What other examples do you find of parallelism used for emphasis, as in the sentences analyzed above? Are elements arranged in climactic order in any of these sentences?

2. What use does Engle make of parallelism in paragraph 2? How does he achieve a sense of climax in the paragraph?

3. How is the essay organized? Is Engle building from less to more important aspects of the fair, or does he use another principle of order?

4. What is his thesis, and where is it first stated? How does he restate it in the course of the essay?

5. What aspects of the fair does Engle focus on, as a way of developing his thesis? What other aspects might he have discussed in more detail if he were developing a different thesis? Can you suggest another?

SENTENCE STUDY

Combine each group of sentences into a single one, using parallelism and subordination where possible. Change the order of ideas if you wish. Here is a sample revision:

> We entered the house. We climbed the stairs. We entered the dark room at the top. We hoped to find a letter. Or we hoped to find some other explanation for the deserted state of the house.

> *Revision:* We entered the house, climbed the stairs, and entered the dark room at the top, hoping to find a letter or some other explanation for the deserted state of the house.

a. We did not want to explore the room further. We were certain there was no explanation to be found in the house. The field behind the house perhaps contained the answer to the mystery.

b. There were signs that someone had entered the garage recently. Not only that, someone else had been searching the field.
c. The garage door had fresh paint marks. There were oil marks on the garage floor. Engine parts were piled in a corner. Tools used to change tires were in another corner.
d. We discussed what he had found in the garage. We searched the field a second time. We decided to call the police. We asked the neighbors whether they had seen anything unusual.

SUGGESTIONS FOR WRITING

1. Describe a county fair or a similar event from your own point of view. Provide enough details so that your readers experience what you did. Remember that you do not have to describe everything. Select your details to fit a thesis, and state this thesis in a prominent place in your essay. Where possible, arrange your details in parallel order to gain conciseness.

2. Compare and contrast two similar events—basketball or football games, school dances, or the like—then develop a thesis relating to them. Comparison and contrast offers an opportunity for parallelism in the construction of sentences and paragraphs. Aim for parallelism in a few of yours.

A TRULY NO NON-SCENTS OUTLOOK

Noel Perrin

Born in New York City in 1927, Noel Perrin was educated at Williams College, Duke University, and Cambridge University in England. He has taught at the University of North Carolina and Dartmouth College, and has written numerous essays, including many on Vermont life. His books include *A Passport Secretly* (1961), *Dr. Bowdler's Legacy* (1969), and *First Person Rural* (1978).

[1] The ads show virile fellows swinging their soap-on-a-rope in a locker room, or standing explorer-like in a rural landscape. They give off almost visible waves of delicious scent: English Leather, or Eau Sauvage, or Acqua di Selva. An admiring and beautiful woman often stands a pace or two behind, though they ignore her. Her nostrils are slightly flared. She has clearly been following her nose to the source of this splendid masculine aroma. It is so intoxicating that she seems likely to spring from behind, and bear the man down to the grass.

[2] I would dearly love to believe the promise of these ads. What could be more agreeable than to have a stream of beautiful women moving upwind, irresistibly drawn by the super-male scent I wear? Surely I would dab myself with Jovan Grass Oil in the morning, splash with Timberline for lunch, and fairly drench with Acqua di Selva as bedtime drew near.

[3] The trouble is that I live in just such a rural landscape as the ads depict. In the course of a normal day I pick up a good many of the rough male scents they describe, not by opening a bottle but just by living. The results for me are so dramatically different from what is about to happen in the ads that I am forced to be skeptical.

[4] Take Acqua di Selva, which calls itself "woodsy" (so is Timberline, I presume), and promises wearers that they will smell as cool and fresh as a rain forest. Two days in three I smell woodsy. We heat our house mostly with wood, and I have about ten cords a year to cut. I have a 50-acre woodlot to cut it on—hilly, rugged terrain that would photograph well. Occasionally I even notch and fell a few saw logs for the mill: Scotch pine, and towering spruces, and wild cherry.

[5] Not only do no women ever follow the woodsy smell to where I am cutting, pluck the chain saw from my hand, and lead me to a patch of ferns; my wife doesn't even let me in the house when I get home. She stops me on the front porch. Nose averted, she combs the wood chips out of my hair. Then she hands me a cake of soap, and suggests I go take a bath in the river. When, as occasionally happens, I cut on a rainy day, and hence come dripping home out of the rain forest, leaving a trail of mud and bark, she has been known to burst into tears.

[6] The smell of leather has proved even less erotic. We have a bright bay gelding named Cinnamon, a fine riding horse. We have

lots of horsy tack, and even a sort of tack room. Leather halters hang from pegs. There are lead ropes and bridles and, sitting on a rack made from wood cut on the place, a saddle of the same shape that is shown in gold silhouette on the English Leather bottle.

[7] The fact that my wife tends to avoid me when I've been cleaning it doesn't prove anything, I admit, since the saddle was made in Japan, and is presumably Japanese leather. But the bridles are both English. And both, I will say it plainly, savor of horse sweat.

[8] Cinnamon loves to canter, and he sweats a lot; also he champs at the bit and gets froth all over. It is true that once when I rode him to a party, a very pretty girl came out and kissed, not me, but him. It is also true that she then went quickly to the bathroom and washed her hands and face.

[9] Then there is the soil itself. Jovan Grass Oil promises to give its wearer the powerful attraction of smelling "earthy," a claim that I find the least plausible of all. I mean, for all I know, men who use Grass Oil may smell earthy, but I don't think that's going to help their social lives much.

[10] We are gardeners. I have a generous supply of rich garden earth on my hands, under my fingernails, on my boots, etc., through most of each May and June, and all it ever gets me is the earnest plea to take my boots off outside and then head straight for the bathroom.

[11] Once I dug a well, and then I was *really* earthy. You could have planted corn on any part of me. At that time I was not married, but engaged. My fiancée's quite serious proposal was that we walk (she didn't want me in her car) to her father's house, and that she then turn the garden hose on me. "You're all over mud," she said in repelled tones.

[12] I frankly don't think *any* male perfume is going to attract women much. They prefer us neutral—if only so as not to collide with their own fragrance. But if I were going to try perfume in a serious way, I would forget all this earthy, woodsy, leathery stuff. In fact, I would forget the whole rural bit. I would aim to have the faint, sweet smell of a single flower in a city square.

COMMENT

Perrin uses parallelism in a less dramatic way than Engle, with sentences and phrases that are often shorter:

> In the course of a normal day I pick up a good many of the rough male scents they describe, not by opening a bottle but just by living.

> Surely I would dab myself with Jovan Grass Oil in the morning, splash with Timberline for lunch, and fairly drench with Acqua di Selva as bedtime drew near.

Perrin modifies these elements just enough to decrease their formality. His parallelism is, in fact, typical of that in everyday speech and writing. Like Engle, he occasionally loosens what might have been a rigid pattern.

QUESTIONS FOR STUDY AND DISCUSSION

1. How does Perrin loosen the parallelism of the last sentence in paragraph 6?

2. What sentences in paragraphs 6 and 8 might have employed parallelism? How would parallelism change the tone of these paragraphs?

3. How does paragraph 1 establish a tone and point of view?

4. Is Perrin developing a thesis, or merely enjoying the absurdity of the perfume ads? Do you think he is commenting implicitly on advertising in general?

VOCABULARY STUDY

1. Perrin chooses words for their connotative meanings, for he is concerned with the feelings they arouse. Two of these in paragraph 1 are *delicious* and *intoxicating*. Locate other words of this kind, and comment on their use in the essay.

2. Perrin points to words like "woodsy" that are chiefly connotative in meaning. Identify words in other magazine ads or TV commercials that are also connotative, and write down how the illustrations help you to understand what feelings and ideas the word is meant to convey.

SUGGESTIONS FOR WRITING

1. The satirist employs a strategy that forces us to recognize the absurdity and humor of an action or idea. Discuss Perrin's strategy in his essay, and compare it to the strategies of E. B. White and James Thurber in their satirical essays in this book.

2. Write your own satirical essay on a different kind of advertisement. Give enough details about the ads to make your readers recognize their absurdity and humor.

3. Examine a series of advertisements for automobiles or lawn equipment or recreational vehicles or equipment, and analyze the images of men and women contained in them. Discuss important similarities and differences in these images, and draw a conclusion from your analysis.

sentence variety

Sentence variety is governed as much by considerations of audience as by the requirements of clear, precise meaning. A string of short sentences, written without connectives, will lose the attention of the reader quickly, owing to their monotony:

> You are watching coal miners at work. You realize momentarily what different universes people inhabit. It is a sort of world apart down there. One can quite easily go through life without ever hearing about that world. Probably a majority of people would even prefer not to hear about it.

Adding connectives and subordinating some of these ideas are ways of removing the monotony and focusing attention on the important ideas:

> Watching coal miners at work, you realize momentarily what different universes different people inhabit. *Down there* where coal is dug it is a sort of world apart *which* one can quite easily go through life without ever hearing about. Probably a majority of people would even prefer not to hear about it.—George Orwell, *The Road to Wigan Pier*

Two of the important connectives in Orwell's original passage have been italicized. Notice that the second sentence of the simplified reduction began with the subject and predicate; Orwell by contrast begins with the modifier *down there* to connect the first two sentences, and he subordinates the third sentence to the second through the word *which*. The more varied sentences are in length and construction, the less monotonous they will seem; however, parallel ideas need parallel construction to highlight their similarities. Too much variation can be as distracting as too little.

WAITING AND WAITING, BUT FOR NAUGHT

Dorothy Rodgers

Dorothy Rodgers was born in 1909 in New York City, and was educated at Wellesley College. She is a sculptor and the author of several books, including *My Favorite Things* and *A Personal Book* (1977). Her husband is the composer Richard Rodgers.

[1] Knowing that I would have to apply for Medicare three months before I reached the marvelous date of becoming 65 years old, I telephoned the Social Security office for information.

[2] I learned that I would have to produce myself in person together with some documents: a photostat of my birth certificate, a W-2 tax form showing Social Security payments made by me and my employer, and an application form which they agreed to mail.

[3] Since I'm self-employed (no one pays any Social Security for me), I didn't have a W-2 form, but I did have two 1099 miscellaneous forms sent me by McCall's and The Ideal Toy Company showing the amount of income I had earned in 1973. I hoped that would do, especially as I wasn't applying for Social Security for the excellent reason that I don't qualify for it.

[4] Armed with these official documents and a book to help pass the time, I set off on a terribly cold morning for the midtown branch of our Department of Health, Education and Welfare where applications for welfare, Social Security and Medicare are processed.

[5] The office is at 1657 Broadway, a building that looks as if it shouldn't be allowed out in daylight.

[6] Next to the entrance was an empty store with double gates

stretched across its front, padlocked to protect God knows what inside.

⁷The sidewalk was littered with the remnants of stuff people use when they wait a lot: cigarette butts, chewing-gum and candy wrappers and crushed paper cups. People were milling around the entrance and I soon found out why. Three polite but firm cops just inside the doors wouldn't let anyone upstairs.

⁸"Social Security?" one of them asked me.

⁹"No," I said, "Medicare."

¹⁰"Same thing," he said. "Get on the bus."

¹¹"What bus? I'm not going anywhere!"

¹²"Lady," he said, "go sit in the bus. It's a waiting room. You'll get a number."

¹³I turned and looked where he was pointing and there were three buses lined up against the curb right in front of the building, so I climbed aboard the first one, which was almost empty.

¹⁴I took the aisle seat in the second row and watched the bus fill up rapidly with all kinds of people: young, old, mothers with cranky children, children with cranky mothers, people who were obviously ill, blacks, whites, one stoned and at least a few eccentrics.

¹⁵The bus was soon totally filled and people were being directed to the other buses. Everyone waited unquestioningly and with complete resignation. At last, one of the policemen approached the bus. He gave us all slips of paper with numbers on them and told us to wait.

¹⁶"Wait" was clearly the name of the game. However, after only a few minutes, the cop came back and told ten people in the front of the bus to get off and go to the second floor.

¹⁷The second floor was enormous. A whole open space was covered by desks at which applicants were being interviewed. Fluorescent lights in the ceiling provided the only relief from the vast gray area. Immediately in front of the elevators there were two waiting rooms. A girl sat at a desk between them. We were told to find seats in the left section and wait for the guard to call our numbers. Mine was 297 and number 258 had just been called.

¹⁸Although I came expecting to wait, an hour and a half had already passed and I realized I was going to be late for my next appointment. I certainly didn't want to leave and have to go through the whole performance all over again another day, so I decided to make a phone call and explain why I'd be late. I got up, tripped over a chair and landed flat on the floor.

[19] People were extraordinarily concerned. "Did you hurt yourself" came at me from applicants and officials in varying accents. Fortunately, I hadn't and, gathering my book, bag, gloves, coat and dignity, I went up to a woman who seemed to be in charge and asked her where the phone booth was. "Downstairs," she answered.

[20] "But if I go downstairs, I might lose my place."

[21] "I'm so glad you didn't hurt yourself! Use my phone." It was kind and unbureaucratic, and I was grateful. Having completed the phone call, I returned to my old seat and moved my legs to make way for a small black woman of indeterminate age who sank into the chair next to mine and gave a great sigh.

[22] I looked at her face; it wasn't black, it was green. She said: "I like to drop dead out there in the cold—buses all filled up. The policeman said for me to come up and sit where it's warm. I got asthma and I got sugar, I can't work and I'm sick. I can't work—I'm 93—oh, I mean 63."

[23] She talked on unintelligibly for a while. All I could do was to make sympathetic sounds. I felt desperately sorry for her, but there was no way I could help solve her overwhelming problems.

[24] Just then the cop called out 279 and I jumped up, dropping my gloves on the floor. Somebody cried: "Lady, wyn'cha put 'em in your pocket so you don't lose 'em?"

[25] I felt like six going on 65—especially as my number was 297, not 279.

[26] I went back to my chair and the woman resumed her talk until at last my number was called. I wished her luck and told her that I hoped things would work out for her.

[27] The next step took me to the girl at the desk. She asked my name, why I was there, and waved me in the direction of the other waiting room where I was to wait until my name was called. After a relatively short time, someone called my name and I was led to a Mr. Wolfe's desk.

[28] He was young and, like everyone else, pleasant and courteous. He went over my papers, took them to be photostated and returned—all in a matter of about five minutes. That was it. I could leave.

[29] I looked around at everyone—the people being quietly interviewed at the desks, the applicants sitting and waiting, waiting with infinite patience.

[30] Undemanding and submissive, confused and afraid to ask questions, sick or destitute—or merely over 65—they wait, in the

cold or on the bus or in the dreary waiting rooms. Wait for Lady Bountiful to hand out our Thanksgiving turkey. Only it isn't Lady Bountiful. It's our own friendly Uncle Sam and it's not a handout. It's a right paid for by the same people, over many years.

[31] No one had been pushed around; no one had been rude or unkind. I went over to the woman who had allowed me to use her phone to tell her how remarkable I thought it was. She said, "We try."

COMMENT

Rodgers' sentences are varied enough so that the short sentences are emphatic. Notice the effect of the one that follows the description of her falling: "People were extraordinarily concerned." And her first sight of the room has the same impact: "The second floor was enormous." If all the sentences in the essay were as short as these, none would convey such impact. The sentence structure expresses feeling in other ways: the statement of the old woman sitting next to the author is punctuated to express her confusion and exhaustion (paragraph 22). Rodgers succeeds in doing more than just stating the facts of the episode: she allows us to feel the experience as she felt it.

QUESTIONS FOR STUDY AND DISCUSSION

1. Where else in the essay are short sentences used for emphasis?

2. How does Rodgers vary her sentences in paragraphs 14–19 so that not all of them begin with "I"?

3. She might have combined some of her short paragraphs. Which of them could be combined? What is gained by not combining them?

4. Rodgers depends on surprise to develop her thesis. How does she build to these surprises? What point is she making?

VOCABULARY STUDY

1. Explain what the connotations of the following words contribute to the experience: *littered, cranky, eccentrics, sympathetic, submissive, destitute.*

2. Find synonyms for the words listed above.

SUGGESTIONS FOR WRITING

1. Describe a similar experience in which your expectations about what would happen were not realized. Make the details of the experience convey your feelings.

2. Zinsser and Rodgers convey different impressions of waiting rooms, and use these settings for different purposes. Compare and contrast the two essays with attention to these points.

PARENTS MUST MAKE UP THEIR MINDS

Sydney J. Harris

Sydney J. Harris was born in London in 1917. He attended the University of Chicago and Central College in Chicago, and was employed in public relations for the legal division of the City of Chicago. He has been a journalist most of his life, writing a column for the *Chicago Daily News* since 1941. His columns have been collected into numerous books, including *Majority of One* (1957), *Last Things First* (1961), and *On the Contrary* (1964).

[1] Parents want two opposite things at once: they want their children to excel, and they want their children to be docile. But the two don't go together, and never have.

[2] Every study made of "achievers" in a genuinely creative sense—that is, people who were truly innovative, whose existence made some positive difference for the human race—has shown that as children these people were anything but docile and conformist.

[3] Almost all were independent, in mind and spirit, if not in body. They began thinking for themselves at an early age, and

either rejected or modified their parents' code of conduct and scale of values. Many were not popular with their peers, and most of them were found either "stupid" or "difficult" by their teachers.

[4] Actually, when parents say they want a child to "excel," what they customarily mean is that they want him to be successful and to be popular. But genuine achievers are often those who fail for a long time, and who rarely attain popularity outside a small circle. And they have often had severe educational problems, from St. Thomas Aquinas, who was called a "dumb ox" at school, to Thomas Edison, who received depressingly poor grades and left school before the age of twelve.

[5] A creative and imaginative child is a great burden to the ordinary parent, and this is why a repressive society produces so few of them; the weaker spirits are crushed, and the hardier ones often overreact in a way that turns them into delinquents, or actual criminals if they happen to live in a squalid environment.

[6] As adults, most of us do not care to tolerate the kinetic qualities of children. We want them to stop wriggling or jumping or sloshing through puddles or dangling from fence posts; and in the same way, we resent agile minds and mercurial temperaments. We don't like to answer silly questions, to respond to anxieties that take fantasy form, or to acknowledge the deeper life of the child's spirit.

[7] He is to be quiet, tractable, unquestioning, unthinking, and invisible if possible. Even the so-called permissive parent is doing the same thing in a different way—giving the child too much money or too much false freedom in order to get him out of the way, to leave time and energy for adult pursuits. The TV set is now what the Bible lesson used to be, only more seductive and more effective.

[8] Nothing in the world is harder than rearing a child who will make a difference to his society. But nothing in the world is more worthwhile, if we are breeding for improvement and not just for dumb survival.

COMMENT

English sentences are built by addition: that is the advantage of the coordinating conjunctions *and, but, for, yet, or, nor*. They join closely related ideas that can stand together:

> Many were not popular with their peers, *and* most of them were found either "stupid" or "difficult" by their teachers.

The semicolon in the single sentence of paragraph 5 also joins closely related ideas. Though the discussion and sentence structure of the essay are formal (the subject is abstract, not concrete, like the experience Dorothy Rodgers describes), the sentences are simple or compound, the kind found most in informal writing. Like Stuart, Harris prefers to break sentences for emphasis rather than connect very long main clauses. If the two sentences of the final paragraph had been combined into one sentence, the final subordinate clause might have been set off in this way:

> Nothing in the world is harder than rearing a child who will make a difference to his society, *but* nothing in the world is more worthwhile—if we are breeding for improvement and not just for dumb survival.

QUESTIONS FOR STUDY AND DISCUSSION

1. What use does Harris make of dashes?

2. How many of his sentences begin with subordinate clauses?

3. Is Harris saying that all delinquent children are creative and imaginative, or that children have trouble in school only for the reasons he gives?

4. Why is the TV set "more seductive and more effective" than the Bible lesson today? Does Harris state or imply the reason?

5. What is the thesis of the essay, and where is it first stated? How does Harris restate it in the course of the essay?

VOCABULARY STUDY

1. Explain the special meanings of *creative* and *imaginative* in the essay.

2. Write a paraphrase of paragraphs 4–6 in language that would be clear to high school students. Add examples to your paraphrase if you wish.

SUGGESTIONS FOR WRITING

1. Develop one of the following statements from your own experience, agreeing or disagreeing with the statement:
   a. "Parents want two opposite things at once: they want their children to excel, and they want their children to be docile."
   b. "A creative and imaginative child is a great burden to the ordinary parent."

c. "As adults, most of us do not care to tolerate the kinetic qualities of children."

d. "The TV set is now what the Bible lesson used to be, only more seductive and more effective."

2. All of us hold contradictory ideas about our parents, our teachers, our world—even ourselves. Discuss one contradictory view that you hold, tracing its origins and its consequences or effects in your life.

concreteness

To make an idea *concrete* is to make it exist for the reader through the senses. The statement "That car's a beauty!" expresses a general attitude and feeling but nothing more. If we want people to share our experience, we must give particulars or details—those physical qualities that make the car beautiful.

Not all abstract ideas can be expressed through physical details. We can, however, show their application to experience or suggest how we came to the idea; or we can give the details that explain it. In a discussion of the emotional makeup of human beings, Desmond Morris says that people enjoy exploring their emotions. Man, he says, "is constantly pushing things to their limit, trying to startle himself, to shock himself without getting hurt, and then signaling his relief with peals of infectious laughter." The abstract idea is here made specific; for we are told what people *do*. But Morris makes the idea even more concrete through the behavior of teenagers when their idols perform on stage. "As an audience, they enjoy themselves, not by screaming with laughter, but screaming with screams. They not only scream, they also grip their own and one another's bodies, they writhe, they moan, they cover their faces and they pull at their hair." From these details he draws a conclusion:

> These are all the classic signs of intense pain or fear, but they have become deliberately stylized. . . . They are no longer cries for help, but signals to one another in the audience that they are capable of feeling an emotional response to the sexual idols which is so powerful that, like all stimuli of unbearably high intensity, they pass into the realm of pain.—*The Naked Ape*

The idea has been made concrete. At the same time, we must be careful not to give more details than we need to make the idea clear. Writing can be so colorful—so crowded with details and descriptive words—that the reader is distracted from the main idea.

CHRISTMAS COMES FIRST ON THE BANKS

William G. Wing

William G. Wing was a veteran correspondent of the *New York Herald Tribune.* He is a specialist on natural resources and conservation, writing for *Audubon Magazine,* the *New York Times,* and other periodicals.

[1] The Christmas sun rises first, in America, on trawlermen fishing the undersea meadows of Georges Bank.

[2] At the moment before sunrise a hundred miles east of Cape Cod, the scene aboard a trawler is so unchanging it can be imagined. The net has been hauled and streamed again. The skipper is alone in the pilot house, surrounded by the radiotelephone's racket and the green and amber eyes of electronic instruments, instruments that are supposed to tell him not only where he is but where the fish are, too.

[3] But this is only hope, not science. Despite the instruments, despite the boat's resemblance to a plow horse, methodically crisscrossing the meadow, her men are not engineers or farmers, but hunters who seek their prey in the wilderness of the sea. The trawlermen are, in fact, the last tribe of nomadic huntsmen left in the East.

[4] The skipper is alone, then, with a huntsman's anxieties: the whereabouts of the prey, the uncertainties of the weather, the chances of hitting a good market.

[5] On deck before him the men are processing the catch just

brought aboard. They sit in a circle of brilliance, the deck lights reflecting from their yellow and Daybrite-orange oilskins and from the brown curve of the riding sail above.

[6] They sit on the edges of the pens, holding the big white and silver fish between their knees, ripping with knives and tearing with hands, heaving the disemboweled bodies into a central basket. Nothing is visible beyond the cone of light but the occasional flash of a whitecap or comber.

[7] There is much noise, though—wind and water and seabirds that have gathered in mobs for the feast of haulback.

[8] There is an appropriateness to Christmas in this scene, east of the sleeping mainland, so marked that it seems quaint. The names of the trawlers themselves—*Holy Family, Immaculate Conception, St. Mary, St. Joseph*—give the flavor. On the engine room bulkhead of the trawler *Holy Cross,* beyond the ugga-chugging Atlas diesel, is a painting of Christ at Gethsemane.

[9] There is an appropriateness, too, among the men. They share alike—equal shares of profit, equal shares of danger. To work together in such small quarters and stern conditions requires a graciousness of spirit that is the essence of Christmas.

[10] The sun is up and the pens are empty. As the deck is hosed down and the trash fish pitchforked overboard, the noise from the birds rises hysterically—barnyard sounds, shrieks, whistles, klaxon horns.

[11] Now the birds can be seen flying in a circle around the boat. Each can hold position for only a few moments beside the point where the remains of fish are washing over. Then it falls astern and has to come up to windward on the other side of the boat, cross ahead and fall backward to the critical point. The birds pumping up the windward side look like six-day bicycle riders, earnest and slightly ridiculous, but when they reach the critical point there is a miraculous moment of aerobatics as the birds brake, wheel and drop in the broken air.

[12] Gulls snatch, gannets plunge, but the little kittiwakes balance delicately, their tails spread like carved ivory fans. There is a column of descending, shrieking birds, a scintillating feathered mass. The birds revolving about the boat have made themselves not only guests at the feast but have formed the wreath as well.

[13] Christmas Day has begun, but for the men it is time to sleep.

They hose each other off and then disappear through the whaleback for a mug-up below.

[14] Boots and oilskins off, they will have a minute or two for a James Bond novel or a crossword puzzle in the bunks, braced against the elevator motions of the hull, not hearing the sounds of Niagara outside. Then the instant unconsciousness that seamen and children know. The skipper alone remains awake, watching Christmas come.

[15] Christmas came first to men on lonely meadows. It will come first again to the men on the lonely meadows offshore, fishing the Bank in boats wreathed by seabirds.

COMMENT

The author tells us that he will seek to make the moment before the sun rises concrete: he will find images that convey the mood and experience of the moment. He does so in the details of the boat, the trawlermen, their relations—"equal shares of profits, equal shares of danger." The seabirds have an unexpected appropriateness, for they wreathe the boats in their circlings. Through careful selection of details, the author succeeds in his purpose; through his description, he is able to make a point without stating it directly.

QUESTIONS FOR STUDY AND DISCUSSION

1. What point is the author making through his description? Is it important to him where the Christmas sun first rises in America?

2. Is the order of details governed by space (moving from one part of the scene to another) or by time, or possibly both?

3. What details or qualities of the scene—stated and implied—suggest Christmas in some way?

4. Is the author saying that the life aboard the trawler and the relations between the men are different during the Christmas season or on Christmas day?

5. How does the author make transitions throughout the essay?

6. What is the point of the concluding comparison?

VOCABULARY STUDY

For each of the following words, list at least two synonyms that suggest a more specific meaning or use. For example, *forecast* is more specific than *foretell* when referring to a weather prediction.

  a. large
  b. small
  c. dirty
  d. clean
  e. law
  f. run

SUGGESTIONS FOR WRITING

1. Describe a scene at a particular moment—for example, the moment of impact in an automobile accident. Select details that contribute to a central impression, but do not state the impression directly.

2. Describe a day of work, showing how the season of the year affects you and your fellow workers. Use your description to develop a thesis.

3. Describe an unusual day in your life—one that perhaps was spent in an unusual setting, away from home. Stress those feelings and details that made the day unusual and memorable.

HOME FOR CHRISTMAS

Carson McCullers

Carson McCullers (1917–67) was born in Columbus, Georgia. She attended Columbia University and New York University. Her many books include *The Heart Is a Lonely Hunter* (1940), *Reflections in a Golden Eye* (1941), *The Member of the Wedding* (1946), *The Ballad of the Sad Cafe* (1951), and *Clock Without Hands* (1961). She received the National Institute of Arts and Letters Award in 1943, and the New York Drama Critics Circle Award in 1950 for her play *The Member of the Wedding.*

¹Sometimes in August, weary of the vacant, broiling afternoon, my younger brother and sister and I would gather in the dense shade under the oak tree in the back yard and talk of Christmas and sing carols. Once after such a conclave, when the tunes of the carols still lingered in the heat-shimmered air, I remember climbing up into the tree-house and sitting there alone for a long time.

²Brother called up: "What are you doing?"

³"Thinking," I answered.

⁴"What are you thinking about?"

⁵"I don't know."

⁶"Well, how can you be thinking when you don't know what you are thinking about?"

⁷I did not want to talk with my brother. I was experiencing the first wonder about the mystery of Time. Here I was, on this August afternoon, in the tree-house, in the burnt, jaded yard, sick and tired of all our summer ways. (I had read *Little Women* for the second time, *Hans Brinker and the Silver Skates, Little Men.* and *Twenty Thousand Leagues under the Sea.* I had read movie magazines and even tried to read love stories in the *Woman's Home Companion*—I was so sick of everything.) How could it be that I was I and now was now when in four months it would be Christmas, wintertime, cold weather, twilight and the glory of the Christmas tree? I puzzled about the *now* and *later* and rubbed the inside of my elbow until there was a little roll of dirt between my forefinger and thumb. Would the *now* I of the tree-house and the August afternoon be the same *I* of winter, firelight and the Christmas tree? I wondered.

⁸My brother repeated: "You say you are thinking but you don't know what you are thinking about. What are you really doing up there? Have you got some secret candy?"

⁹September came, and my mother opened the cedar chest and we tried on winter coats and last year's sweaters to see if they would do again. She took the three of us downtown and bought us new shoes and school clothes.

¹⁰Christmas was nearer on the September Sunday that Daddy rounded us up in the car and drove us out on dusty country roads to pick elderberry blooms. Daddy made wine from elderberry blossons—it was a yellow-white wine, the color of weak winter sun. The wine was dry to the wry side—indeed, some years it turned to vine-

From *The Mortgaged Heart* by Carson McCullers. Reprinted by permission of Floria V. Lasky.

gar. The wine was served at Christmastime with slices of fruitcake when company came. On November Sundays we went to the woods with a big basket of fried chicken dinner, thermos jug and coffee-pot. We hunted partridge berries in the pine woods near our town. These scarlet berries grew hidden underneath the glossy brown pine needles that lay in a slick carpet beneath the tall wind-singing trees. The bright berries were a Christmas decoration, lasting in water through the whole season.

[11] In December the windows downtown were filled with toys, and my brother and sister and I were given two dollars apiece to buy our Christmas presents. We patronized the ten-cent stores, choosing between jackstones, pencil boxes, water colors, and satin handker-chief holders. We would each buy a nickel's worth of lump milk choc-olate at the candy counter to mouth as we trudged from counter to counter, choice to choice. It was exacting and final—taking several afternoons—for the dime stores would not take back or exchange.

[12] Mother made fruitcakes, and for weeks ahead the family picked out the nut meats of pecans and walnuts, careful of the bitter layer of the pecans that lined your mouth with nasty fur. At the last I was allowed to blanch the almonds, pinching the scalded nuts so that they sometimes hit the ceiling or bounced across the room. Mother cut slices of citron and crystallized pineapple, figs and dates, and candied cherries were added whole. We cut rounds of brown paper to line the pans. Usually the cakes were mixed and put into the oven when we were in school. Late in the afternoon the cakes would be finished, wrapped in white napkins on the breakfast-room table. Later they would be soaked in brandy. These fruitcakes were famous in our town, and Mother gave them often as Christmas gifts. When company came thin slices of fruitcake, wine and coffee were always served. When you held a slice of fruitcake to the window or the firelight the slice was translucent, pale citron green and yellow and red, with the glow and richness of our church windows.

[13] Daddy was a jeweler, and his store was kept open until mid-night all Christmas week. I, as the eldest child, was allowed to stay up late with Mother until Daddy came home. Mother was always nervous without a "man in the house." (On those rare occasions when Daddy had to stay overnight on business in Atlanta, the chil-dren were armed with a hammer, saw and a monkey wrench. When pressed about her anxieties Mother claimed she was afraid of "escaped convicts or crazy people." I never saw an escaped convict,

but once a "crazy" person did come to see us. She was an old, old lady dressed in elegant black taffeta, my mother's second cousin once removed, and came on a tranquil Sunday morning and announced that she had always liked our house and she intended to stay with us until she died. Her sons and daughters and grandchildren gathered around to plead with her as she sat rocking in our front porch rocking chair and she left not unwillingly when they promised a car ride and ice cream.) Nothing ever happened on those evenings in Christmas week, but I felt grown, aged suddenly by trust and dignity. Mother confided in secrecy what the younger children were getting from Santa Claus. I knew where the Santa Claus things were hidden, and was appointed to see that my brother and sister did not go into the back-room closet or the wardrobe in our parents' room.

[14] Christmas Eve was the longest day, but it was lined with the glory of tomorrow. The sitting-room smelled of floor wax and the clean, cold odor of the spruce tree. The Christmas tree stood in a corner of the front room, tall as the ceiling, majestic, undecorated. It was our family custom that the tree was not decorated until after we children were in bed on Christmas Eve night. We went to bed very early, as soon as it was winter dark. I lay in the bed beside my sister and tried to keep her awake.

[15] "You want to guess again about your Santa Claus?"

[16] "We've already done that so much," she said.

[17] My sister slept. And there again was another puzzle. How could it be that when she opened her eyes it would be Christmas while I lay awake in the dark for hours and hours? The time was the same for both of us, and yet not at all the same. What was it? How? I thought of Bethlehem and cherry candy, Jesus and skyrockets. It was dark when I awoke. We were allowed to get up on Christmas at five o'clock. Later I found out that Daddy juggled the clock Christmas Eve so that five o'clock was actually six. Anyway it was always still dark when we rushed in to dress by the kitchen stove. The rule was that we dress and eat breakfast before we could go in to the Christmas tree. On Christmas morning we always had fish roe, bacon and grits for breakfast. I grudged every mouthful—for who wanted to fill up on breakfast when there in the sitting-room was candy, at least three whole boxes? After breakfast we lined up, and carols were started. Our voices rose naked and mysterious as we

filed through the door to the sitting-room. The carol, unfinished, ended in raw yells of joy.

[18] The Christmas tree glittered in the glorious, candlelit room. There were bicycles and bundles wrapped in tissue paper. Our stockings hanging from the mantlepiece bulged with oranges, nuts and smaller presents. The next hours were paradise. The blue dawn at the window brightened, and the candles were blown out. By nine o'clock we had ridden the wheel presents and dressed in the clothes gifts. We visited the neighborhood children and were visited in turn. Our cousins came and grown relatives from distant neighborhoods. All through the morning we ate chocolates. At two or three o'clock the Christmas dinner was served. The dining-room table had been let out with extra leaves and the very best linen was laid—satin damask with a rose design. Daddy asked the blessing, then stood up to carve the turkey. Dressing, rice and giblet gravy were served. There were cut-glass dishes of sparkling jellies and stateliness of festal wine. For dessert there was always sillabub or charlotte and fruitcake. The afternoon was almost over when dinner was done.

[19] At twilight I sat on the front steps, jaded by too much pleasure, sick at the stomach and worn out. The boy next door skated down the street in his new Indian suit. A girl spun around on a crackling son-of-a-gun. My brother waved sparklers. Christmas was over. I thought of the monotony of Time ahead, unsolaced by the distant glow of paler festivals, the year that stretched before another Christmas—eternity.

COMMENT

Time organizes the author's memory of a childhood Christmas: the sense of Christmas approaching, in the early fall; the rising excitement of the days before Christmas; the long waiting for five o'clock of Christmas morning; the "thought of the monotony of Time ahead" and "the year that stretched before another Christmas." The details and impressions the author records are therefore not presented at random: she connects them to give us the concrete world of a Georgia childhood. This one corner of her life tells us much about her, without our needing other details. Just as one well-chosen example may explain an idea fully and memorably, a few well-chosen details about the experience of Christmas allows the reader to know the world of the author in more than bare outline.

QUESTIONS FOR STUDY AND DISCUSSION

1. In how many ways is the reader reminded of time and its importance to the experience of Christmas?

2. How does the final word of the essay—"eternity"—imply meanings that the whole essay explores?

3. The author gives details of some aspects of Christmas but not of others. Why does she tell us what she thought about in bed? Why does she tell us what she ate for breakfast, instead of describing all the gifts she received? Why does she describe the experiences of September?

4. What other aspects might she have described in more detail? What would have been gained or lost if she had provided these details?

5. What do you discover about the author through this one experience?

6. How is the essay different in tone and purpose from William Wing's description of Christmas on the Banks?

VOCABULARY STUDY

Explain how the connotations of the following phrases contribute to the concreteness of the essay: *heat-shimmered, jaded yard, slick carpet, nasty fur, raw yells of joy, satin damask, stateliness of festal wine.*

SUGGESTIONS FOR WRITING

1. Describe a Christmas morning or another holiday morning and select your details to convey what was special about this day. Let your details reveal what was special. Don't tell your reader directly.

2. Compare the ways William Wing and Carson McCullers make their feelings about Christmas concrete.

3. Write a description of the objects and slogans associated with a national holiday, perhaps Thanksgiving or the Fourth of July. Explain how these contribute to your experience of the holiday from year to year.

figurative language

Much of our language is *figurative*—that is, not literal but metaphorical—sometimes without our realizing it is. Certain figures of speech may once have called a picture to mind but have become stale. Here are a few examples:

blaze of glory   *drunk with power*   *hard as nails*

The first of these is a *metaphor*—a figure of speech in which one thing is talked about as if it were something else. The metaphor does not tell us that glory is like a fire: it speaks of glory as if it were a fire. "Drunk with power" is also a metaphor: it specifies that power acts like an intoxicant. "Hard as nails" makes the comparison directly through the word *as,* and we therefore call it a *simile.* Another important figure of speech is *personification,* which gives animate or human qualities to something inanimate or nonhuman:

The tree *cowered* in the storm.

Figurative language is one way of conveying our feelings about an object or experience.

In exposition and argument, figurative language can make an idea or attitude concrete and persuasive. Here is a surgeon describing the tools of his art:

The scalpel is in two parts, the handle and the blade. Joined, it is six inches from tip to tip. At one end of the handle is a narrow notched prong upon which the blade is slid, then snapped into place. Without the blade, the handle has a blind, decapitated look. It is helpless as a trussed maniac. But slide on the blade, click it home, and the knife springs instantly to life. It is headed now, edgy, leaping to mount the fingers for the gallop to its feast.— Richard Selzer, *Mortal Lessons*

Metaphor, simile, and personification here are combined in a highly effective way; the description conveys the excitement of the surgeon as he holds the scalpel and prepares to use it.

UNTYING THE KNOT

Annie Dillard

Annie Dillard was born in 1945 in Pittsburgh and attended Hollins College. A sensitive and close observer of nature, she lived in the Roanoke Valley of Virginia for ten years and then moved to Puget Sound in the Pacific Northwest. She has written three books: *Tickets for a Prayer Wheel* (1974), a book of poems; *Pilgrim at Tinker Creek* (1974), for which she received a Pulitzer Prize; and *Holy the Firm* (1978), a meditation.

[1] Yesterday I set out to catch the new season, and instead I found an old snakeskin. I was in the sunny February woods by the quarry; the snakeskin was lying in a heap of leaves right next to an aquarium someone had thrown away. I don't know why that someone hauled the aquarium deep into the woods to get rid of it; it had only one broken glass side. The snake found it handy, I imagine; snakes like to rub against something rigid to help them out of their skins, and the broken aquarium looked like the nearest likely object. Together the snakeskin and the aquarium made an interesting scene on the forest floor. It looked like an exhibit at a trial— circumstantial evidence—of a wild scene, as though a snake had burst through the broken side of the aquarium, burst through his ugly old skin, and disappeared, perhaps straight up in the air, in a rush of freedom and beauty.

[2]The snakeskin had unkeeled scales, so it belonged to a non-poisonous snake. It was roughly five feet long by the yardstick, but I'm not sure because it was very wrinkled and dry, and every time I tried to stretch it flat it broke. I ended up with seven or eight pieces of it all over the kitchen table in a fine film of forest dust.

[3]The point I want to make about the snakeskin is that, when I found it, it was whole and tied in a knot. Now there have been stories told, even by reputable scientists, of snakes that have deliberately tied themselves in a knot to prevent larger snakes from trying to swallow them—but I couldn't imagine any way that throwing itself into a half hitch would help a snake trying to escape its skin. Still, ever cautious, I figured that one of the neighborhood boys could possibly have tied it in a knot in the fall, for some whimsical boyish reason, and left it there, where it dried and gathered dust. So I carried the skin along thoughtlessly as I walked, snagging it sure enough on a low branch and ripping it in two for the first of many times. I saw that thick ice still lay on the quarry pond and that the skunk cabbage was already out in the clearings, and then I came home and looked at the skin and its knot.

[4]The knot had no beginning. Idly I turned it around in my hand, searching for a place to untie; I came to with a start when I realized I must have turned the thing around fully ten times. Intently, then, I traced the knot's lump around with a finger: it was continuous. I couldn't untie it any more than I could untie a dough-nut; it was a loop without beginning or end. These snakes *are* magic, I thought for a second, and then of course I reasoned what must have happened. The skin had been pulled inside-out like a peeled sock for several inches; then an inch or so of the inside-out part—a piece whose length was coincidentally equal to the diameter of the skin—had somehow been turned right-side out again, making a thick lump whose edges were lost in wrinkles, looking exactly like a knot.

[5]So. I have been thinking about the change of seasons. I don't want to miss spring this year. I want to distinguish the last winter frost from the out-of-season one, the frost of spring. I want to be there on the spot the moment the grass turns green. I always miss this radical revolution; I see it the next day from a window, the yard so suddenly green and lush I could envy Nebuchadnezzar down on all fours eating grass. This year I want to stick a net into time and say "now," as men plant flags on the ice and snow and say, "here." But it occurred to me that I could no more catch spring by the tip of

the tail than I could untie the apparent knot in the snakeskin; there are no edges to grasp. Both are continuous loops.

⁶I wonder how long it would take you to notice the regular recurrence of the seasons if you were the first man on earth. What would it be like to live in open-ended time broken only by days and nights? You could say, "it's cold again; it was cold before," but you couldn't make the key connection and say, "it was cold this time last year," because the notion of "year" is precisely the one you lack. Assuming that you hadn't yet noticed any orderly progression of heavenly bodies, how long would you have to live on earth before you could feel with any assurance that any one particular long period of cold would, in fact, end? "While the earth remaineth, seed-time and harvest, and cold and heat, and summer and winter, and day and night shall not cease": God makes this guarantee very early in Genesis to a people whose fears on this point had perhaps not been completely allayed.

⁷It must have been fantastically important, at the real beginnings of human culture, to conserve and relay this vital seasonal information, so that the people could anticipate dry or cold seasons, and not huddle on some November rock hoping pathetically that spring was just around the corner. We still very much stress the simple fact of four seasons to schoolchildren; even the most modern of modern new teachers, who don't seem to care if their charges can read or write or name two products of Peru, will still muster some seasonal chitchat and set the kids to making paper pumpkins, or tulips, for the walls. "The people," wrote Van Gogh in a letter, "are very sensitive to the changing seasons." That we are "very sensitive to the changing seasons" is, incidentally, one of the few good reasons to shun travel. If I stay at home I preserve the illusion that what is happening on Tinker Creek is the very newest thing, that I'm at the very vanguard and cutting edge of each new season. I don't want the same season twice in a row; I don't want to know I'm getting last week's weather, used weather, weather broadcast up and down the coast, old-hat weather.

⁸But there's always unseasonable weather. What we think of the weather and behavior of life on the planet at any given season is really all a matter of statistical probabilities; at any given point, anything might happen. There is a bit of every season in each season. Green plants—deciduous green leaves—grow everywhere, all

winter long, and small shoots come up pale and new in every season. Leaves die on the tree in May, turn brown, and fall into the creek. The calendar, the weather, and the behavior of wild creatures have the slimmest of connections. Everything overlaps smoothly for only a few weeks each season, and then it all tangles up again. The temperature, of course, lags far behind the calendar seasons, since the earth absorbs and releases heat slowly, like a leviathan breathing. Migrating birds head south in what appears to be dire panic, leaving mild weather and fields full of insects and seeds; they reappear as if in all eagerness in January, and poke about morosely in the snow. Several years ago our October woods would have made a dismal colored photograph for a sadist's calendar: a killing frost came before the leaves had even begun to brown; they drooped from every tree like crepe, blackened and limp. It's all a chancy, jumbled affair at best, as things seem to be below the stars.

[9]Time is the continuous loop, the snakeskin with scales endlessly overlapping without beginning or end, or time is an ascending spiral if you will, like a child's toy Slinky. Of course we have no idea which arc on the loop is our time, let alone where the loop itself is, so to speak, or down whose lofty flight of stairs the Slinky so uncannily walks.

[10]The power we seek, too, seems to be a continuous loop. I have always been sympathetic with the early notion of a divine power that exists in a particular place, or that travels about over the face of the earth as a man might wander—and when he is "there" he is surely not here. You can shake the hand of a man you meet in the woods; but the spirit seems to roll along like the mythical hoop snake with its tail in its mouth. There are no hands to shake or edges to untie. It rolls along the mountain ridges like a fireball, shooting off a spray of sparks at random, and will not be trapped, slowed, grasped, fetched, peeled, or aimed. "As for the wheels, it was cried unto them in my hearing, O wheel." This is the hoop of flame that shoots the rapids in the creek or spins across the dizzy meadows; this is the arsonist of the sunny woods: catch it if you can.

COMMENT

Metaphor is particularly appropriate to the ideas of this essay. Dillard uses the knotted snakeskin as a metaphor for existence. She makes her point directly: she can no more "catch spring by the tip of the tail" than she can untie the knot—"there are no edges to grasp. Both are continuous loops." She builds carefully to this statement, the full meaning emerging in the details of her account. The open feeling of spring stands for a larger experience: the sense of "open-ended time." Dillard wants to see the world anew at each moment, though she knows that experiences repeat themselves. That is why she does not want to "catch spring by the tip of the tail." It would fix the experience instead of keeping it open. Having explored these ideas, she can finish her analogy—"Time is the continuous loop"—and she thinks also of a divine power that is everywhere always. It is the oneness and at the same time the variousness of nature that she seeks to express through figurative language.

QUESTIONS FOR STUDY AND DISCUSSION

1. The power of nature, and its openness, are symbolized in many ways in the essay. How is it symbolized at the end?

2. The author moves from ordinary experience to the extraordinary. What words and phrases suggest the extraordinary and mysterious qualities of life as the essay proceeds?

3. What use has the author made of the Bible (Daniel 4:25) in paragraph 5?

4. In how many ways is the knotted snakeskin used in the essay? That is, how many references do you find to entanglement and overlapping?

5. How does the author characterize herself through her response to the snakeskin and the world of Tinker Creek?

6. What use does the author make of personification?

VOCABULARY STUDY

Write a paraphrase of the final paragraph, translating similes, metaphors, and other figures of speech into literal language.

SUGGESTIONS FOR WRITING

1. Write about your feelings and thoughts concerning a season of the year. Focus your discussion on an object you associate with this season. You may want to explore the various qualities of the object and what these tell you about the season.

2. Develop one of the ideas of the essay from your point of view and personal experience.

THE BREAKFAST OF HEROES

Madora McKenzie

Madora McKenzie grew up in Los Angeles, went to high school in London, and later attended Bennington College and Boston University. For several years she has been a staff writer on the arts for *The Christian Science Monitor*. In this brief essay she is able to present some complex ideas simply and concisely, through apt examples and figurative language.

[1] Until the advent of video and telstar with their instant access to success, or at least, publicity, famous people didn't much know they were famous. Only their biographers knew for sure. When there weren't so many media to contend with, we weren't so self-conscious or as conscious of other selves. Whereas once we kept diaries, now we make movies. The content has for the most part remained constant, but the audience has grown. Considerably.

[2] Theodore Roethke said we learn by going where we have to go; a parallel truism is that we almost never know where we are until we get there. Hindsight is a convenient book binder. It gathers up all the loose folios of the past and stacks them neatly for all to read. But the pages rarely get to read each other and it's hard to draw conclusions while the print is still wet. Living legends are a legacy of the twentieth century.

[3] Knowing what you are is of course an essential and ongoing discovery. However, knowing what other people think you are can keep you from being what you are. It's never been advisable to live out an assumption, no matter how flattering that assumption might be. In a certain sense it's better not to know what you seem to be, at

least not entirely. As the poet Rilke once advised a young writer, "the creative individual must always remain unconscious, unsuspecting of his best virtues, if he would not rob them of their ingenuousness and untouchedness."

[4] But even if you do know, it is never particularly smart to publicize the fact. Let it spread by word of mouth, but not your words and not your mouth. Which brings me to the inevitable question: When did it become so all-fired important for other people to know about us? True, recognition is nice, and starving is not, but is mass acceptance really a viable ambition? Is ambition really all that viable, or even enviable? Somewhere between the invention of the tabloid and the television the act of seeing fell second place to the aura of being seen. Suddenly everyone wants to be on stage and nobody wants to be seated. Once the limelight was a searchlight—it sought out the artist whether he liked it or not. Now it's hard to tell the spotlights from the flashlights being held by and up to the face of every fame seeker.

[5] Sometimes biographies offer clues as to how talented people got that way. More often the critical fine points have either been air brushed or blown out of proportion. Either there's no mention of someone like Virginia Woolf even being aware of laundry, or such relentless attention is paid to every undarned sock that it all begins to sound like one's own unsorted heap. This is not really the affinity one is striving for. One thing is certain: when Virginia Woolf signed the backs of her checks, the writing did not come out in italics, nor were the sums large enough to warrant italics.

[6] It doesn't matter, you see, whether or not James Joyce liked Wheatena for breakfast. It's just helpful to remember that, like the rest of us, he did eat breakfast. It puts into perspective the fact that, unlike the rest of us, after breakfast he sat down and wrote "Finnegan's Wake." Extraordinary people start out ordinary every morning and achieve a day's worth of greatness only through consistent and persistent hard work. This effort is not assuaged by their love of what they do. It is the love.

COMMENT

This essay shows how effectively figurative language can serve the purposes of exposition. The metaphors used by the author carry the weight of discussion, beginning with the title of the essay, which refers to ideas in the final paragraph. The use of metaphor in paragraph 4 deserves special comment: McKenzie employs a familiar, even "dead," metaphor—the limelight—in a highly original way. The result is that the reader must think about the idea contained in the metaphor in light of the ideas being developed. Though the vocabulary is sometimes abstract, the writing has the ring of spoken sentences. We hear a distinctive voice as we read, not the dead tone of so much formal writing on subjects such as this.

QUESTIONS FOR STUDY AND DISCUSSION

1. How does McKenzie develop the metaphor in her sentence "Hindsight is a convenient book binder" (paragraph 2)? What do the "pages" and "print" refer to in the life of the "living legend"?

2. What is the meaning of Roethke's statement "We learn by going where we have to go"? What is metaphorical about this statement and the parallel truism McKenzie cites?

3. How does she explore the metaphor of the limelight? How do the various kinds of light differ for her?

4. How do you interpret the metaphor in the statement "More often the critical fine points have either been air brushed or blown out of proportion"? What in the concluding sentence of paragraph 5 is metaphor, and what does it mean?

5. Where does McKenzie first state her thesis, and how does she restate it? What transitions does she employ to make changes in topic or point of view or example?

VOCABULARY STUDY

1. McKenzie uses familiar words and metaphors in new ways. In paragraph 4, for example, she contrasts the popular jargon word *viable* with the word *enviable*. Discuss their difference in meaning, then discuss other examples of this play with words in the essay.

2. Explain the meaning of the following words as they are used in the essay: *advent* (paragraph 1); *truism* (paragraph 2); *assumption, ingenuousness* (paragraph 3); *tabloid* (paragraph 4); *extraordinary* (paragraph 6).

SUGGESTIONS FOR WRITING

1. Develop one of the following ideas from your point of view and experience, disagreeing with it in part or in whole if you wish. In the course of your essay, use metaphor and other figures to develop your ideas:

   a. "We almost never know where we are until we get there."
   b. "Hindsight is a convenient book binder."
   c. "It's never been advisable to live out an assumption, no matter how flattering the assumption."
   d. "Suddenly everyone wants to be on stage and nobody wants to be seated."

2. Discuss the extent to which McKenzie agrees with the assumptions and conclusions in Eric Hoffer's essay "Dull Work."

A GUIDE FOR THE PERPLEXED

Max Apple

Max Apple lives in Houston, Texas, where he teaches at Rice University. He has written *The Oranging of America and Other Stories* (1976) and *Zip: A Novel of the Left and the Right* (1978). His humorous essay on the blues, like Noel Perrin's on perfume ads, looks at our popular culture and its language from an unusual and interesting point of view.

[1] Galen called it Head Melancholy. If afflicted, he said, there was too much black bile in your system. He recommended sunshine, fresh air, or a diversion like choler or lust. This is the very Galen who treated the Emperor Marcus Aurelius, the Galen whose medical theories were in vogue for close to 2,000 years.

[2] In my own youth at the middle of this century, people no longer called it Head Melancholy, but respectable adults, even parents and teachers, spoke very seriously about getting up on the wrong side of their bed. Such awareness of bedsidedness was one of the things, I always knew, that distinguished adults from children.

[3]Children, all taken up with mathematics and telling right from left and deciding whether they wanted to be doctors or firemen, children couldn't be bothered with sides of the bed. In all of our polymorphous perversity we just rolled around and yet we grew to adulthood accepting the validity of bedsidedness.

[4]It was a wonderful short cut. When my mother told me about the wrong side of the bed she was apologizing in advance for any unparent-like behavior that might follow. An entire generation grew up learning subtlety from such hints. We too expected in adult life to be able to offer splendid nonspecific arraignment of our moodiness. We could not suspect that the world would outgrow the metaphor of bedsidedness, that the bed itself would become the central symbolic presence of our generation.

[5]Notwithstanding all the niceties of psychiatry, there still is, I think, a state of modest misery distinguishable from neurosis. It is a condition that may be akin to depression, only peripherally associated with identity crises, and probably has nothing at all to do with interpersonal peer relationships. Kharma is not an issue. Class strife and economic necessity function merely as deep background.

[6]Still, when I get up on the wrong side of the bed, I don't announce it. To do so would put me at the mercy of the generation gap. Instead, by systematic examination I ferret out distress and overcome it. I don't let this malaise, this tricky Head Melancholy, this wolf in sleep's clothing get me down. I reach for my biorhythm calculator.

[7]At my bedside, preprogrammed with my natal information down to the minute, it projects the Dow-Jones average for my day. I am lucky. As it happens, I am today in the midst of two highs marred only by a single low. On a day like this, Evel Knievel could do all of his stunts. With only a single low like mine, trapeze artists throw kisses to the invisible deities and mount their pedestals fearlessly. One low is as safe as new radials, so long as you're absolutely sure of your birthday.

[8]This means, then, that my mood is deeper than destiny. Having looked outside I must now go in. A soft chair, a straight spine, and ten deep breaths catapult me from modern technology to the simple contentment of the Hindu mystic. My third eye glows. Above me is the eternal sun of knowledge, at my side lies the blue lake of peace. My third eye scans the landscape the way a tourist takes in Paris, then it settles down to concentrate on Nothing. The Empti-

ness enters me. I am a pit without dirt, an upside-down Coke bottle, an eye of a hurricane. My mantra crackles in the cold universe. Ambition, fear, desire and hope scatter like roaches.

[9] Then, slowly I re-enter this muddy vesture of decay, this me of pipes and pouches, this pulpy organic unity. I slap my hands to be certain of the material world, then I shave and shower.

[10] Yet even thus cleansed, meditated and biorhythmed, I am still nagged by that nonspecific old-fashioned melancholy. I am grateful at such times for my track shoes which lie at the ready. I lace my spikes, scare the neighborhood shoppers with the sound of my steps upon the cement. At the track I earn twenty aerobic points and luxuriate in the fresh sweat of such effort.

[11] After another shower and a breakfast of bran and yogurt buttressed by kelp wheat-germ oil and Vitamin C, I am ready to face, then ultimately to transcend, the approaching crises of this stage of my life. I am ready to cross streets, greet friends, answer telephones, read letters, make decisions and have lunch. If I am not gnawed by indigestion, aroused by lust, or overcome by envy of my colleagues, I may even have a nice day.

[12] When I return home, my children peek out from beneath their pyramids. "Were your biorhythms sound, Dad, and your diet low in saturated fats?" They offer me a share of their bee pollen.

[13] My wife, also a veteran of such battles, puts aside "The Hite Report" to heat dinner. She who has studied Yoga and body language reads the slope of my shoulders, perceives the relative intensity of my breath. "Stand on your head for a few minutes," she recommends. She joins me. Our bloods rush upside down, our children hold hands and dance to the music of Zoom. From our perspective they are strange and powerful creatures.

[14] "Passages," she says.

[15] "Ships in the night," I answer.

[16] "Tomorrow," she says, "be a *mensch*. Stay home and sulk."

COMMENT

Apple is playing with the fashionable jargon of recent years—phrases and terms used to describe how people behave and feel. For example, the phrase "polymorphous perversity" is a Freudian term used to describe the capacity for many kinds of physical pleasure in infants and children; people who use this phrase hope to find in it a cure for adult malaise and other ills. Apple points out that we outgrow some metaphors and adopt others, hoping to give a name to states of mind that elude exact definition. He thus plays with the language of meditation and other pursuits of mental satisfaction. He also alludes to ways of describing mental states in the writings of the past; the phrase "this muddy vesture of decay" is Shakespeare's description of the human body, in *The Merchant of Venice*. The success of his satire, like Noel Perrin's and Woody Allen's, depends on our recognition of similar foibles and pursuits in our own lives.

QUESTIONS FOR STUDY AND DISCUSSION

1. Does Apple directly state the symptoms of the "modest misery distinguishable from neurosis," or does he let the reader infer them from other details?

2. What current clichés does Apple use in the essay? What purpose do these serve?

3. How many targets of satire do you find in the essay? What general strategy has Apple employed in reaching them?

4. What is the point of his wife's comment "be a *mensch*" (a Yiddish term for a mature, unselfish, and responsible person)? What is the meaning of the metaphors you notice in their conversation?

5. Has Apple developed a thesis? Or is his purpose merely to be humorous?

VOCABULARY STUDY

Use the following words in sentences of your own. After each sentence, state how the word fits your meaning: *subtlety, arraignment, nicety, pulpy, buttress, slope, perspective.*

SUGGESTIONS FOR WRITING

1. Write an analysis of one of Apple's paragraphs, showing how tone is established through figurative language.

2. Analyze current advertisements for a product to determine how much of the language used is figurative. Discuss how certain of the similes and figures help to shape an attitude toward the product.

usage

We earlier mentioned the formal and informal uses of English. Each of us has a formal and informal language, each suited to specific occasions. At such formal occasions as weddings, funerals, and interviews with deans and employers, we speak a language different from our language at home or with our friends. Though the standards of formal and informal language are sometimes different from one group of people and one part of the country to another, there is agreement on extreme differences—for example, that the language of insurance policies is formal, and that the language of television comedy is informal. One important measure of the difference is sentence structure. Formal sentences are often complex, sometimes with considerable subordination and use of parallelism, as in this passage:

> In defying nature, in destroying nature, in building an arrogantly selfish, man-centered, artificial world, I do not see how man can gain peace or freedom or joy. I have faith in man's future, faith in the possibilities latent in the human experiment: but it is faith in man as a part of nature, working with the forces that govern the forests and the seas; faith in man sharing life, not destroying it.— Marston Bates, *The Forest and the Sea*

In the first sentence a series of modifiers builds to the core sentence. An informal sentence, by contrast, is usually looser, perhaps starting with the core sentence and ending with the modifying phrases, as in this sentence you are reading. Or it may coordinate the three main ideas instead of subordinating:

> We have defied nature, and destroyed it, in building an arrogantly selfish, man-centered, artificial world, and I do not see how man can gain peace, freedom, or joy.

A sentence whose core idea comes at the end is sometimes called *periodic*. By contrast, a *loose* sentence begins with the core idea and finishes with modifying or explanatory phrases and clauses:

> Usually sharks stay at a respectful distance, for after all you are nearly as big as they are, but this one apparently liked people, because he came right up to the diver, whose only recourse was to bat him over the nose with the plastic slate used for note taking.— Marston Bates, *The Forest and the Sea*

The concrete subject matter and colloquial phrases like *bat him over the nose* contribute to the informality of the sentence. The more abstract the ideas, the greater the sense of formality a passage will convey. Formal English often deals with specific concrete ideas and experiences, and uses a simple vocabulary; informal English usually does.

Slang and jargon associated with particular jobs or sports are more common to informal discussions. People who work on assembly lines or repair telephone equipment or automobiles share a special language—in particular, special terms and expressions. So do teenagers, jazz musicians, college professors, and baseball fans. This language is less common in formal writing, mainly because the audience for that writing is usually a very general one. It is important for writers to keep in mind what terms or expressions their audience knows. Expressions associated with rock music will be understood by an audience of rock fans, but a general audience will need these terms explained.

Unless we know that our audience will be a special one, it is a good idea to think of it as general—representing many kinds of backgrounds and interests. This advice bears especially on diction, for it is vocabulary that gives readers the most trouble—especially inexact and overblown words and expressions that conceal, rather than clarify, our thoughts.

AUTOMOTIVE JARGON

Brooks Atkinson

Brooks Atkinson was born in 1894 in Melrose, Massachusetts, and graduated from Harvard in 1914. He was associated with the *New York Times* through most of his career, serving as reporter, book reviewer, drama critic, and critic at large. During the Second World War he was a war correspondent for the *Times* in China and Russia, and in 1947 he received the Pulitzer Prize for Foreign correspondence. His numerous books include *Once Around the Sun* (1951) and *Tuesdays and Fridays* (1963).

[1]The man said that if the car needed attention it should be driven into dealership. If there was trouble with the underbody torque box, dealership would fix it. Dealership, he said, is equipped with sensitive oscilloscopes, hypervelocity guns and all the tools and car components that assure six happy smiles in fun cars that have plenty of stretch-out comfort.

[2]Dealership? Last year it, or he, was the dealer, concerned exclusively with customer acceptance, which on the whole was good. Now his status has been raised from human being to institution. No temperament now; no human errors, no jokes such as: "Hey, mister, what have you been doing with this car? Driving it?" On both sides we rise into a bright aura of automation, the customer representing complaintmanship; dealership representing friendship, fellowship and companionship. Also, salesmanship.

[3]In view of the nature of the problem this is the right thing to do. Don't forget that your shooting-brake is a complex problem with more than 2,500 moving parts, including a courtesy light-group and a diode-rectified A.C. generator. No human being should be permitted to lay a wrench on it. He has been made obsolete by advanced energy conversion concepts that, car-wise, can be mastered only by trained personnel.

[4]It still takes considerable drivemanship to get into the garage where the trained personnel perform acts of research and correction. The laboratory is so full of cars and car components that only light observation helicopters can get inside. A convalescent car protrudes through the exit on to the sidewalk, and one lane of the street is

blocked by cars that are chaperoned by trained customership waiting for a chance to get in. Ignorant people might think that something had gone wrong. Dealership looks like an accident. Ease of entry and exit have collapsed. But dealership knows best. Under the vast pleasure-dome of the auto laboratory, dealership personnel are keeping the megatane rating high and the climate controlled. Don't be vulgar.

⁵ Dealership knows the value of a car. A pretty car is like a melody. In the showroom the cars are displayed like goddesses with a tub of blooming laurel at the head and a vase of roses at the rear. The salesmen wear dark jackets and striped pants, and display carnations in their buttonholes. It may be a fun car on the road. In the showroom it is a prestige car. Dealership performs suitable rites of worship.

⁶ And rightly. For the arrival of new cars at dealership is not like a shipment of nails or shirts, or books—trivial things that can be stored and forgotten. Dealership at the right number of outlets in the right locations, stimulated by the prospect of adequate profit opportunity, owes something to the honor and spirit of the nation, and must keep faith with the master designing that has produced this symbol of an expanding economy.

⁷ Last year's model was, if not a fraud, at least a dud. Let's not even discuss it. Since then, advanced thinking in Detroit has brought us brakes of light-alloy racing calipers and disks with sintered-metallic linings (either that, or power-grip caliper disk brakes), a tri-posed power engine mounting and the brushed-chrome instrument panel with built-in tachometer. (What, no built-in opisometer?) Aerodynamically derived, the car is action-packed and geared to high performance. It has terrific lift on acceleration like a startled gazelle.

⁸ Human beings, inevitably marred by imperfections, are not qualified to take charge of such a celestial creation. Even dealership must feel inadequate on occasion. But the transfiguration of human being into dealership is a move in the right direction. We proudly stand on the threshold of the promised land.

COMMENT

Where Trillin leaves much to be inferred about Reedman's, Atkinson states his attitude directly about how cars are now sold and serviced. He states his thesis concerning the car dealer in paragraph 2—"Now his status has been raised from human being to institution"—and develops it through important changes in language and performance. He is attacking the new jargon that has consequences for the sale and service of the car.

QUESTIONS FOR STUDY AND DISCUSSION

1. How does Atkinson expose the implications of the word *dealership?* What other jargon does he identify and criticize?

2. What is the tone and meaning of the statement, "In view of the nature of the problem this is the right thing to do"?

3. What is the tone of the final paragraph? What clichés has Atkinson introduced, and to what purpose?

VOCABULARY STUDY

Make a list of the special terms or jargon of a profession or trade with which you are familiar. Note special meanings that are not given in the dictionary. Write down the etymology of those words listed in the dictionary, and suggest possible etymologies for several of the words not listed.

SUGGESTIONS FOR WRITING

1. Atkinson wrote this essay in 1963. Discuss the extent to which the automotive jargon he identifies is still current, and mention other jargon that has arisen.

2. Analyze the jargon of another business or profession—perhaps that of doctors and hospitals, or policemen, or football players.

JOB HUNTING

Art Buchwald

Art Buchwald was born in Mount Vernon, New York, in 1925, and was educated at the University of Southern California. During the Second World War he served in the Marine Corps. He has written for many newspapers; his satirical columns have been collected into many books. His chief target has been the Washington scene but he has also written about contemporary social problems.

Vice President of Development
Glucksville Dynamics
Glucksville, California

DEAR SIR,

I am writing in regard to employment with your firm. I have a BS from USC and PhD in physics from the California Institute of Technology.

In my previous position I was in charge of research and development for the Harrington Chemical Company. We did work in thermonuclear energy, laser beam refraction, hydrogen molecule development, and heavy-water computer data.

Several of our research discoveries have been adapted for commercial use, and one particular breakthrough in linear hydraulics is now being used by every oil company in the country.

Because of a cutback in defense orders, the Harrington Company decided to shut down its research and development department. It is for this reason I am available for immediate employment.

Hoping to hear from you in the near future, I remain

Sincerely yours,

EDWARD KASE

DEAR MR. KASE,

We regret to inform you that we have no positions available for someone of your excellent qualifications. The truth of the matter is that we find you are "overqualified" for any position we might offer you in our organization. Thank you for thinking of us, and if anything comes up in the future, we will be getting in touch with you.

Yours truly,

MERRIMAN HASELBALD
Administrative Vice-President

From *I Never Danced at the White House* by Art Buchwald. Copyright © 1971, 1972, 1973 by Art Buchwald. Reprinted by permission of G. P. Putnam's Sons.

Personnel Director
Jessel International Systems
Crewcut, Mich.

DEAR SIR,

I am applying for a position with your company in any responsible capacity. I have had a college education and have fiddled around in research and development. Occasionally we have come up with some moneymaking ideas. I would be willing to start off at a minimal salary to prove my value to your firm.

Sincerely yours,
EDWARD KASE

DEAR MR. KASE,

Thank you for your letter of the 15th. Unfortunately we have no positions at the moment for someone with a college education. Frankly it is the feeling of everyone here that you are "overqualified," and your experience indicates you would be much happier with a company that could make full use of your talents.

It was kind of you to think of us.

HARDY LANDSDOWNE
Personnel Dept.

To Whom It May Concern
Geis & Waterman Inc.
Ziegfried, Ill.

DERE SER,

I'd like a job with your outfit. I can do anything you want me to. You name it Kase will do it. I ain't got no education and no experience, but I'm strong and I got moxy an I get along great with peeple. I'm ready to start any time because I need the bread. Let me know when you want me.

Cheers
EDWARD KASE

DEAR MR. KASE,

You are just the person we have been looking for. We need a truck driver, and your qualifications are perfect for us.

You can begin working in our Westminister plant on Monday. Welcome aboard.

CARSON PETERS
Personnel

COMMENT

Buchwald writes in a clearly satirical voice when he writes in his own person. He is not writing in his own person in these letters, but we do hear him indirectly—in the language he has given the correspondents. Buchwald's humor arises in the changes we see in Kase's letters and in the situation itself. Humor must develop out of real problems in the world we know: we will not find humor long in invented qualities and situations. Those problems may be serious—the problem Buchwald deals with is a serious one today. We can laugh with Buchwald because we are laughing not at Kase but at ourselves and at the dilemma of our world.

QUESTIONS FOR STUDY AND DISCUSSION

1. How do Kase's letters change in language? What are the most important changes? What changes do you notice in sentence structure?

2. What situation is the source of Buchwald's humor? What exactly is he satirizing?

3. What do Kase and his correspondents reveal about themselves in the impressions they give of themselves?

VOCABULARY STUDY

Find substitutes for the formal diction in the letters to Kase. Discuss how their substitution would change the humor or point of the letters.

SUGGESTIONS FOR WRITING

1. Write three letters of application for the same job. Change your language to give a different impression of yourself. Use these letters to make a satirical point, as Buchwald does.

2. Write an exchange of letters like Buchwald's, satirizing a current social problem through them. Fit the language of each letter to the character and attitude of the writer.

THE FINE ART OF PUTTING THINGS OFF

Michael Demarest

Michael Demarest was born in Long Island, New York, in 1924, and was educated in England at Rugby and Oxford. Since World War II, when he served in the U.S. Merchant Marine, he has written for newspapers and magazines. In nearly twenty years at *Time*, he has been a foreign correspondent, editor, and senior writer. He won the John Hancock Award in 1973 for financial and business reporting, and the J. C. Penney University of Missouri Award for his 1974 *Time* cover story on American pets. Demarest is a member in good standing of the Procrastinators' Club of America, Inc.

[1] "Never put off till tomorrow," exhorted Lord Chesterfield in 1749, "what you can do today." That the elegant earl never got around to marrying his son's mother and had a bad habit of keeping worthies like Dr. Johnson cooling their heels for hours in an anteroom attests to the fact that even the most well-intentioned men have been postponers ever. Quintus Fabius Maximus, one of the great Roman generals, was dubbed *"Cunctator"* (Delayer) for putting off battle until the last possible *vinum* break. Moses pleaded a speech defect to rationalize his reluctance to deliver Jehovah's edict to Pharaoh. Hamlet, of course, raised procrastination to an art form.

[2] The world is probably about evenly divided between delayers and do-it-nowers. There are those who prepare their income taxes in February, prepay mortgages and serve precisely planned dinners at an ungodly 6:30 P.M. The other half dine happily on leftovers at 9 or 10, misplace bills and file for an extension of the income tax deadline. They seldom pay credit-card bills until the apocalyptic voice of Diners threatens doom from Denver. They postpone, as Faustian encounters, visits to barbershop, dentist or doctor.

[3] Yet for all the trouble procrastination may incur, delay can often inspire and revive a creative soul. Jean Kerr, author of many successful novels and plays, says that she reads every soup-can and

jam-jar label in her kitchen before settling down to her typewriter. Many a writer focuses on almost anything but his task—for example, on the Coast and Geodetic Survey of Maine's Frenchman Bay and Bar Harbor, stimulating his imagination with names like Googins Ledge, Blunts Pond, Hio Hill and Burnt Porcupine, Long Porcupine, Sheep Porcupine and Bald Porcupine islands.

[4] From *Cunctator's* day until this century, the art of postponement had been virtually a monopoly of the military ("Hurry up and wait"), diplomacy and the law. In former times, a British proconsul faced with a native uprising could comfortably ruminate about the situation with Singapore Sling in hand. Blessedly, he had no nattering Telex to order in machine guns and fresh troops. A U.S. general as late as World War II could agree with his enemy counterpart to take a sporting day off, loot the villagers' chickens and wine and go back to battle a day later. Lawyers are among the world's most addicted postponers. According to Frank Nathan, a nonpostponing Beverly Hills insurance salesman, "The number of attorneys who die without a will is amazing."

[5] Even where there is no will, there is a way. There is a difference, of course, between chronic procrastination and purposeful postponement, particularly in the higher echelons of business. Corporate dynamics encourage the caution that breeds delay, says Richard Manderbach, Bank of America group vice president. He notes that speedy action can be embarrassing or extremely costly. The data explosion fortifies those seeking excuses for inaction—another report to be read, another authority to be consulted. "There is always," says Manderbach, "a delicate edge between having enough information and too much."

[6] His point is well taken. Bureaucratization, which flourished amid the growing burdens of government and the greater complexity of society, was designed to smother policymakers in blankets of legalism, compromise and reappraisal—and thereby prevent hasty decisions from being made. The centralization of government that led to Watergate has spread to economic institutions and beyond, making procrastination a worldwide way of life. Many languages are studded with phrases that refer to putting things off—from the Spanish *mañana* to the Arabic *bukra fil mishmish* (literally "tomorrow in apricots," more loosely "leave it for the soft spring weather when the apricots are blooming").

[7] Academe also takes high honors in procrastination. Bernard

Sklar, a University of Southern California sociologist who churns out three to five pages of writing a day, admits that "many of my friends go through agonies when they face a blank page. There are all sorts of rationalizations: the pressure of teaching, responsibilities at home, checking out the latest book, looking up another footnote."

[8] Psychologists maintain that the most assiduous procrastinators are women, though many psychologists are (at $50-plus an hour) pretty good delayers themselves. Dr. Ralph Greenson, a U.C.L.A. professor of clinical psychiatry (and Marilyn Monroe's one-time shrink), takes a fairly gentle view of procrastination. "To many people," he says, "doing something, confronting, is the moment of truth. All frightened people will then avoid the moment of truth entirely, or evade or postpone it until the last possible moment." To Georgia State Psychologist Joen Fagan, however, procrastination may be a kind of subliminal way of sorting the important from the trivial. "When I drag my feet, there's usually some reason," says Fagan. "I feel it, but I don't yet know the real reason."

[9] In fact, there is a long and honorable history of procrastination to suggest that many ideas and decisions may well improve if postponed. It is something of a truism that to put off making a decision is itself a decision. The parliamentary process is essentially a system of delay and deliberation. So, for that matter, is the creation of a great painting, or an entrée, or a book, or a building like Blenheim Palace, which took the Duke of Marlborough's architects and laborers 15 years to construct. In the process, the design can mellow and marinate. Indeed, hurry can be the assassin of elegance. As T. H. White, author of *Sword in the Stone,* once wrote, time "is not meant to be devoured in an hour or a day, but to be consumed delicately and gradually and without haste." In other words, *pace* Lord Chesterfield, what you don't necessarily have to do today, by all means put off until tomorrow.

COMMENT

Demarest's sentences and diction are mostly formal, although his essay deals with everyday experiences. He does not chat with us about the art of putting things off: he prefers to deal with the subject seriously. But the serious point he has to make about procrastination does not prevent him from being humorous, as his frequent play on words shows: "Even where there is no will, there is a way." Thus the formality of the language invites us to consider Demarest's ideas seriously, but he manages to avoid a sober attitude toward the subject, toward his reader, and toward himself.

QUESTIONS FOR STUDY AND DISCUSSION

1. Demarest mixes abstract with concrete words, often for humorous effect. What examples of this mixed diction can you cite?

2. Why does Demarest refer to visits to the barber, the dentist, and the doctor as "Faustian encounters"?

3. What point is he making about bureaucratization? Is he making this point seriously?

4. What points is he making about putting things off?

5. What shifts in tone do you notice, and how are they managed?

VOCABULARY STUDY

1. Identify words that you would expect to find in formal speech and writing. State what words might be used in their place in informal speech and writing.

2. Use your dictionary to find out whether the following pairs of words are different in meaning or in level of usage or possibly both:
   a. *ruminate, ponder*
   b. *echelons, ranks*
   c. *reappraisal, revalue*
   d. *rationalizations, excuses*
   e. *assiduous, hard-working*
   f. *truism, platitude*

SUGGESTIONS FOR WRITING

1. Demarest distinguishes two classes of people in his second paragraph. Describe your attitude toward putting things off and state the class you belong to and why you do.

2. Organize an essay for a specific audience on one of the following statements. Use your experience and observations to qualify it or to support it fully:

a. "The best liar is he who makes the smallest amount of lying go the longest way—who husbands it too carefully to waste it where it can be dispensed with."—Samuel Butler

b. "One of the most striking differences between a cat and a lie is that a cat has only nine lives."—Mark Twain

c. "One can never pay in gratitude; one can only pay 'in kind' somewhere else in life."—Anne Morrow Lindbergh

d. "You might as well fall flat on your face as lean over too far backward."—James Thurber

INDEX OF AUTHORS AND TOPICS

Where there are several page numbers for a topic, italics indicate the main discussion.

333